ISLAM:

A THREAT OR A CHALLENGE

(From Ancient Mecca to Modern Baghdad)

ISLAM:

A THREAT OR A CHALLENGE

(From Ancient Mecca to Modern Baghdad)

BY

ANIS A. SHORROSH, D.min, D.phil
Author of Best Seller, <u>Islam Revealed</u>

Published by:
Nall Printing
755 Middle Street
Fairhope, AL 36532
Phone 251-928-1139
nallprnt@bellsouth.net

Cover Design by: Sam Noerr

ISBN: 0-9759897-0-7
Library of Congress Control Number: 2004096139

Islam: A Threat or A Challenge (From Ancient Mecca to Modern Baghdad)

First Edition
Printed and bound in the United States of America by Nall Printing.
1 2 3 4 5 6 7 8 9 10

Other Works by Dr. Anis A. Shorrosh

ISLAM REVEALED

THE EXCITING DISCOVERY OF THE ARK OF THE COVENANT

JESUS, PROPHECY AND THE MIDDLE EAST

WHERE JESUS WALKED

SUBJECT OF THE LIBERATED PALESTINIAN

THE FIG TREE

THE ULTIMATE REALITY

AN AMBASSADOR FOR JESUS

THE GLORY OF CHRIST: A COMMENTARY ON EPHESIANS (IN ARABIC)

INTERPRETER OF THE TRUE FURQAN

Some of these books are available at:
www.islam-in-focus.com

This book is dedicated to the following friends whose instructions, information, suggestions and inspiration have meant so much to me personally and to this ministry:

Robert, Kamal, Lucius, Dale, Marshal, Sparkie, Gene, Walter, Nathan, Georges, Sam and Mark.

CONTENTS

INTRODUCTION 11
   A. The making of the book *Islam: a Threat*
   or a Challenge 11
   B. The purpose of this document 15
   C. Why must we determine the true global
   goals of Islam 16

I. THE TWO FACES OF ISLAM 18
   A. Peacemakers 18
   B. Warmongers 20
   C. General Muhammad is the crucial clue! 22
   D. Early life—570-595 27
   E. Years of maturity—595–610 28
   F. Call to proclaim monotheism—610-622 34
   G. General Muhammad the conqueror—623-632 .. 40

II. BATTLE OF THE AIRWAVES 45
   A. Is President George W. Bush an astute
   diplomat, a political powerhouse, a
   sensational strategist or a repeater of
   Islamist slogans? 45
   B. Is oil politics the supreme ruler in the
   world today? 49
   C. Human rights in Islamic countries 51
   D. Shock and awe statistics 59
   E. Islam presents another God and a
   counterfeit Gospel 66

III. SOURCES OF ISLAM 75
   A. Biblical Sources of Islam 77
   B. Extra-Biblical sources 80
   C. Arabian fairy-tales 81
   D. Internal problems with **The Quran** 82
   E. Major ethical problems 84
   F.   In defense of **The Quran** 87
   G. Early advances of Islam by the
       sword—623-732 88
   H. Later advances of Islam 90

IV. WHO ARE THE BLACK MUSLIMS 95
   A. Early Islam in America 95
   B. Black Islam is an American phenomenon 97
   C. The Nation of Islam and Elijah Muhammad ... 101
   D. Malcolm X and his journey of discovery 103
   F.   The ramifications of the One-Million Man
       March on Washington 113
   G. Muslim organizations in America 115
   H. What attracts people to Islam? 116
   I.   Theoretical questions 118

V. SEPTEMBER 11ᵀᴴ 2001 AND THE
   AFTERMATH 122
   A. America's false sense of security 122
   B. Seven causes for the Attack on America
       on 9/11/2001 135
   C. Who was involved in the demonic and
       diabolical terrorist plot? 137
   D. The political invasion of America by Muslims .. 139

VI. QAEDA'S HISTORY AND GOALS 149
   A. Osama Bin Laden 149
   B. Moderate Islamic governments targeted 156
   C. The U.S. a mortal enemy of the
       Islamists and Jihadists 160

D. The ultimate goal of Muslims is world
   supremacy 162

VII. PRESS RELEASES OF UTMOST INTEREST . . 169
   A. The September 11, 2001, full press
      release on Exposing Islam, **The Quran** and
      Fanatic Muslims 169
   B. Can a devout Muslim be an American
      patriot and loyal citizen? 181
   C. What can Muslims do to demonstrate their
      loyalty to America? 183
   D. Twenty-year plan for USA—Islam targets
      America 185
   E. Additional revelations 189
   F. Political and media penetration 190
   G. Honest and enlightening articles 196
      1. Capetown, South Africa Tribune—
         July, 1991, by Brian King 196
      2. Jerusalem Post—April 21, 1993 198

VIII. THE HEARTBREAKING ARAB-ISRAELI
   CONFLICT 203
   A. Ancient history of the land and Israel 204
   B. Roman occupation 205
   C. Islamic invasion 205
   D. Are the Palestinians descendants of the
      Philistines? 205
   E. British mandate 206
   F. Modern history of the Israeli-Palestinian
      conflict 207
   G. Issues and answers 225
   H. What is the second intifadah (the shaking)? . . . 230
   I. The heartbreaking Arab-Israeli problem can
      be resolved 233

IX. IRAQ-YESTERDAY, TODAY, AND

    TOMORROW 238
    A. Iraq's brilliant past 239
    B. Iraq's troubled times 242
    C. Iraq's bright tomorrow 261
    D. What about the Weapons of Mass
        Destruction? 268
    E. Biblical prophecy and the future of the
        Middle East 277

CONCLUSION 283

BIBLIOGRAPHY 287

INTRODUCTION

A. The making of the book *Islam: a Threat or a Challenge*

A*mazingly enough*, three weeks before the attack on America of September 11, 2001, this writer was prompted to prepare a video tape. The introduction of the riveting video began with some footage of the first attack on the Twin Towers by Muslim militants in 1993. Imagine the overwhelming shock which reverberated through his mind, heart and soul on September 11, as he watched on television at 7:40 CST, the diabolical and demonic attack on the Twin Towers in New York City. The shock was the more powerful because he and his wife had visited the world-renowned trade center a week earlier. The title chosen was "Islam: a Threat or a Challenge." The urgency to complete the one-hour project was due to several factors. One of them was the determination to have the presentation ready to share with the largest Messianic congregation in North America, August 30, 2001. Another reason was a vision of showing it on television to expose, explore and explain both the threat of Islamists and the challenge of sharing the Gospel with the Muslim world.

This author had his wife drive him to Houston, Texas, for a speaking engagement at a university only two days after the attack. Because the airports were closed and the airplanes were grounded, only land transportation was feasible. Everything went well at the University's scheduled meeting. The students sang with mixed feelings which expressed the sorrow Americans were experiencing at the horrendous attack. The topic was "Life is a series of journeys." To tell them of his tragic past, and of his father's attack by non-Christian fanatics in Palestine for trying to hand out New Testaments in Arabic, might help the students better cope with the calamity. In order to uplift them further, he explained how he was enabled to overcome the bitterness and vengefulness that crippled him for years by learning from Jesus, the Nazarene, how to forgive one's enemies. He felt very much at ease while telling of his family's escape from war-torn Nazareth on camel-back in 1948. His father, who disappeared during the battle over Nazareth, inadvertently stepped on a land mine a few weeks later at the border-crossing into Jordan, where the family had taken refuge. Of course, he was blown to bits and pieces. The author never found out where his father was buried until many years later.

The anger, hate and vengeful spirit did not begin to vanish or diminish easily. The Holy Spirit convicted him in graduate school that his failed grade in the second course of Hebrew was due to his inner sense of rebellion at the "ridiculous" idea of forgiving the atrocities of the Israelis against the Palestinians, who were his enemies. Having sailed through five years of high school and four years of college in just thirty-two months, and going to school summer and winter—taking double courses, that singular failure prompted him to seek a lasting solution. How can an Arab love a Jew? With help from his seminary counselor, the decision was made to begin praying for the Jews generally, and the Israelis specifically, as Jesus taught in Matthew 5:54 and by example on the cross when He prayed for his enemies. The next four years this author faithfully prayed every Saturday, the Jewish Sabbath, for the Jews. On returning to New Orleans Baptist Theological Seminary, Dr. Strange, the Hebrew professor was still there and was deeply moved by the disciplined spirit of Mr. Shorrosh, who took Hebrew again and happily passed it. The strategy of relating such a personal experience was to encourage the students to pray for their enemies, whom the Heavenly Father can help anyone to forgive and even to love.

The following minutes rang out with laughter and sheer delight as he shared how, after being saved at age eighteen, he worked for a while at the Baptist Mission Hospital in Jordan as a lab technician. Missionaries recommended his coming to America. At age twenty, he felt like the proverbial "fish out of water." "Hi" caused him to look upwards, not taking it as a colloquial greeting. "Hot dogs" frightened him as he thought of cooked dog meat and objected vehemently to the despicable idea. The new word he heard at the dinner table "holler" did not necessarily mean to shout or speak very loudly when the hostess told him, "When you need anything 'holler.'"

He continued his presentation by detailing God's call to the ministry, the graduation from Clarke Junior College with honors, then Mississippi College, with a B.A., and New Orleans Baptist Theological Seminary, with a Master of Divinity degree. It was there that he met Nell, the Alabama "Southern Belle", who captured his heart completely, and would become his wife within a few months on August, 31, 1957. The hazel-eyed beauty was visiting the campus one day with other student nurses preparing to engage in missionary work overseas. In 1959, along with an eight-week old son, the Shorrosh family returned to Jordan for a total of seven years. They came back to America five months before the Six-Day War of June, 1967. They now had three sons. Later in 1971 a daughter was born. The involvement in international evangelism continued for thirty-five years. But the last fifteen years focused much on debating Muslims on every continent from 1985 until now and concluded the entire address.

So far, everything went well. However, Mr. Shorrosh had previously agreed to a question and answer period after the presentation. But looking back at that incident, anyone would have realized that it was a gross miscalculation on the university's and his part, considering the volatile atmosphere throughout the U.S.A.—especially on college and university campuses. During the twenty-minute exchange, one student inquired whether Muhammad was a true prophet. Shorrosh gave Biblical references to the student body of 1200 as an answer. (There were nearly 100 Muslims present.) He referred to II Corinthians 11:14, which indicates that Muhammad did not actually see the angel Gabriel, but Satan disguised as an angel. Moreover, in I John 2:22, one can surmise that Muhammad can be labeled as an anti-Christ because he denied that God is a Heavenly Father and that Jesus is the Son of God.

The uproar was tremendous, yet predictable. Instead of the Baptist University faculty taking a stand for the Truth, the speaker was scandalized, scolded and stigmatized for being politically incorrect. An article appeared in the largest Baptist weekly paper in the world, "The Baptist Standard" of Texas, entitled, "Faculty apologizes for speaker." It also appeared on the internet for the world to see the hypocrisy of the Baptist leadership, who six months later, through a two-page letter from the president apologized and humbly asked for forgiveness. Several doors were closed in his face including a major invitation in Texas, due to the unfair article. This writer was vilified publicly, but vindicated privately. Is this America's way these days of doing business for Christ?

The day after the speaking engagement, the writer felt led to express-mail a package including a copy of the video, "Islam: A Threat or a Challenge," an audio of the book **Islam Revealed** and a copy of the new historic document **The True Furqan** to President George W. Bush in Washington. On Sunday, the same materials were mailed to each of the 100 U.S. Senators in Washington, D.C. It was arranged through a phone call to one of the Alabama U.S. Senator's office that once the books arrived his staff would distribute them. Two weeks later the same materials were also sent by Federal Express to the 437 members of Congress. It was a labor of love and the project was nicknamed "Informing Washington about Islam." Somehow, the author's mind went back to a notable statement by President John F. Kennedy. His famous words still challenge Americans, *"Ask not what your country can do for you—ask what you can do for your country."* The huge and costly project was a demonstration of the deep love and appreciation the Shorrosh family has for the United States of America, its leaders and its people, their fellow American citizens.

B. The purpose of this document

It is apparent to the average intelligent American citizen that a gigantic conspiracy is in motion aggressively "buying off" the media outlets to deceptively propagate the line that "Islam is a peaceful religion!" Subsequently, he was compelled to produce this document to expose this fallacy. This is the question to American's first, then to the entire world: *"Is Truth being sacrificed for tolerance and is the soul of America being sold for cheap crude oil?"*

C. Why must we determine the true global goals of Islam

One cannot fight an enemy without knowing the plans and purposes which that enemy harbors for him, his defeat and destruction. It is incredible that the bloody history of Islam for the past 1400 years is glossed over. Additionally, the sixty-six battles which General Muhammad himself led in the last ten years of his life (from 623-632) are ignored. Furthermore, the colonization by Islamic powers of other countries, during the first one hundred years after Muhammad's death, is neglected. The above three facts of history are totally overlooked by the administration of the United States and the general public. Somehow, the spin-masters have painted a picture for the White House, the two houses of Congress, and the general public that "Islam is a peaceful religion and Muslims are a non-violent peace-loving people." Yet one wonders as he watches the daily television news, hears the radio and reads the newspapers and magazines, *"How can the news of ruthless atrocities throughout the world carried out by fanatic Muslim terrorists relate to what pundits, spin-masters and talking heads tell us every day in America?"*

The naked and absolute truth is the realization that the Quranic injunctions and General Muhammad's orders to Muslims everywhere is that they should never rest until the whole earth is subjugated to Allah and the **Quran** by deception, persuasion, immigration and military invasion. In short, the goals of fanatic Muslims are two. First, they want to Islamize the peoples of the world. Second, they want to take over their countries and rule them by the "Sharia,"—the laws of Islam from archaic Arabia's seventh-century culture. Today, December 4, 2003, news from Canada tells how

Muslims are trying to incorporate "Sharia" into Canada for the Muslim population.

Historically, whenever Muslims are small in numbers, as they are currently in the United States of America, they are docile, delightful and dedicated citizens. However, when they grow in numbers one had better look out. Isn't it astonishing that every Muslim country in the world today is neither a democracy nor a freedom-loving country and free exercise of religion is available to Muslims only, while others are given limited freedom of worship! Do Americans envision this way of life for the future? Can Americans allow their country to become a "mullahcracy—one nation under Allah, **The Quran** and the Mullah?" How many Americans are willing to live under a political power which is a religious and social order at the same time? There has never been a time in the 1400 years of Islamic history that religion and the state, within a Muslim country, were separate. Neither was there ever a country called a Muslim country that did not ruthlessly persecute Christians, Jews, other religionists and Animists or give much freedom to any opposition. Democracy and Islam cannot co-exist!

"To surrender to Our will completely" and "to obey Our commandments freely" is genuine faith. For Our ultimate will is mercy and peace. Our supreme commandments are unconditional love and sacrosanct brotherhood. How then dare you oppose Our will and kill, kill, kill and transgress Our command in order to avenge yourselves! (The True Furqan "Peace" 4:10)

1

THE TWO FACES OF ISLAM

t is of utmost importance that one does not lump all the 150 Muslim sects into one monolithic group. There are Secular Muslims, Sincere Muslims and Savage Muslims.

However, like it or not, it is their book **The Quran**, which they say is their fundamental, eternal, unchanging and divinely-inspired document, which is the basic source of terrorism. A number of these "killing verses" as well as the peaceful ones will be presented to the reader in the following pages. Therefore, one must realize that Islam, in reality, is both a peaceful and a violent religion. Muslims can become, according to their interpretation of **The Quran**, either peacemakers or warmongers. Statistics and surveys have concluded that 10-15 percent, of the world's one billion Muslim population, are Islamists, terrorists or sympathizers of Holy War.

A. Peacemakers

"Lo ! Those who believe (in that which is revealed unto thee, Muhammad), and those who are Jews, and Christians and Sabaeans—whoever believeth in Allah and the Last Day and doth right—surely their reward is with their Lord, and there shall no fear come upon them neither shall they grieve." (surah 2:62)

Here is another delightful passage which gives one a sense of encouragement and an affirmation that Islam is a peaceful religion.

"They are not all alike. Of the People of the Scripture there is a staunch community who recite the revelations of Allah in the night season, falling prostrate (before Him). They believe in Allah and the Last Day, and enjoin right conduct and forbid indecency, and vie one with another in good works. They are of the righteous." (surah 3:113-114)

The Muslim propagandist will neither debate, nor get involved in an interview without proudly quoting, ". . .*there is no compulsion in religion.*" (surah 2:256)

Consequently, anyone reading these passages and several others like them would certainly conclude that "Islam is a peaceful religion."

Imagine the inspiration one would experience when he reads from surah 29:46,

". . .We believe in that which hath been revealed unto us and revealed unto you; our God and your God is One and unto Him we surrender."

However, this writer believes absolutely that in many ways Islam is like a coin with two sides. Or like the god "Janus," (which is the origin of our month of January) of the ancient Romans, who had two faces. One will have to ask sooner or later, as he researches deeper into Islam's fourteen hundred years of history, if Islam is actually a schizophrenic religion!

B. Warmongers

Believing that the reader is sufficiently intelligent to analyze the subject matter at hand, the writer will simply present some quotations directly from **The Quran** which demonstrate forcefully and formidably how ruthless, enslaving and victimizing the religion of Islam is!

"Fight against such of those who have been given the Scripture as believe not in Allah nor the Last Day, and forbid not that which Allah hath forbidden by His messenger, and follow not the Religion of Truth, until they pay the tribute readily, being brought low." (surah 9:29)

"O ye who believe! Take not the Jews and Christians for friends. They are friends one to another . . . ." (surah 5:51)

" . . . I will throw fear into the hearts of those who disbelieve. Then smite the necks and smite off them each finger." (surah 8:12)

As if the above verses are not gruesome enough, please consider the following verse in which Muhammad puts a curse on the Christians and the Jews.

"And the Jews say: Ezra is the son of Allah, and the Christians say: The Messiah is the son of Allah. That is their saying with their mouths. They imitate the saying of those who disbelieved of old. Allah (Himself) fighteth against them. How perverse are they!" (surah 9:30)

Surprisingly enough Yousef Ali translates "Allah fighteth against them," into "Allah curseth them," meaning Allah curses both Jews and Christians.

If one thinks that the above statement brutalizes and betrays the Jews and Christians, please contemplate the following statement. ". . .*But if they turn back (from Islam) take them and kill them wherever you find them.*" (surah 4:89)

In other words, Islam becomes a prison with no exit whatsoever. Once a Muslim, always a Muslim; there is no freedom of choice in Islam. The author has maintained for many years that Islam is a victimizing and enslaving religion and the above is another proof of this conviction.

The people of the Western World are made to believe that the mosque is just like a church building or a synagogue, used simply as a house of worship. The media propagates that; so do church leaders and particularly Muslim clerics. Astonishingly, from the days of Muhammad until now, they serve other purposes. Mosques have also been used for storing weapons, making military plans, as well as preparing religious, social and economic strategies to take over their communities and other non-Muslim countries. Whenever one visits some mosques in America, he will quickly realize that most of them are built like fortresses, much more than houses of worship. You could say the mosque's role is much like the White House, the Supreme Court and the Pentagon all in one building.

One of my best friends is Dr. Mark Gabriel, who is a brilliant former Muslim teacher at Al-Azhar University in

Cairo, Egypt. He related to me that during his days as a student one of his teachers was Sheikh Omar Abd El Rahman. The professor shocked him one day with his response to Mark's question, *"Why is it that you are always teaching us about Jihad, whereas* **The Quran** *talks also about peace and forgiveness?"* Mark told me that the infamous terrorists, who later in 1986 masterminded the assassination of President Sadat of Egypt, and in 1993 the attack on the Twin Towers in New York City, became red with fury. His response was revealing, as well as startling. *"My brother, there is a whole surah called 'Spoils of War' but none called peace. Jihad and killing are the head of Islam, without them you cut the head of Islam."* See <u>Against the Tides</u> by Mustafa Ramadan. (Third printing, by World-Wide Printing, Minsk, Belarus, Russia, 1999)

Now this brilliant, physically and spiritually blind Muslim leader languishes in a prison cell in New York for the terror he inflicted on the people of New York in 1993. He and his accomplices should have been executed for their vile and violent deeds. Americans should advocate a second trial and pass death sentences on each of the mass murderers.

C. General Muhammad is the crucial clue!

Muhammad was born to Abd Allah and Aminah in Mecca in 570 A.D. His father's name indicates that some Arabs believed in a god called "Allah." "Servant or slave of Allah" is the meaning of "Abd Allah." Muhammad's father died on a mercantile trip and never saw his son. Additionally, his mother, Aminah also died when the child was six. Biographers of Muhammad tell that the first few years of his life were spent in the care of a Bedouin woman called Halimah who expressed great trepidation because the child experienced epileptic episodes.

Eventually Abu Talib, Muhammad's uncle, took him into his household and raised him with his own children for sixteen years. Since this uncle was a traveling merchant, Muhammad left his shepherding work and began to travel with Abu Talib. For three years, Muhammad was employed by Khadijah, a twice-widowed woman of Mecca. His business carried him to Syria, Persia and Egypt. Had he continued in this business, the entire course of history would have been radically different.

The handsome, articulate and successful camel-caravan leader caused Khadijah to offer him marriage. He was twenty-five, but she was forty-five! He accepted. Obviously, it was a socially and economically motivated decision because Muhammad was a "nobody," an impoverished orphan.

For the next fifteen years, Khadijah's uncle, Waraqah Bin Nawfal, took Muhammad to the Hira caves, on the outskirts of Mecca, and spent one month each year teaching the inquisitive young man Biblical history and Christian traditions. Since the old man was the Bishop of Mecca, he was grooming Muhammad to take over the Nestorian church in Mecca. Whenever anyone reads the early Quranic passages of Mecca, one is totally impressed at how they express the longing of anyone for divine truth and the earnest desire for a meaningful life. The surahs (or chapters) contain Biblical themes of prayer, reverence for God, biographies of prophets and an attitude of deep respect and honor towards Christians and Jews.

In 610 Muhammad had begun to proclaim that he had seen a vision of an angel calling himself Gabriel at the Hira Cave who instructed him to begin reciting messages from Allah. Waraqah encouraged Muhammad to believe it was an angel who called to him, not a demon, as he had first feared.

Allah was one of the greater deities in Mecca, whose name is a combination of "Elah," a god and "Alelah," the personalization of the object. Thus Allah means "the god." Muhammad added the word "Akbar", meaning greater. It was the title for the moon god at that time among some Arab tribes. One must conclude that "Allahu Akbar" meant that this god "Akbar" is greater than the 360 idols and gods at the Kaabah in Mecca's temple.

One must wonder what went wrong in the grand long-term plans of the old preacher. The author is absolutely certain first of all, that Waraqah could not have anticipated the consequences of the epileptic seizures Muhammad was experiencing. In a new book entitled **Life Alert**, published in 2001 by Winepress Publishing and authored by Dede Korkut, M.D., the reader is startled at the revelations. Muhammad suffered from two neurological deficiencies, the doctor declares on pages 171-177. One was hydrocephalus, due to his being the first born to Aminah through her narrow birth canal causing extra pressure on the baby's head at birth. The other was complex partial seizures. Even the entire list of symptoms of such afflictions matches Muhammad's life and actions 100 percent.

1. Auditory illusions—which may involve misperception of tempo, loudness or distance.
2. Visual illusions—which may in comparison distort familiarity, strangeness and unreality.
3. Emotional illusions—which may involve fear, sorrow, sadness, depression, even leading to suicidal wishes.
4. Familiarity illusions—which includes the unreal perception.

It is indeed extraordinary to learn that Julius Caesar, Emperor of Rome, and Lord Byron, the English poet, suffered from the same deficiencies.

Secondly, Muhammad's inner longing to overcome his tragic upbringing, as an impoverished orphan, probably prompted him to strive to excel in everything that he did to prove to himself and to the world that he was somebody important and not gripped with the inferiority complex which may afflict 90 percent of the Arabs in the world. Interestingly, Arabs try to camouflage their affliction by expressing a spirit of superiority complex and being ostentatious and loud in public and in private.

Muhammad knew that Arabs of that period considered the greatest hero to be either a poet or a warrior. Therefore, he set these two goals for himself and accomplished them very impressively in twenty-three years. One tradition relates how Muhammad on one occasion challenged all the poets of Arabia by declaring, *"I am the best orator of Arabia, none can match my eloquence. Try it if you can."*

In surah 2:23 of **The Quran** we are told:

"And if ye are in doubt concerning that which We reveal unto Our slave (Muhammad), then produce a surah of the like thereof, and call your witnesses beside Allah if ye are truthful.

Again, in surah 10:38,

"Or say they: He hath invented it? Say: Then bring a surah like unto it, and call (for help) on all ye can besides Allah, if ye are truthful."

Additionally, we read in surah 1:18,

"Or they say: He hath invented it. Say: Then bring ten surahs, the like thereof, invented, and call on everyone ye can beside Allah, if ye are truthful!"

It is of utmost significance to go on record that a friend of mine and I have produced an entire Quran, not just ten surahs, and published it in 1999. It is entitled The True Furqan.

Because he could not persuade them and other Arabs by the eloquence of **The Quran**, Muhammad began his ten-year plan to take over all of Arabia by the sword. Consequently, in the year 623 the Battle of Badr became the initial salvo. Eventually, General Muhammad launched sixty-six battles within ten years—incredible! (I stand to be corrected, but) I have not found any military leader in history who waged that many battles in such a short time! Historically, he lost as many as he won, but he won the most crucial ones, especially the battle for Mecca.

Ten thousand warriors followed General Muhammad as he advanced on the capital of Arabia, his former hometown. Besieged by such an overwhelming force, Khalid ibn el Waleed tried to stand up to them but lost forty-five fighters. Realizing the futility of it all, the leaders of Mecca surrendered quickly to save their lives. In other words, Muhammad took vengeance on the city which tried to kill him, and made him a refugee by forcing him to leave his home. How? He obligated the entire citizenship to bow down to "Allah" and the new religion of Muhammad, now named Islam. Subsequently, General Muhammad became the absolute authority for religious faith and practice of Islam by the violence of the sword, not the volitional will of the people. Dictatorship became the system to rule in Islam—not democracy.

Let this writer state the following for all posterity: **"Without the Scimitar of Steel, Muhammad and his savage, ruthless army of illiterate Arab Bedouins, neither his name nor his religion would have spread throughout the earth. Both would have been buried under the searing, wind-swept sand dunes of ancient Arabia, forgotten by time and ignored by humanity!"**

D. Early life—570-595

Much of the information that comes to us is found in **The Quran** itself, the Hadith (Traditions) and two biographies by Ibn Ishaq and Ibn Hisham. Ibn Ishaq collected two volumes of stories about Muhammad after Muhammad's death in 767. Ibn Hisham condensed them into one volume in Arabic between 767-834 A.D. The German translation was done by Professor Gustaf Weil in 1864 and the English translation from German and Arabic in 1997 by Abd al-Masih. It was printed by Light of Life in Villach, Austria.

Although the Gospels were written within the first ninety years of the birth of Christ, by his own disciples and other witnesses, there is no such record in Islam's history concerning Muhammad. In fact, the earliest document, which deals exclusively with the life of Muhammad, was written between 150 to 200 years after his death. In other words, we have no eye witnesses who captured the activities, teachings, speeches and battles of Muhammad. The famous "Traditions, the Hadith," were orally transmitted long before the nine volumes were written. These materials are exactly what the name means, "The lore and folklore of Muhammad." All in all they are tales and fairy tales, facts mixed with fiction, about General Muhammad's practices, prowess's, powers and activities. Muhammad was much like Proteus, the Greek god. Proteus had the faculty of assuming different shapes and changing his form and principles; Muhammad demonstrated the same characteristics from age forty until his death at age sixty-two!

E. Years of maturity—595–610

Inasmuch as a summary of his life was incorporated in the previous point, it is sufficient to mention that from 575-600, he was practically an orphan boy for eight years, then an orphan adopted by his uncle, from eight to sixteen, then an apprentice on mercantile trips by his uncle, Abu Talib, from sixteen to twenty-five. Of course, the beginning of his so-called visions of 610 A.D. was preceded by the most significant event in his entire life, which was marrying Khadijah, the Nestorian Christian widow, an aristocratic lady of Mecca.

It is unfortunate that historians overlook and underestimate this event in his career as general and prophet. It must be emphasized that had he not married Khadijah, who was twice widowed (with the control of her two deceased husbands' wealth) which became available to Muhammad, he would never have had the opportunity to go to the Hira Caves for an entire month every year during the first fifteen years of his marriage of twenty-six years. Neither would he have joined the Hanifa group.

Subsequently, Muhammad became a part of the aristocracy of Mecca by the sheer reason of marrying Khadijah plus his charming personality. One must never forget that it was Khadijah, and no one else, who was the first to support him as a prophet of Allah.

This writer is categorically certain that had Muhammad been a contemporary of Jesus the Messiah and had met him personally, he would have become a fervent, fierce and fiery disciple and an enthusiastic Christian evangelist.

Muslims today, and particularly for the past one hundred years or so, have been enchanted with the **Gospel of Barnabas.** For the past fourteen hundred years

Muslims generally, and their theological scholars specifically, have been eagerly probing into the Biblical records and extra-Biblical ones to find any proof-text whatsoever to justify their **Quran** and authenticate their General as to his prophethood. That is why Barnabas' Gospel is so significant to them.

Whenever anyone reads the **Gospel of Barnabas** in Arabic or in English, he quickly discovers chronological, geographical, Biblical and historical blunders. A misleading statement on page 57 tells that Jesus announced that the Messiah would come through the lineage of Ishmael, not Isaac. On page 58-59, one is told that Jesus gave a prophecy about Muhammad and declared that Jesus himself wished to be worthy to untie Muhammad's sandals! Furthermore, Job is called "a friend of God" several times, while the Bible calls only Abraham by such a title in II Chronicles 20:7, Isaiah 41:8 and James 2:23. Another blunder is found on page 91 where the reader is told that Barnabas was the disciple who asked Jesus to identify his betrayer at The Last Supper and not the Apostle John, as the Gospels relate. The writer of the **Gospel of Barnabas** records on pages 117-118 that Jesus himself told the multitudes that he was a mere man and only a prophet. On page 123, one is told that Jesus predicted that Muhammad is the name of the coming Messiah! On page 277 Barnabas is identified as a disciple of Jesus. However, Acts, chapter nine, presents him as an early Jewish convert to Christianity at Antioch, who became a leader of the young church and befriended Paul.

Muslims boast that Muhammad's great achievement was that he proclaimed monotheism to his pagan Arab relatives in Arabia courageously and boldly and thereafter to the rest of the world. The impression is that no one else had done such preaching before him. Historically, there were several intellectual men who gathered in Mecca frequently to debate religious, poetic, literary, and philosophical subjects called Hanifites. Muhammad attended these discussions during the first fifteen years of his marriage to Khadijah very often. He no longer had to work in order to make a living by traveling as a caravan leader to Syria, Egypt and other mercantile centers. Therefore, the first fifteen years of his marriage to his wife, Khadijah, were spent in research and study in preparation for his book, **The Quran**.

Additionally, Muhammad began by declaring that he was sent as a messenger of "Allah," who some Meccans worshipped as their main deity, to simply remind people of Abraham's religion. Therefore, one is astonished to find the words "reminder," "remind," "remember" and so forth 247 times in **The Quran**. The book, **A Concordance of the Qur'an**, pp. 388-394, by Hanna E. Kassis, Associate Professor of Religious studies at the University of British Columbia, contains them all. It was printed at the University of California Press in 1983, covering 1444 pages. The reader should not be surprised when this author expounds that **the best title for the Quran is "The Reminder."** To those of you who recognize that **The Quran** has fifty different titles, it is remarkable indeed that one of them is 'The Reminder." One reads terms like, "and remember Noah," "and remember Jonah," "and remember Joseph," "and remember Mary" and "remember Jesus, son of Mary," very frequently in **The Quran**.

Nevertheless, this author's extraordinary logical question is: "Why should any Muslim boast that the miracle, which authenticates the prophethood of Muhammad, is **The Quran**, when they firmly hold to the belief that Allah, through Gabriel, inspired it? Such conviction is called mechanical inspiration.

During the second debate with Mr. Ahmed Deedat of South Africa, which took place in Birmingham, England, in August, 1988, this writer declared to the nearly twelve thousand attendees that practically seventy-five percent of **The Quran** is plagiarized from **The Bible**. The author has never backed down from that declaration and will be publishing two new books to prove this truth very soon. One will be entitled, **Biblical Plagiarism in the Quran**, while the other will be **Ninety-nine Excellent Reasons Why Muhammad Is Not A Prophet of God**. The first book will clearly present every Biblical story, event, personality and teaching which the Quran has borrowed from **The Bible**. Alas, one will find them minced, mixed up and mangled—at times beyond recognition. The second will powerfully verify the title and definitely vilify Islamic claims of fourteen hundred years, as to Muhammad's claims to prophethood. If one were to take the Biblical references out of **The Quran**, what would be left could hardly fill a booklet of seventy pages.

At the conclusion of twelve years of mentoring by Bishop Waraqah bin Nawfal, forty five followers were all that Muhammad could claim in Mecca. Suddenly the old preacher expired and Muhammad had no advisors and only two encouragers—his wife and Abu Bakr. He plunged himself into a bottomless pit of pity and self-doubt. He even proclaimed on a Friday, at the weekly public meeting, that the three goddesses of the Meccans could become a part of his system of religion. It was a brilliant tactical move which won immediate and positive response from the pagan Meccans. "Al-lat," "Uzza," and "Manat," were the three leading goddesses of the Meccans out of the 360 gods and goddesses found in and around the famed Kaabah Temple.

In the pagan mythology of the Meccans at that period in history, these were the daughters of the moon and the sun. Muhammad announced that since they were the daughters of the moon, which had two names, "Allah," and "Akbar," their intercession was valid and ought to be sought by his followers. However, Muhammad could not have predicted the consequences and the uproar by his early followers, the Sahabah. They demanded to know what happened to the doctrine of the one God. He had to back down, which at once pleased his followers, yet enormously enraged the Meccans.

Consequently, the Meccans plotted to kill him and he had to escape for his life. He sent his other followers to Abyssinia (the ancient Christian Kingdom of Ethiopia), as well as other cities and neighboring countries, to escape the murderous wrath of his town's manipulated and angry Meccans. In other words, they felt that he had deceived them in order to win them over to his new religion.

Amazingly enough, Muslims declare that he "migrated" to Medina because there were 175 followers there. They even call that tragic event of 622 A.D. "Al-Hijrah", "the migration" and mark the date as the year Islam was borne! But they rarely relate the blunder of their prophet into polytheism, which is the belief in multitudes of gods. Is it not obvious that Muhammad, at one time in his so-called twenty-three years of ministry, was a polytheist? Did he not encourage his earlier followers who were nicknamed "Al Sahabah," to seek intercession of the three goddesses of the pagan Meccans?

F. Call to proclaim monotheism—610-622

According to Islamic history and Muslim historians, Muhammad's real life began in 610 when he rushed to his beloved wife with unbelievable news. He related to her with great anguish and sense of terror that he came from the Hira Caves. He tried to explain, while he was begging her to cover him with something because he was shaking, cold, foaming at the mouth and very agitated. Khadijah, the faithful wife of sixteen years, tried to calm him down enough so she could understand his plight. Muhammad was forty years of age when he declared that he had seen either a demon or an angel who terrified him so badly that he was tempted to jump off the cliff to his death. We are told that she excused herself and ran to her uncle, Waraqah bin Nawfal. She felt he was the only spiritual and religious man in Mecca who could explain the phenomenon. But who was Waraqah?

Waraqah was the man who performed the public wedding ceremony and declared her and Muhammad husband and wife. Waraqa was the leading Christian citizen in Mecca and pastor of the Nestorian Church. As an Arab, Waraqah's delight was obvious, according to Muslim authorities, because he informed her that since all the previous prophets of God were Jews, it was time for God to send an Arab to be a prophet to the Arabs.

Consequently, he assured her that what Muhammad experienced was an appearance of an angel, not a demon.

For the following ten years Muhammad claimed that he was a warner, a preacher and a messenger from Allah to revive the religion of Abraham. In short, he did not come to bring a new religion but to rejuvenate the Abrahamic concept of God. As far as Muhammad was concerned, the original purpose of the Kaabah was to worship the Creator God and that is why it was originally built without a roof. The leaders of the Meccans decreed that the Kaabah must have a roof on it, because during the rainy season people would get wet as they came inside to worship. The Kaabah has been covered ever since. Originally, whenever the worshiper went in, he would look up to the heavens and praise the Almighty, or worship the stars if he were a Sabean. Over the centuries paganism had taken hold and the few believers in the one God were basically the intellectuals of Mecca. Muhammad met with them, after he married Khadijah and continued to do so for the following fifteen years. They were known as Hanifites. In other words, the so-called twenty-three years of inspiration originated with Waraqah bin Nawfal and this group because no one ever saw the angel!

It is believed by Muslims in general that the twelve years following this first vision, Muhammad was receiving a stream of messages from Allah through the angel Gabriel. This angel, who supposedly had announced to Muhammad that Gabriel was his name and that he was the messenger of Allah, was sent specifically to Muhammad with Allah's revelations. Surprisingly enough, the so-called revelations ceased in the twelfth year and the dry spell practically ended Muhammad's ministry, commencing precisely with the death of his mentor, the preacher Waraqah. Was Waraqah one and the same angel, Gabriel?

Another question erupts in one's mind when he discovers that Muslims believe that **The Quran** was sent from heaven overnight. If one is to believe this declaration, then why did it take Muhammad twenty-three years to spell out the 114 chapters, 6140 verses, 77,639 words and 323,015 letters? Furthermore, 75 percent of the so-called revelations were already recorded in the Bible centuries before Muhammad was born! So, where is the revelation in the Quran?

To the illiterate Bedouins of Mecca, including himself, the Biblical stories were new to them because there was no Arabic translation of **The Bible** at that time. Additionally, Preacher Waraqah Bin Nawfal apparently was not interested in evangelism. Neither were members of his small congregation.

What this writer is attempting to articulate is this—Muhammad's revelations were simple sermons uttered in the Bedouin's classical Arabic, prose and poetry from the Old Testament Biblical records, pagan's traditions, Persian tales, mythical stories, Nestorian Christian teachings and contemporary Sabean religious practices.

It is obvious to any reader of **The Quran**, who is the least familiar with Jewish traditions and Biblical scriptures, that there was not any "new" revelation given to Muhammad, as Muslims proclaim. All the so-called messages, with few exceptions, are repetitions of the lives and works of Adam, Noah, Abraham, Moses, Joseph, David, Solomon, Jonah, John the Baptist, Mary the mother of Jesus the Messiah and others. It was not a totally jarring experience for this writer to hear a Jewish theologian, while lecturing on Islam announce: *"Islam for all practical purposes is Judaism in Arabic."*

Therefore, it is very intriguing to any observer to take notice of Muslim and Jewish dress, the ceremonial washing before worship, the covering of the head by men, the separation of the sexes during worship services, the bowing down in worship and the particular direction when one is praying. One quickly recognizes more fully how the two religions are truly similar. Nevertheless, the deep-seated animosity of Islam toward Judaism is due to the competition between the offspring's of Isaac and Ishmael, the desire for international political power and the negative Quranic opinion concerning the Jews.

Furthermore, today there is also a desire to control Arabia which is supposed to be sacred property due to Allah's revelations there. The Jews are accused of controlling the world through their tremendous acumen in finances, along with the powerful political influence in Washington. The Arabs are accused of trying to do the same with three methods: oil as a tool of control, the spread of the religion of Islam and the Sword of Islam. In these modern days, the latter has turned into a diabolical and fanatic war of Islamic terrorism throughout the world—World War III.

There must be a way to reconcile the two most vicious antagonists on the planet for the past 100 years. It is not a matter of Israeli and Palestinian, neither of international Jews nor Gentile Arabs. It is deeper than that. Many rational Christian theologians are convinced that **The Bible** reveals to us, in both the Old and New Testaments, that man is an incorrigible sinner. Moreover, he is at the same time an incorrigibly religious person. However, religions of the world have never solved man's spiritual problems, on an individual basis–yes, collectively– never.

This week as these words are being penned, a dear friend by the name of Dr. Martha Myers was gunned down Monday, December 30, 2002, along with two others, at the Baptist Hospital in Jibla, Yemen. A fourth missionary survived. One wonders why a militant Muslim would murder a godly and saintly physician! Dr. Myers had spent nearly twenty-five years of her life loving the people of Yemen, healing their sick and caring for the dying. That mission hospital was the first hospital ever built in Yemen thirty-five years ago. The personnel, who are mainly international, along with native help, treated around forty-thousand people every year. This writer was very deeply struck last year when he conversed with Dr. Myers over the phone in Montgomery, Alabama, at her fantastic commitment to the Lord and Yemen's people. She asked for prayer for the International Mission Board of the SBC to not hinder her from going back after her furlough. Because of their concern for her security, after the attacks of 9/11/2001 and the bombing of the famous battleship, the Cole, they felt it was too risky for her to go back. She was delighted to return to minister among the people she loved so much, despite the risks involved—apparently, she had a date with destiny. The martyr's lifeless body, with a savage bullet in the head, was laid in the ground in Yemen, a land she loved. Jesus' words must echo in the memory corridors of any Christian's mind, "Greater love has no one than to lay down his life for his friends." (John 15:13)

The news media carried the tragic story world-wide. To the credit of Baptists in general, her friends and relatives in particular, not a single sentence of animosity or desire for vengeance was ever uttered. The love and forgiveness of Jesus seemed to be real in their hearts and on their lips. Furthermore, any news observer would have been struck by the response of the murderer as to why he shot the four saints. The entire world was reminded of the Attack on America of 9/11 because he declared joyfully, *"I shot these Americans to get closer to Allah."* Certainly, one should conclude, something is terribly wrong in the wiring of the brain of any individual who believes the deity is pleased with murderers, unless the deity is Satan himself, who came to kill and destroy.

It is refreshing that within the Christian context we desire a closer walk with God, the Heavenly Father, our walk is characterized by loving God first, others second and ourselves last. We are to forgive our enemies, bless them who curse us and pray for them who abuse us. (Matthew 4:44) Christians have suffered at the hands of Muslims for fourteen hundred years. With the exception of the Crusades, Christians have tried to carry the loving message of Jesus of Nazareth by opening hospitals and clinics. They have built children's schools as well as colleges and universities. They often operate special training centers for nursing mothers, initiate agricultural projects and organize adult education. Their aid programs for the poor and hungry have sent millions of tons of food, clothing and medicine to the ends of the earth, especially during natural or man-made disasters.

Christianity is a compassionate and caring faith. Therefore, it must be boldly stated that the hope of Muslims and everyone else on the planet is Jesus Christ, the man from this author's hometown of Nazareth. He can change anybody's heart and life, and set him on a course of a new life of love and liberty for himself, as well as for others who may hear the message and trust Jesus the Messiah as their Savior and Lord. In 2003, records show that one million short term volunteers left America's shores to share this message throughout the world. Now, that is true love.

Please realize that this writer is speaking from personal agonizing and traumatic experiences. Jesus Christ changed his aimless, hopeless, fatherless life at age eighteen. He taught him first to tolerate his enemies, then to forgive them and finally to love them! Admittedly, it took ten years of earnest prayer to reach such a marvelous point in his seventy years. While at Oxford Graduate School, in Dayton, Tennessee, among the many lasting lessons impressed upon this eager student was Dr. Basil Jackson's statement: *"One powerful sign of being human is the ability to change."* Subsequently, with the help of the Holy Spirit the impossible, which is loving one's enemies, can become possible.

G. General Muhammad the conqueror—623-632

It was explained earlier under point C why Muhammad became a warrior, but it was not mentioned that the unparalleled thrill of victory, the rush of racing horses, the rattle of swords and the den of battle were intoxicating. Much like a drunkard can never be satisfied with one drink, Muhammad ended up waging sixty-six battles in ten years. Because of these battles fear and terror spread throughout Arabia much like Attila the Hun had done 150 years earlier in Asia. Eventually, Muslim armies conquered the entire Arabian Peninsula by 632 A.D.

Of course, the main attraction to the warrior in that time and place was not just the thrill of victory. It was ultimately the plunder of war, enslavement of captured enemies and the sensual delight of adding more virgins and widows to the warrior's household. The impoverished and illiterate Bedouins had never known of anything so fantastically glorious to equal fighting for General Muhammad! Furthermore, Muhammad announced that Allah from on high had instructed him to command that each warrior must give one-half of the spoils of war to Allah's messenger while the warrior keeps the rest.

As if these were not enough, enticement to fight for Muhammad, the brilliant General, assured the warrior of two lucrative rewards. If one were to be killed in battle he would go straight to paradise without ever having to be punished for any of his misdeeds. Secondly, vast rewards await him in Paradise. Here are Muhammad's unbelievable revelations concerning paradise:

> *"A similitude of the Garden which those who keep their duty (to Allah) are promised: Therein are rivers of water unpolluted, and rivers of milk whereof the flavour changeth not, and rivers of wine delicious to the drinkers, and rivers of clear-*

*run honey; therein for them is every kind of fruit,
with pardon from their Lord . . . . "* (surah 47:15)

A very pertinent and serious question must be asked, "Who can ever stop such a fighting machine with every warrior convinced wholeheartedly that his is a win-win situation"? To survive a battle you would receive 80 percent of the plunder, with 20 percent for Allah and his messenger. To be slain in battle you would be welcomed into such a sensual paradise of wine, women and song, that it could hardly be rejected by illiterate, impoverished and pagan Bedouins of the desert.

It is necessary to conclude this chapter by reminding the reader that once a recognized leader proclaims to you that he is the messenger of God Almighty, receiving special revelations from an angel of God, who are you to defy such a powerful man and hope to continue living? Do you remember Guyana in South America, and the infamous Jim Jones massacre? Once again, it is necessary to clarify that the ultimate success of Muhammad was not only due to his articulation of some Biblical truths in the classical Arabic of the time, but also to his brilliant military strategies as the greatest warrior the Middle East has ever known.

If the opponents were not convinced by Arabic oratory and articulation of the so-called divinely inspired messages, they certainly could be convinced by the edge of the sword. One is very intrigued when he looks at the flag of Saudi Arabia, the heart of Islam, because he notices not only one sword on the flag, but two. The words on the flag declare, *"There is no God but Allah and Muhammad is his messenger."*

Facts, evidence and truth show that it is impossible for anyone to characterize Muhammad by any other justifiable title than a "General." Not to sound extremely critical of a fellow Arab who has influenced millions of people throughout the world for the past 1400 years, it must be underscored that "Truth should overarch any tradition, or loyalty to ones race, color or national origin."

A positive note can still be nailed down here. If Muhammad, before the age of forty, had lived in the days of Jesus, he would have made an excellent disciple. He was never a prophet according to the Biblical or theological definition of a prophet. A prophet or a prophetess was a person who talked to God and God talked to him. To bestow such a lofty and honorable title, Muhammad should have spoken to God and God spoken to him on a person to person level. Yet all the information from his biographers, **The Hadith** and **The Quran** itself indicates that it was always the so-called angel Gabriel who communicated with Muhammad, not the Almighty God, as in the case of Moses. Besides, what prophecy does the entire **Quran** contain?

Furthermore, no one else ever heard or saw the angel Gabriel speaking to him. There were no witnesses to the revelations, neither to the appearance of the angel. Throughout the Biblical record, angels appeared to individuals, as well as to groups of people. But the remarkable thing is that upon the testimonies of two or more eye-witnesses, an event, statement, or declaration is substantiated as fact or fiction. Therefore, one can conclude that it was the inner voice of Muhammad's ambition to become the Emperor of Arabia which he accomplished in twenty-three years. The outstanding Iranian journalist, Mr. 'Ali Dashti, wrote a book entitled **23 Years—A Study of the Prophetic Career of Mohammad,** published in London by George Allen and Unwin, in 1985, in which he expressed the same sentiment. There is another reason for the rise of Muhammad and the emergence of Islam on the horizon of history, which we will discuss later.

Let us be very clear on these matters. We never reward the work of murderers and enemies of peace. Rather, their punishment will be the eternal torments of hellfire. Once they arrive there, they will be cast into the very bottom of that horrible pit. (The True Furqan "Peace" 4:15)

||

BATTLE OF THE AIRWAVES

A. Is President George W. Bush an astute diplomat, a political powerhouse, a sensational strategist or a repeater of Islamist slogans?

mericans who dearly admire and love Mr. Bush, whose riveting life story (**George and Laura** by Christopher Andersen) this writer and his wife are reading at this moment, is nicknamed "Bushie" by his loveable wife, Laura. Yet none of us evangelical Christians were prepared for the startling declaration which was made in his address to the nation concerning Islam, immediately following the attack on America. He repeated what Muslim leaders told him: *"Islam is a peaceful religion and Muslims are a peace-loving people."*

To add insult to injury in the minds of Christians everywhere, the spin-masters in the liberal media began to theorize to the terrorized and anguished American public various causes for the attack. One of their theories was that the "nineteen" Arab Muslim hijackers, who incinerated themselves within the four commercial jet liners, along with three thousand others on the ground, had hijacked Islam and scandalized the entire Muslim world! The Muslim Mullahs originated this deception.

Because very few Americans throughout the U.S.A. have studied Arabic or read **The Quran** and Islamic history to know the truth about Islam, the lie became a true statement to the public because of the sheer repetition by the media pundits and the politically-correct talking heads. Of course, any surveyor of Islamic history will quickly discover that the fourteen hundred years of Islamic history is more or less a churning sea of human body parts in millions of gallons of human blood! It is of utmost importance to emphasize and reemphasize that, due to the so-called revelations from Allah to Muhammad and his followers in **The Quran**, Islam became a blood-thirsty religion. The instructions to subdue the world to Allah and the laws of **The Quran** have never been revoked by any Fatwa or by any Muslim sheikh or theologian during the past fourteen hundred years. "Fatwa" is an Arabic word which means an Imam's legal declaration or judgment concerning a political or religious issue. As for the crusades, as wrong as they were, they lasted for less than two hundred years and were the Christian nations' justified response to Muslim's invasion of their European countries. The Muslim Jihad has been going on for fourteen hundred years, unabated.

If the media cacophony was not convincing enough, Americans were subjected to viewing on their T.V. screens Muslim mullahs, Christian leaders and Jewish Rabbis on the same platform decrying the diabolical and demonic attack on America. Americans were told that the entire horrific attack was perpetrated by Muslim hijackers who were not true Quranic Muslims, because Islam is a peaceful religion.

As a grateful Palestinian Arab Christian American, this author watched our popular president take off his shoes and stand on the ground of the American Muslim's leading mosque in Washington, D.C., and practically hug and greet the Muslim leaders as if they were next of kin. It was extremely incongruous of his convictions and mine as born-again Christians. **The Bible** clearly declares that there is nothing common between darkness and light. The so-called commonality of our Christian faith with the Islamic faith, because it claims that Islam was established on the ancient faith of Abraham and the same supreme being of God, is historically, linguistically, philosophically, intellectually and spiritually not true.

It must be clarified, first of all, that President Bush, a very caring and compassionate individual, was trying to avert a backlash by the majority of the American public of 286 million Americans against the five million, seven hundred eighty thousand Muslims in America (**The World Almanac and Book of Facts 2002**, published by World Almanac Books, New York, NY). He succeeded in a phenomenal manner. (By June of 2004 the population reached 290 million). There were very few incidents reported across America in which Muslims were abused or attacked because of their religious affiliation, dress, manners or names. It must be concluded therefore that Mr. Bush's move was a magnificent stroke of an astute diplomat by extending an olive branch of peace towards the Muslims in America and the rest of the world.

Not only has President Bush demonstrated his savvy as an astute diplomat, but secondly, he has also proved himself a political powerhouse. The reason for that is his convincing the thirty-nine Muslim governments of the world that he does not hold them responsible for the actions of the Muslim terrorists on that Black Tuesday. Yet you need to be reminded that America has been under assault by Muslim groups since the year 1969 with the hijacking of three U.S. airliners and blowing them up in the Jordanian desert not far from Amman, the capital of Jordan. See the exhaustive list of attacks since 1914, included in this book in chapter VII, "The Heartbreaking Arab-Israeli Conflict."

Thirdly, by demonstrating a reconciliatory attitude toward Muslims and Islam and by not identifying Saudi Arabia, (as the major supplier of cheap oil for us in America) as our most ruthless enemy, who has been far more cunning than Iraq, Mr. Bush guaranteed the continuous flow of cheap oil.

Fourthly, one is impressed to learn that the administration of Mr. Bush was also able to keep the lid on the 10-15,000 sleeping cells in America. The Homeland Security needed time to discover them one by one before they did us any more harm. It was most encouraging to hear, during the first week of January, 2003, the FBI director, Mr. George Tenent, (who resigned in May before this book was completed) announce a very revealing statement to the American public. He exclaimed that since the attack on 9/11/ 2001, the combined efforts of the FBI, CIA, the Justice Department, the military and allies overseas, we have been able to thwart 150 terror attacks in America and abroad. Yes, one can conclude that the popular president is a skilled strategist, an astute diplomat and a powerful political powerhouse.

B.   Is oil politics the supreme ruler in the world today?

The world would have never heard of Muhammad or of his religion, if it were not for his brandishing the scimitar of steel in the year 623. Nor would the world have ever heard of Saudi Arabia or seen the expansion of Wahabhism and militant Islam throughout the world in the twentieth century, if it were not for the discovery of "black gold," upon which the entire economy of the West is dependent. Most of the economies of the Western democracies of the world would come to a standstill without oil in less than six months.

The setbacks of Islam and Muslim countries, which took place in World War I and II, were swiftly exchanged for successes once the oil was discovered under the sand dunes of Arabia, Iraq, Iran, Kuwait, Bahrain, Qatar and the United Arab Emirates. Any research into the history of Islam and Muslim governments of the twentieth century will conclude with the incisively astonishing discovery that culturally, educationally, and scientifically every one of them practiced repressive Arabian Middle Ages lifestyle! Only the tiny country of Lebanon in the Middle East was becoming a beacon of liberty, justice, educational and economic opportunities. Lebanon was nicknamed, "Jewel of the Middle East," "Paradise of the Arab world," and "Little Switzerland." Eventually Lebanon was decimated and destroyed by Muslim militants in a fourteen-year civil war against the only Arab Christian country on the planet, whose ancient Arab Christian population had no other country to claim as their own. Tragically, one hundred fifty thousand men, women and children were killed. Five hundred thousand more were injured for life. Out of the four and one-half million population, one million fled for safety to many countries!

Nevertheless, the ascendancy of oil's incredible and international importance started to take shape after World War I. Then the industrial revolution began to use oil in its manufacturing of goods, generating electricity, providing fuel for automobiles, air transportation and locomotives. Saudi Arabia produces the largest number of barrels of oil a day (8.7 million). America produces the second largest (8 million) But, according to Associated Press business writer, Bruce Stanly, America needs 16 million barrels a day. (Mobile Register, June 12, p 5B) Some of the readers will be quite surprised to learn that Iraq has richer oil reserves than Saudi Arabia. Therefore, in 2002-2003, the war drums were not beating because of Iraq's chemical and biological WMD's (weapons of mass destruction) only, but many believe because of America's insatiable appetite for cheap oil also. OPEC produces 17.3 million barrels a day.

To the credit of wise leaders in the American administrations, the U.S. has reduced its dependency on foreign oil from 71 percent in 1973 to 41 percent by the year 2002. The environmentalists need to get some sense into their minds and hearts, by getting out of the way for more Alaska oil exploration. When Americans utilize the many other alternative sources of energy such as solar, atomic, coal, ethanol, hydrogen, wave dispersion, and windmills, America can reduce its need for oil to 10 percent or even 0 percent within ten to twenty years. Sputnik orbited the globe in 1959. America's spacemen landed on the moon in 1969, only ten years after President Kennedy's challenge to the nation to do so!

Therefore, the U.S. is a nation of "can do." It is interesting to learn that we have 438 atomic reactors throughout the world and America has the most—104!

However, just as America's economical relationship with China is due to the fact that the Chinese can produce manufactured goods at a fourth or a third of America's costs, whenever the U.S. can purchase oil cheaper from foreign suppliers than produce it from its own oil wells, why not? It makes perfectly good economical sense. Interestingly enough, ancient commanders of the armies of the world, as well as today's commanders, believe that any army marches on its stomach. Not surprisingly, in the twenty-first century the entire world's economies (including the armies) march to the empowering tune of petroleum, the king of fuels. How long can America's public travel or its infrastructure operate without foreign oil is a very serious question! Very few knowledgeable experts are capable of answering this question accurately. Nevertheless, it is estimated by some pundits in the U.S. government that the answer is "a maximum of six months."

C. Human rights in Islamic countries

Throughout the history of nations and peoples, the fact is that people had to fight and shed their blood to acquire freedom from their masters, governments and rulers. Human rights, as basic as they are universal, have somehow been ignored by the elite in most modern Muslim societies of the world. Prior to the emergence of Christianity and the eternal teachings of Messiah Jesus about human rights, concern for our fellow man and compassion for the poor in any society, the Greeks surprised the known world. Their philosophers advanced the idea of individual and collective freedom in the name of democracy. Socrates, Aristotle and Plato were joined by the famous orator, Sophocles, in proclaiming that freedom should be enjoyed by all humans and that slavery is inhumane.

Although the dawning of a new day for human beings, and their rights, loomed on the horizon, the flame of freedom was extinguished by their military power. Democracy was exchanged for dictatorship, and the Roman law made everybody else a slave except a Roman citizen. Historians tell us that at the time of the preaching of the Gospel by Paul and the other Apostles, 90 percent of the people under the control of the Roman Empire were officially slaves. The riveting motion picture "Sparticus" tells such stories graphically. It is obvious to anyone searching historical documents that the struggle for freedom burns in the heart of every thinking human being, no matter where he lives. Jesus of Nazareth proclaimed that "If the Son has made you free, you are free indeed." (John 8:36) He also declared, "I have come that you may have life and have it more abundantly." (John 10:10)

The sand storm of Islam swept over the known world within one hundred years (632-732) after the death of General Muhammad. The clouds covered the nations and the peoples of the world by what became known throughout history as "The Dark Ages." There were only two groups of people living under the Muslim rulers. The first group was those who were Muslims by volition or by violence, who had all the rights matching those of the rulers themselves. The only difference between them was the importance of the citizen, his wealth, family connections, political position or educational training.

The second group was called "Dhimah." This Arabic word comes from an expression used by the Arabs to express a situation in which a friend or a relative leaves his children as a trust in the hands of another friend or relative to care for them because of an upcoming long journey or his approaching death. It also refers to monetary or valuable property that is left in the hands of a neighbor, relative or friend as a trust to watch over. The reasons could be that the individual is on a journey for business or pleasure or he is approaching death and the children are not of age to assume responsibility. In other words, the individual who is taking this responsibility upon himself is basically an overseer of the property or the family left behind.

Researchers of Islamic history are quite surprised that Muslims considered Christians, Jews and other adherents to other religions as "Dhimah," but with a twist. Those people, as far as the Muslims were concerned provided a source of monetary income. In short, rather than killing them for not accepting Islam, they would allow them to live and practice their faith, provided they pay 29 percent of their annual income to the Muslim rulers. To this day both scholars and non-Muslim human rights observers cannot accept this practice in any Muslim country.

As recently as three years ago in Nigeria, West Africa, it was very traumatic to notice what happened. Nigeria has the largest black population of any country on the planet—126 million. The population is evenly divided between Christians and Muslims. When some of the predominately Muslim states voted to practice the "Sharia," instead of the constitution of the government of Nigeria, the Christian president did not send armies to force them to renounce that decision. However, what was most disturbing was not the constant flow of news that Muslims and Christians were clashing, to the tune of thousands killed and hundreds of houses of worship burned. It was the discovery that now, the governments of these Islamic states decreed that the Islamic law must be applied to Muslims as well as to Christians.

The fact is, with extremely few exceptions, Muslim countries do not allow much freedom of religion for the minority adherents of other religions in their midst. For the past five years some of the non-Muslim islands of Indonesia have gone through agonizing experiences of Muslim Jihad being declared on them, because they were Christians. Only a few months ago a terrible bombing accident took place in the legendary Bali Islands by Muslim fanatics who had determined that night clubs should not operate on the island and that foreigners are a religiously justifiable target for execution. Two hundred were killed and many more maimed and mutilated. A few months ago the Indonesian government brought the criminals to justice and gave each a stiff prison sentence including executions for some.

According to the annual report of human rights by the United Nations in 2003, seven out of ten countries where people are persecuted and their human rights are ignored are always Muslim countries. It must be repeated that whenever a Muslim citizen, in Saudi Arabia, Egypt, Somalia, Syria and any other Muslim country, decides to change his religious affiliation, and particularly to

Christianity, he faces immediate persecution. Constant harassment by the ordinary citizens, as well as the government, is frequently concluded with execution by Jihadists. The constant flow of incredibly gruesome information, by survivors from Muslim countries, would cause any freedom-loving individual to cry out for justice and fair play in the arena of human rights.

Islam seems to be the solitary repressive religion that maintains a grip on the idea of denying human rights to its people and specifically to non-Muslims. But that is not all. Women's rights are non-existent in numerous Muslim countries. Even **The Quran** does not permit a widow to receive either the inheritance, or half of it, but only one-third of it. As for the children of a departed father, the males get twice the inheritance of the females. One would hope that, with the dawning of the twenty-first century, the promulgation of education, transportation, communication and the internet superhighway such governments would change for the better. People can stand enslaving oppression and religious aggression for so long and when change is not forthcoming, what one will end up with is revulsion, rebellion and revolution.

At this moment in time, Muslim terrorists advocate the overthrow of what they perceive as corrupt governments in Saudi Arabia, Iraq, Syria, Libya, Somalia, Bahrain, Qatar, Kuwait,Yemen, Bangladesh, Morocco and most of the current Muslim administrations. Yet, when one looks at the results of this philosophy in the countries of Iran and Somalia, a shock of disbelief takes over. If, indeed, the Shah of Iran and his administration were corrupt up until 1979, then history records that the new so-called religious administration of Ayatollah

Khomeini and his successors, the "Mullahcracy" is ten times as corrupt. What shall one say of the atrocities of the Taliban regime of Afghanistan and the reduction of Somalia to a backward war-lord controlled castaway?

To any freedom-loving person in the world it is very encouraging to hear reports of demonstrations on university campuses, in the streets and even in the Iranian hometown of the departed Khomeini himself, demanding that the clergy return to the mosques and let an elected civilian government run the country. One does not have to be a philosopher, a historian, a theologian or a contemporary student of current events to figure out that this business of a theocratic government and the going back to the days of Muhammad just does not cut it. "Mullahcracy" is hypocrisy, not democracy.

Whenever a human being becomes a Muslim, he becomes a slave of Allah and gives up all his human rights, whether he knows it or not. There is no freedom of speech, choice, expression or questioning one's religion of Islam. Here are some intriguing examples:

Twenty-five years ago I met Bilkis Sheikh in Pakistan. She was animated, excited and exuberant in detailing for me her conversion to Messiah Jesus from Islam. But that joy of finding eternal life, salvation from sin and a purpose for the rest of her life on earth was clouded by the rejection she experienced from her husband, who was a general in the armed forces. Eventually her entire family isolated her and some even persecuted her, which culminated in her desperate fleeing from Pakistan to the West. Her life story is a riveting, dramatic and moving record of God's grace, entitled, **I Dared to Call Him Father**.

Timothy Abraham, an Egyptian national, came to Christ Jesus through the one-month visit of a pen-pal from Pennsylvania, a study of the scriptures and a vision of Christ Jesus in the dead of night in his bedroom. As a result of this American friend giving him a copy of the book **Islam Revealed,** Timothy began to correspond with me, since I wrote that book. Five years later, the president of a Baptist Seminary and I spent weeks and months in a feverish effort to rescue him from Egypt before the authorities imprisoned him because of his conversion from Islam to Christ. For the first couple of years he lived in fear, although he was in America, because he knew of other Muslim converts who were followed by Libyan and Egyptian agents who eliminated them. Joyfully, he is now a fearless and effective witness for Christ Jesus in person, and in public meetings, from North Carolina to the ends of the earth—through the internet!

Dr. Mark A. Gabriel is the new name for a former professor of the world-renowned Al-Azhar University in Cairo, Egypt. He taught Islamic history and culture for a number of years before deciding to follow Messiah Jesus as Lord and Savior of his life ten years ago. The result of his decision was the immediate loss of his job, harsh imprisonment and inhumane torture for eighteen days by the secret police. So far, with seven attempted assassinations on his life, Mark has survived. He had to flee the country, establish residency in South Africa and finally immigrate to the U.S.A. and write a very readable, informative book entitled **Islam and Terrorism**. It was published by Charisma House of Lake Mary, Florida, at the end of 2002. It is a must-read book. Mark's latest effort is entitled <u>Islam and the Jews</u>, published by the same publishers, 2003.

Author Naguib Mahfouz is still a Muslim. He won the 1988 Nobel Laureate in literature. In 1994 Muslim fundamentalists attacked him on his way home from his lecture at a nearby University. He was stabbed and left in the street in a pool of blood. Although Dr. Mahfouz was eighty-three years old, neither mercy nor compassion was shown to him at that old age. Surprisingly, he survived to tell what happened. The reason for the attack was the fact that he wrote openly about the oppression, mistreatment and the loss of human rights of the poor and neglected people of Cairo, Egypt.

Dr. Farag Foda was shot to death in 1992 because he exposed the atrocious activities of the Islamic fundamentalists. As a moderate Muslim he warned the Egyptians specifically, and the Arab Muslim countries generally, plus people of the world, concerning the seriousness of the problem of fundamentalist Islam. He went as far as declaring that their literalist philosophy and militant actions were in fact a cancer which needed to be surgically removed.

Finally, some of you may not be aware of the most renowned of these insightful "Islamic" personalities, whose name is Salman Rushdie. He is an Indian national, But a British citizen, who has made a name for himself as an able and articulate novelist. Interestingly enough, he rote **The Satanic Verses** in 1988 with the anticipation of winning a Pulitzer Prize for literature. What he ended up getting was totally different. Ayatollah Khomeini, the spiritual and political leader of Iran after the Islamic Revolution of 1979, promised three and one-half million dollars (later raised to five million) to anyone who would murder Mr. Rushdie. The public outcry reverberated from one end of the earth to the other. The outraged British government closed its embassy in Iran and ended up spending one million dollars annually for the following ten years in providing a twenty-four hour security detail for Rushdie whenever he traveled. Recently, Rushdie remarried and immigrated to the U.S.

The above are very few examples of the thousands of similar cases, which would take an entire volume to detail, of oppressive and repressive fundamentalist Muslims. Thus, Islam and fanatic Muslims demonstrate their antagonism and aversion to political human rights, freedom of speech and freedom of religion.

D. Shock and awe statistics

The following statistics would be of interest to any student of current events, religion and societies in our world today. In **The World Almanac and Book of Facts 2002** one finds that the Muslim population of the world is estimated at one billion. As far as Muslims, in the United States of America are concerned, they number five million, seven hundred eighty thousand.

According to the "2003, 30 Days Muslim Prayer Focus," the following nations have a Muslim population of at least 10 percent or with more than 1 million Muslims per nation (in millions):

Afghanistan	22.24	India	126.71	Pakistan	150.35
Albania	1.21	Indonesia	171.03	Palestine	2.94

Algeria	30.47	Iran	67.04	Philippines	3.80
Azerbaijan	6.47	Iraq	22.39	Qatar	0.48
Bahrain	0.51	Israel	0.75	Russia	14.99
Bangladesh	110.56	Italy	1.38	Rwanda	0.81
Benin	1.22	Jordan	6.42	Saudi Arabia	20.06
Bosnia	2.39	Kazakstan	9.81	Senegal	8.73
Brunei	0.21	Kenya	2.41	Sierra Leone	3.40
Bulgaria	0.98	Kuwait	1.72	Singapore	0.53
Burkina Faso	5.97	Kyrgyzstan	3.67	Somalia	10.09
Cameroon	3.77	Lebanon	1.96	Sri Lanka	1.51
C. African Rep.	0.56	Liberia	0.41	Sudan	19.07
Chad	4.21	Libya	5.41	Suriname	0.11
China	25.43	Macedonia	0.51	Syria	14.56
Comoros	0.58	Madagascar	1.12	Tajikistan	5.54
Cote d'Ivoire	5.71	Malawi	1.42	Tanzania	10.66
Cyprus	0.18	Malaysia	12.90	Thailand	3.22
Djibouti	0.60	Maldives	0.28	Togo	1.11
Egypt	59.24	Mali	9.77	Tunisia	9.55
Eritrea	1.85	Mauritania	2.67	Turkey	66.35
Ethiopia	19.40	Mauritius	0.19	Turkmenistan	4.10
France	5.91	Morocco	28.18	Uganda	1.31
Gambia	1.16	Mozambique	3.56	UAE	1.60
Georgia	0.99	Myanmar	1.73	United Kingdom	1.18
Germany	3.04	Nepal	1.20	USA	4.18
Ghana	4.24	Niger	10.47	Uzbekistan	20.31
Guinea	6.35	Nigeria	45.72	Yemen	18.10
Guinea Bissau	0.52	Oman	2.36	Yugoslavia	1.72

One hears frequently the phrase, "Islam is the fastest growing religion in America." There are no statistical numbers to prove that glibly repeated statement whatsoever. It is the opinion of this writer that the statement was concocted by evangelical Christian leaders a dozen years ago to generate a more zealous and enthusiastic evangelistic approach by the churches to reach out to Muslims. It is apparent that their ploy has backfired.

Nevertheless, the growth of Muslims in America is basically due to these factors:
1. Annual immigration of 100,000 Muslims to the U.S.A. since 1961.

2. The birthrate of Muslim families which far exceeds any ethnic religious group in the U.S.A.—five children per family. As of 2003 statistics show that 31 percent of the Muslim population living in America were born here.

3. The marriage of eight to ten thousand Muslim men to American women annually and then Islamizing them, then add them to the growing list of Muslims in America!

4. The gigantic effort of Louis Farrakhan, the charismatic and persuasive Muslim leader in convincing uneducated and unemployed African-Americans that Islam is the answer to their problems with white, racist, discriminatory Christianity.

5. The success of militant Muslim mullahs in converting alienated and angry African-Americans in the prison system to Islam.

It must be noted here and now that statistics have shown throughout the countries of the world that Christian adherents double in fifty-four years while Muslims do the same every twenty-seven years. Yet, six million Muslims have turned from Islam to Christianity every year since 1991, according to "Al Jazeera" T.V. report of December 2003.

Now, according to an extensive article entitled "Why I Chose Christ", printed in "Mission Frontiers" monthly magazine by the US Center for World Missions of Pasadena, California, on March 2001, the following statements should be considered seriously. According to them, two main attractions drawing Muslims, by the droves, are the personality of the God-man Jesus (Isa) and a spiritual book which stands out above all others, the

Bible. Figures presented in the 2000 edition of The World Christian Encyclopedia show that each year 950,000 people convert to Islam from other persuasions. By contrast, Christianity sees some 2,700,000 each year shift their affiliation to the Christian faith!

1. One's eternal destiny haunts many who long for the hope of heaven and the certainty of salvation from hell.
2. The incomparable character of Jesus the Christ is recognized as a most powerful compelling element in attracting anyone. Christ's humility, refusal to retaliate when persecuted and his crucifixion overwhelm the seeker.
3. The teachings of Christ, in the Sermon on the Mount, the reading of the New Testament, the love of Christ and his followers for the poor, the downtrodden and the outcasts, is another magnetic tool.
4. Many Muslim-background believers discovered that the Bible is really the true Word of God because of its plausible logic and answers to lifelong questions which are reasonable and relevant to any time, place or society.
5. Encounters, such as visions and dreams, either by a figure of an angel or Jesus himself, convince many to follow Him. Others are drawn by supernatural healings in His name. An Egyptian Muslim was reading Luke 3, where the Holy Spirit descended on Jesus in the form of a dove. A stormy wind suddenly blew into his room, and a voice spoke to him saying, "I am the Messiah, whom you hate. I am the Lord whom you are looking for." He testified that he wept uncontrollably, and accepted Jesus as his Lord from then on. These unconventional means are used by the

Holy Spirit in numerous non-Christian cultures to draw people to Jesus frequently and powerfully.

6. Nearly 50 percent of the surveyed Muslim-background believers affirmed that the love of God was the most critical key in their decision.

7. Love by example of the followers of Jesus, who present a living proof that Jesus does change lives and makes a difference for time and eternity, is another marvelous attraction.

8. As many as 10 percent of Muslim-background believers declared that the particular attraction of a personal relationship with God was the strongest factor in their conversion.

9. Some Christian scholars refer to this last attraction as the eighth beatitude namely, persecution and suffering. A sizeable number of Muslim-background believers experience persecution, rejection and physical suffering. Yet, the psychological wounds, which are inflicted upon those who have been counted as dead by their families, are underestimated. Additionally, national churches have not arrived at the point of accepting believers with such background readily. The steadfastness, in the face of persecution, elucidates the extraordinary role that persecution plays in the spiritual growth of the Muslim-background believer.

Suffice it to say, the Holy Spirit is definitely at work in a very incredible way throughout humanity in dramatic means. The dynamic methods explain how Christ's hand is extended to Muslims throughout the world in these remarkable days of enthusiastic and dedicated ministry of evangelism and missions.

I wish there was space enough to relate to you the inspiring story of "Barnabas", his conversion, persecution, survival, miraculous healing and becoming a powerful voice for Jesus among Israeli Arab Muslims! During the years 1999 to 2003, close to 2000 Muslim believers were baptized in Israel. Baptism in the Middle East for adults is the most significant sign for any convert, thus demonstrating his clean break from his traditional religion or denomination.

As more Muslims are discovering the appeal and necessity of formal education, they are opting for two things. First, they are postponing the years of their marriage to fulfill their dream of a good education without the burden of wife and children. Secondly, they are realizing that considering the nature of the economy, both in America and the rest of the world, in the twenty-first century, a couple would condemn themselves to poverty if they decide to have more than one or two children. As a result, it is the guarded opinion of the author, that the biological growth of Muslims will be halted very predictably from now on.

In contrast to what has been presented so far, it will benefit the reader to recognize that there are slightly over one billion Catholics in the world, with seventy-one million of them in North America. As for evangelicals in the U.S.A., there are eighty-six million of them. But the total world Christian population is over two billion. There are three hundred and sixty million Buddhists in the world today, nearly one billion Hindus and fifteen million Jews.

Let us hope that the 1948 United Nations Universal Declaration of Human Rights will become a reality in the 219 countries of the world. Happily, one of the definitions of that statement is, "*A person's religion is what he or she says it is.*" Now, that is true religious freedom!

It is eminently crucial that the question of how this can be achieved should be answered. Whenever Christians are a minority, they should seek to entertain dialogues, discussions and debates with the majority religion. It is a universal belief that truth is promoted far beyond ones geographical boundaries or intellectual understanding. In Acts 17:1-32 and Romans chapters 1-3, we find that the Scripture illuminates the fact that the natural man has some knowledge of God as well as some spiritual matters. Messiah Jesus predicted, according to Matthew 8:11, "*And I say to you that many will come from east and west, and sit down with Abraham, Isaac, and Jacob in the kingdom of heaven.*"

Moreover, the Apostle Paul declares something very similar in Ephesians 2:18-19, "*For through Him [Jesus] we both have access by one Spirit to the Father. Now, therefore, you are no longer strangers and foreigners, but fellow citizens with the saints and members of the household of God.*" It is heartening to read the story of Cornelius in the book of Acts that he was "god-fearing, and devout," despite the fact that he was a non-Jew.

A model for what we are discussing, as well as interfaith dialogue, can be discovered in the Apostle Paul's encounter with the Athenians. In Acts 17:16-34 one learns of the genuine interfaith encounter in which Paul builds on the religiosity of the Athenians to the extent of quoting from their own poets concerning the unknown God. He explained to them that he was proclaiming that the true God, Jesus Christ, was the name of the statue, which they had dedicated to the unknown God, for whom they were looking.

E. Islam presents another God and a counterfeit Gospel

For the past nineteen years, this writer has used several brochures to distribute among those who attend seminars on Islam, sending through the postal service information to people who write seeking help in understanding Islam and witnessing to Muslims. The following material has been used very effectively under the title of "Islam—Another God? Another Gospel?" with comparison at the end of the brochure.

Islam—Another God? Another Gospel?

The Six Pillars of Islam

Affirmation: "There is no God but Allah and Muhammad is his messenger" which is recited constantly by devout Muslims.

The Fast: Faithful Muslims fast from dawn through sunset every day during the ninth month of the Islamic calendar, Ramadan, which is sacred.

Almsgiving: A Muslim is expected to give 2.5 percent of their income to the poor.

Prayer: Muslims are required to pray five times a day, facing Mecca.

The Pilgrimage: Muslims are expected, at least once in their lives, to journey to Mecca.

Jihad: Holy war

The Six Beliefs of Islam

God: There is only one true God, named Allah.

Angels: They are the servants of God, through whom he reveals his will. The greatest angel is Gabriel who appeared to Muhammad. Everyone has two "recording angels"—one to record his good deeds, the other to record his bad deeds.

The Prophets: Allah has spoken through many prophets, but the final and greatest of these is Muhammad. Other great prophets were Noah, Abraham, Moses and Jesus.

The Holy Books: The Quran is the holiest book of Islam, believed to be Allah's final revelation to mankind and superceding all previous revelations. It is believed to come from the "preserved tablet" in heaven, passed on orally to Muhammad by the angel Gabriel. It contains 114 chapters or "surahs." Muslims also recognize the Law of Moses, the Psalms and the gospels, but consider them to be corrupted.

The Day of Judgment: A terrible day on which each person's good and bad deeds will be balanced to determine his fate.

The Decree of God: Allah ordains the fate of all. Muslims are fatalistic. "If Allah wills it," is the comment of the devout Muslim on almost every decision he makes.

Islam and Christianity
Agreement

God: There is one God who is creator and sustainer of the universe. He is infinite, all-knowing, all-powerful and the sovereign judge.

Jesus: Jesus was God's prophet and was without sin.

The Scriptures: The writings of Moses and the Old Testament prophets, and the New Testament gospels are divinely inspired.

Salvation: God will judge all men according to their earthly life. Some will spend eternity in Heaven; others will spend eternity separated form God in Hell.

Disagreement

God in the Quran: God is so far above man in every way that He is virtually unknowable. The absolute power of God to do as He wills is stressed.

Jesus in the Quran: Jesus was a messenger of God, but not the Son of God. To the Muslim, the unforgivable sin is that of *shirk*, or associating anyone or anything with God. The very idea of God becoming man is evil to a Muslim. Almost all Muslims believe that Jesus did not die on the cross, but that Judas died in his place.

The Scriptures in the Quran: The Bible has been corrupted over the years and contains error. However, the Quran is God's final word and supercedes all other scriptures.

Salvation in the Quran: On the Day of Judgment, God will weigh each man's good deeds against his bad deeds, in deciding his eternal destiny. God reserves the absolute right to send individuals to Paradise or Hell as he chooses. The Muslim can never be sure whether or not he will reach Paradise. Most expect to spend some time in Hell being punished for his sins.

God in the Bible: God exists in three distinct Persons, Father, Son and Holy Spirit and it is possible for men to have a personal relationship with Him. God is loving and gracious as well as just.

Jesus in the Bible: Jesus was the Son of God—God became man. He was conceived miraculously by the Holy Spirit and born of the Virgin Mary. Jesus died on the cross to pay the penalty for man's sin. He rose from the dead, ascended into heaven, is alive today and one day will return

The Scriptures in the Bible: The Old Testament in Hebrew and the New Testament in Greek as handed down are trustworthy and the final authority in all matters of faith.

Salvation in the Bible: Salvation is by God's grace, not by man's works. Jesus paid the penalty for man's sin by His death on the cross and His resurrection. All who put their trust in Jesus' finished work on Calvary are instantly "born again" into God's Kingdom. The Christian who trusts Christ can be sure of Heaven, and will never enter Hell.

How to Become a Christian

& Humbly confess to God that you are a sinner (Romans 3:23) and that you know Jesus only can save you (I Timothy 2:5 & Acts 4:12)

& Tell Him sincerely that you repent of your sins, and are willing to turn away from them and submit to God's will. (Luke 13:5)

& Confess that the Lord Jesus Christ died on the Cross and shed His blood to pay the price for your sins, and that He arose and will come again (Romans 10:9-10)

& Simply ask God to save you from hell—ask Jesus to be your Savior. (Romans 10:13)

& Finally, ask Jesus to be the Lord of your life and take control of it. (Romans 12:1-2)

What do Muslims Say About Jesus?

They deny that He is Almighty God come in the flesh. (I John 4:1-2)

They deny that He is the Son of God. (John 10:36)

They deny that He died on the cross for our sins. (Matthew 26:28, John 19:30)

They deny that He rose from the dead. (Luke 24:38-39)

They deny that He is the final, definitive revelation of God. (Hebrews 1:1-2)

What did Jesus Say of Himself?

Verily, verily, I say unto you, Before Abraham was, I am. (John 8:58)

Say ye of him, whom the Father hath sanctified, and sent into the world, Thou blasphemest: because I said, I am the Son of God? (John 10:36)

I am the resurrection, and the life; he that believeth in me, though he were dead, yet shall he live. (John 11:25)

Ye call me Master and Lord: and ye say well; for so I am. (John 13:13)

I am the way, the truth, and the life: no man cometh unto the Father, but by me. (John 14:6)

I am the true vine, and my Father is the husbandman. (John 15:1)

Which God is Allah? Is He Yahweh or Another God?

History records that in Muhammad's day (c. 570 AD), there were some 360 gods worshiped in the Kaabah, the large stone cube in Mecca which is now Islam's holiest shrine. Allah was one of these gods, and the tribal deity of the Quraish tribe, the tribe of Muhammad's family. Ultimately, Muhammad overthrew all of the idols in the Kaabah except Allah, which he kept and lifted up as the one true God. (See Baar, *The Unholy War*, p. 59)

From a pagan temple of hundreds of gods, Muhammad transformed the Kaabah into a temple of just one, Allah; and commanded every Muslim to make a pilgrimage to the Kaabah once in their life time. (surah 22:26-37)

Is this stone idol the God of Abraham, Isaac and Jacob? Just because Muhammad tells us it is the true God does not make it so. We need to measure Allah against the Bible. There are important differences between the God of the Bible (Yahweh or Jehovah) and Allah:

& Allah chose Hagar and her son Ishmael for the covenant. The God of the Bible chose Abraham's other son, Isaac, as heir to the covenant. (Genesis 21:12, 22:2-18)

& Allah is an impersonal being, impossible to approach or comprehend. The Bible's God befriends men like Abraham (Isaiah 41:8), talks with them and even allows them to haggle with Him (Genesis 18:23ff). Men can even complain to God and He receives their cries with compassionate firmness (Jeremiah 12:1ff, Jonah 4:2-9).

& Allah is a god of fear and terrorism that commands destruction upon those who refuse to convert to Islam. The Bible's God delights to show His boundless mercy (Micah 7:18, Psalms 108:4) and wishes to prolong the lives of people (Lamentations 3:22-23, Luke 9:56). His Gospel is the "Good News" of peace and forgiveness.

& Allah requires obedience to Islam and weighs the works of people. But Jesus is relegated to just a prophet below the authority of Muhammad by the Quran. The Bible's God can only be reached through Messiah Jesus, and trust in Him is the only way to Heaven. (John 14:6)

In the light of Allah's dubious past and his radical difference from Yahweh, we are forced to conclude that he is just another false god who cannot save anyone. Rather, through his false prophet, Muhammad, he leads hundreds of millions into eternal darkness.

Inasmuch as this book began in December 2002, and concluded in June 2004, we are very impressed to see some changes in Saudi Arabia concerning the problem of terrorism. It is very likely that millions of prayers, pressure from the American administration, Gulf War II, and the bombing attacks in Riyadh in May and November, 2003, may have brought about the following drastic change in the government. Over two thousand Wahabbi Muslims have been imprisoned because of inciting opposition to the royal family. It is also believed that over a thousand Imams have been reeducated to stop them from preaching radical Islam. Interestingly enough, the Saudi government is now monitoring the sermons that are preached throughout the land in the mosques during the Friday services. As a result, there has been a marked change of attitudes toward Americans and the West from negative in May 2003 to positive in October 2003. It is hoped that this change will continue and become a part of the thinking of the entire population. Unfortunately, now, a year after this paragraph was written, foreign workers have been killed and kidnaped and many are fleeing the country for safety after numerous bombings and shoot-outs throughout the country.

Perhaps the most extraordinary development of the 21st century throughout the Middle East is the willingness to overcome living and acting emotionally, but rationally. Living in the past has caused the people of the Middle East to lag behind technologically, educationally, agriculturally, scientifically, economically and politically. Therefore, one can claim optimism for the first time in centuries as he looks at Iraq, Jordan, with the new King Abdullah II, Kuwait, Qatar, and even Palestine as they are experiencing positive and drastic changes in these fields.

Out of the heart of the righteous emerge goodness, love, purity, peace, truth and faith. (The True Furqan "Truth" 6:6)

III

SOURCES OF ISLAM

uslims have maintained, during the past fourteen hundred years that in the beginning was the Word, and the Word became a book. They assert that Allah did not reveal himself in the person of Muhammad, but in the book called **The Quran**. In fact, one should not be surprised when he finds that the word "book" is mentioned in **The Quran** over two hundred times. The Gospel of John emphasizes that truly in the beginning was the Word. But the Word became Flesh, not a book. Therefore, God reveals himself most clearly in the person of Jesus the Christ.

Even in the days of Muhammad, his countrymen accused him of telling tales. **The Quran** itself has this intriguing verse from chapter 25, verse 5,

"And they say Fables of the men of old which he hath had written down so that they are dictated to him morn and evening."

We are told in 29:48,

". . .And thou (O Muhammad) wast not a reader of any Scripture before it, nor didst thou write it with thy right hand, for then might those have doubted who follow falsehood."

One of the most interesting debates which I had with Muslim leaders involved Dr. Jamal Badawi. He is a native of Egypt with an earned Ph.D. in Economics and taught at St. Mary's University in Halifax, Nova Scotia, Canada. He is the best known spokesman for Islam in North America. While holding three debates, at the University of Kansas in 1989, he informed me that he had produced one hundred fifty T.V. and radio programs under the title of "Islam in Focus." One of the three debates covered the subject of "**The Quran**: Word of God or Muhammad's," a title he suggested to pull me into the debate. (Both audio and video of this debate are available from our ministry.) A year later he was attacked physically in South Africa, during a lecture tour, because he suggested such a title for a debate with me. Subsequently, the result of the attack caused the producers of the video to change the title to "**The Quran**: Word of God or Man?"

At any rate, the conviction of this writer, as a result of years of serious study and probing research concerning the nature of **The Quran**, is that it is no more than a book of sermons authored by Muhammad in seventh-century Arabic written in prose and poetry.

A. Biblical Sources of Islam

The names of Old Testament prophets and Biblical events are very definitely reproduced in **The Quran**. The individual who is familiar with **The Bible** discovers that the stories are garbled and confused. Although **The Quran** mentions twenty-eight prophets, basically Adam, Noah, Abraham, Moses, Isaac, Jacob, Ishmael, Joseph, David, Solomon, Elijah, Elisha and Jonah are singled out. Much of **The Quran** deals with the Pentateuch, the first five books of Moses and Psalms, but to a great degree the book of Genesis.

Allah, Muhammad, Mecca, the black stone at Kaabah and the many ceremonies in the practice of Islam should be found in the Old Testament, if Islam is truly traced back to Abraham. But such is not the case. It is safe to assume that Islam grew from the polytheistic and animistic culture of Muhammad's surroundings. History tells us that in Mecca there were three hundred sixty idols within and without the Kaabah which were worshiped by the people of the Arabian Peninsula. It will behoove the reader to compare the following passages from **The Quran** and **The Bible** which will show extreme similarity, if not flagrant plagiarism.

We have written in the Scripture, after the Reminder My righteous slaves will inherit the earth. (surah 21:105) The righteous shall inherit the land, And dwell in it forever. (Psalm 37:29)

Show us the straight path. (surah 1:6) Teach me Your way, O Lord, And lead me in a straight path. (Psalm 27:11)

The Night of Power is better than a thousand months. (surah 97:3) For a day in Your courts is better than a thousand. (Psalm 84:10)

He is the First and the Last, and the Outward and the Inward; and he is the Knower of all things. (surah 57:3) I am the First and I am the Last; Besides Me there is no God. (Isaiah 44:6)

Please compare surah 11 of **The Quran** and Psalm 14; surah 12 with Psalm 16; surah 14 with Psalm 35; surah 15 and Psalm 5; and surah 18 and Psalm 34. It is worthy of consideration that Muhammad himself proclaimed to his listeners that he had not come to bring a new religion, but to revive the religion of Abraham. In fact, when in his old age a son was born to him from the Ethiopian slave-girl, Maryam, he called him Abraham. The child died when he was only fourteen months old. And most Muslims do not know this because the fame of Muhammad's oldest daughter, Fatima, and his conniving young wife, Ayisha, eclipsed everyone else in the family.

Amazingly enough, **The Quran** mentions Jesus ninety-seven times in ninety-three Quranic verses. Muhammad knew much more about Christianity than the rest of the Arabs around him, because he also tells of Zachariah and his renowned son, John the Baptist, as well as the disciples of Jesus. Recent research has uncovered the fascinating connection of Muhammad to his wife's uncle, Waraqa. It is now believed that this man, the Bishop of the Nestorian Church in Mecca, apparently spent the first fifteen years of Muhammad's marriage to Khadijah, instructing him in the Biblical history and traditions. It is no wonder, therefore, that Muhammad knew much more about the Bible than the rest of his contemporaries. Imagine that **The Quran** refers to the Law of Moses, the Psalms of David and the Gospels one hundred and thirty-one times.

There is a major problem in **The Quran** when one discovers that the Gospels, which were already canonized centuries before the Arabian prophet was even born, are not mentioned as a plural word. Why did Muhammad use the word "gospel" as a singular whenever he referred to the New Testament? Here is the reason. His mentor, Waraqah bin Nawfal, who performed the marriage ceremony when Muhammad married Khadijah, knew Hebrew. He had translated a so-called **Gospel of Matthew**, not the Biblical Matthew, from Hebrew into Arabic. Since that was the only gospel Muhammad could read in Arabic, and no other portion of the Bible was translated into Arabic at that time, Muhammad thought that was the only gospel. Somehow, he believed that God gave Moses a book and David another, so God gave Jesus a third book called the Gospel. Furthermore, because the author of that particular gospel was an unconverted Jew who did not believe in the divinity of Jesus, neither His death, resurrection nor the Trinity of God, these doctrines are very strongly reflected in **The Quran**.

Had any portions of the New Testament been translated into Arabic, the story of Muhammad would have been totally different. In a way, Muhammad's experience at this period of his life reminds me of Apollos in the book of Acts, who had heard about John the Baptist and was preaching the message without realizing that the missing link was the death and resurrection of Jesus, whom John proclaimed. In other words, he was preaching half of the message of the Gospel, because that's all he knew at that moment in time. Muslim scholars are at a loss to explain why **The Quran** uses the word "gospel" when they claim it refers to the entire New Testament.

It must be mentioned here that numerous passages in **The Quran** closely parallel passages in the New Testament, signifying the fact that Muhammad borrowed these thoughts for his so-called revelations from the New Testament Scriptures. Compare surah 44:56 with Revelation 2:11; surah 7:40 with Matthew 19:24; surah 7:50 with Matthew 16:24; surah 61:6 with John 14:24-26; and surah 22:47 with II Peter 3:8. Inasmuch as these passages are part of **The Quran**, this writer has a valid theory. Muhammad must have learned Hebrew at the hands of Bishop Waraqah, who during the fifteen years must have translated and explained these passages from an existing Hebrew translation of the New Testament. Furthermore, he must have felt that the Jews of Yathrub or Medina would accept him as their Messiah because he knew Hebrew, and some of his followers believed he fulfilled Deuteronomy 18:18. He was rejected because he could not perform a miracle and because of his fighting with the sword to enforce Islam.

B. Extra-Biblical sources

The Apocryphal Fables were not understood by Muhammad to have been fables, but authentic stories. In the Family of Imran's surah 3:35-37, one is amazed to see practically the exact quotations from the second century **Protevangelion's** James the Lesser 4:2, 5:9 and 7:4.

Therefore, it is impossible to believe that **The Quran** is inspired by God Almighty. Another extra-Biblical source is of course the Nestorian heresy, which taught that Jesus had only one nature which was human, but not another which was divine.

C. Arabian fairy-tales

The pagan Arabs, besides having three-hundred-sixty idols in the Kaabah, had seven celebrated temples throughout Arabia. Each was dedicated in honor of the seven planets. This writer wonders seriously if the idea of the seven layers of heaven, mentioned in **The Quran**, originated with the idea of the seven planets. Incidentally, after being in Baghdad twice in 2003 and 2004 and visiting two of Saddam Hussein's palaces, I have come up with an interpretation for all of his fascination with opulence. I think Saddam had a very deep fantasy of reliving the famous One Thousand and One Arabian Nights and his being that famous potentate!

Stones with various shapes were worshiped even in ancient Petra, which is a fabled archeological site located in the southern part of Jordan. Some of the readers may recall the fabulous scene from Indiana Jones' movie "The Last Crusade." It was Petra's facade which appears at the end of the movie where finally the cup of the Last Supper is found. Many believe that the stone, which is embedded in the structure of the Kaabah, shaped like an egg, and seven inches long, was originally one of the idols in pre-Islamic Arabia. Muslims believe that Allah sent it from heaven to identify the place of worship long, long ago. They say that originally it was whiter than milk, but it had become black from the sins of those who touched it.

Al-lat was the chief idol at Taif, which means in Arabic "the goddess." Al-Uzza and Manat were the two sisters of Al-lat, and all three were worshipped by the Meccans. Tradition has it that when the moon (a male deity in pagan Arabia), married the sun (the female deity), the three daughters were born from this union.

D. Internal problems with **The Quran**

When one reads in surah 2:59 the incredible story of Ezra or Uzair and his donkey, one becomes quite incredulous. The exaggeration becomes very obvious when one reads that the man and his donkey were dead for one hundred years and then Allah raised them up. Personally, I have no problem with God raising a dead human being. But with the large number of donkeys in the Middle East, they do not need any more additions to their numbers!

In the Biblical narrative of the Ten Commandments in Exodus 20, we are told that God gave them to Moses on Mount Sinai. In **The Quran**, surah 7:171, as well as in 5:60, we are told that actually Mount Sinai was a "covering" over the heads of the Israelites in Sinai!?

The contradiction of science is glaringly obvious in surah 18:86. We are told that Alexander the Great discovered that the setting of the sun was in a muddy spring! The superstitious and the illiterates, in the days of Muhammad, would believe such a story. But to claim it as a revelation from God is nonsense.

The worst problem is abrogation or annulment. When Muslims encounter Quranic contradictions, they resolve them by claiming the doctrine of Nasikh and Mansukh. That means the verses, which are supposedly revealed chronologically later than the others, annul the previous ones—surah 2:106. We wonder, why would Allah abrogate "or cause to be forgotten" certain verses, if **The Quran** is an unchanging eternal book? In explaining the Jihad doctrine, one is astounded and mystified when he learns that one solitary verse, in surah 9, verse 5, annuls 124 verses which originally encourage tolerance.

"Then, when the sacred months have passed, slay the idolaters wherever ye find them, and take them (captive), and besiege them, and prepare for them each ambush. But if they repent and establish worship and pay the poor-due, then leave their way free. Lo! Allah is Forgiving, Merciful."

Such a doctrine is unacceptable and foreign to an all-wise God. God is presented in this context as an ignorant God who dictates wrong commands and latter corrects them because they do not work. We must ask a logical, not a theological question. If this doctrine is from God, how come we still have all the recognized abrogated verses in the Quran?

The fickle faith of Islam is seen in the direction of the daily prayers of Muslims. When Muhammad began his campaign, to win over the people of Mecca, he taught that the physical direction of their prayers (Qibla) should be directed to the Kaabah. Angered by their rejection of him as a prophet, and having fled to Medina, he now changed his direction (Qibla) towards Jerusalem. Seventeen months later, Allah changed his mind again. Now the command was to again pray toward Mecca, and no longer toward Jerusalem. This writer has asked Muslim friends if Allah had two **Qurans,** which could explain the doctrine of abrogation.

Surah 6:34 announces, ". . .*There is none that can alter the words of Allah.*"

Upon careful research into the life of Muhammad, one has to conclude that the so-called messages from heaven through Gabriel were originating from his vast imagination to justify his political and moral conduct. Wives added, territories annexed, battles fought and wholesale executions were inflicted under the pretext of Allah's revelation through the angel Gabriel.

E. Major ethical problems

Women are inferior to men according to surah 2:228 (also 24:31).

". . .*And women shall have rights similar to the rights against them . . .but men have a degree over them.*"

Anyone who visits a mosque on Friday prayers will also notice that men sit in the front, boys behind them and if women are allowed, then they must sit behind everyone else. Churches in the Middle East have been so influenced by Islamic culture that only recently have they allowed men to sit on one side while women sit on the other. At least equality is demonstrated because they are side by side of the aisle. What about the veil in some Muslim countries? It is another method to curb the social and political power of half the human race in Islam.

In inheritance a woman's share is half that of a man's. Surah 4:11 proclaims, *"To the male a portion equal to the portion of two females . . . ."*

In a court of law, the witness of two women equals the witness of one man. (surah 2:282) *". . .and if there are not two men, then a man and two women such as you chose for witness . . . ."*

A wife can be beaten by her husband according to surah 4:34. *". . . As for those from whom ye fear rebellion, admonish them and banish them to beds apart, and scourge them . . . ."*

The worst indication of women's inferiority in Islam, as a major ethical problem, is seen in surah 4:3. *"And if ye fear that ye will not deal fairly by the orphans, marry of the women, who seem good to you, two or three or fo*ur . . . ." In other words, marriage for a woman becomes actually sex on demand by her husband. Women are sex objects on earth and in Paradise. (Surah 2:223) Turkey and Tunisia do not allow polygyny (The practice of having more wives than one at the same time). Egypt, however, passed a new law in 1985 allowing men to marry up to four wives. The same country recorded 1,208 marriages with four wives, 9,000 with three and 12,000 with two in the year 1995.

Have you heard of the humiliating practice of clitoridectomy? This barbaric practice erroneously called female circumcision, removes a young girl's clitoris and frequently the inner and outer labia. The most terrible psychological outcome is that the girl grows up to be docile and submissive because her mother is usually the one who sanctions the assault on the girl's physical integrity. Furthermore, when the girl's source of pleasure in her intimate relation with her future husband has been eradicated, her spirit will be broken forever.

Muhammad was given a slave by the name of Zayd, by his first wife, Khadijah, as a wedding gift. Although Muhammad instructed Muslims to treat slaves kindly, Muslims were not under any obligation to release them. In surah 4:36 this idea is expounded upon. In 1453, when the Turks finally captured Constantinople, they enslaved 50,000 Byzantines according to Iben Waraqa's book, Why I am Not a Muslim, page 231. History provides evidence that when the Christian nations of Europe were trying to suppress slavery, Muslims were its greatest supporters and were involved in slave trade. Arab Muslims captured blacks in Africa and sold them as slaves to Europeans.

The Dictionary of Islam notes that Thomas Patrick believes that Islam and slavery go hand in hand, while Christianity abhors it. Thanks to President Lincoln, who freed the slaves in 1865, the Christian principles won over the practice of slavery. Although only 25 percent of Southerners owned slaves at that time, still it was a black page in America's history as a Christian nation.

Thirty-two years earlier the British parliament passed the Abolition Act on July 26, 1833, freeing 700,000 slaves in the West Indies colonies alone. Seven years later England outlawed slavery throughout the British Empire.

Even in the 21ˢᵗ century, Sudan, Senegal and Mauritania, along with Saudi Arabia, still practice slavery. Christian Solidarity, besides encouraging persecuted Christians throughout the world, has redeemed more than 20,000 slaves in the years 1995-2003, in the Sudan alone. These people were mainly black Christians who were captured by Muslim militia.

Perhaps the most far-reaching and terrible ethical problem in Islam is the idea of Jihad. What can any individual in the twenty-first century understand from reading surah 4:84, *"So fight (O Muhammad) in the way of Allah . . . and urge on the believers . . . ."* or surah 4, verse 74, *"Let those fight in the way of Allah who sell the life of this world for the other, whoso fighteth in the way of Allah, be he slain or be he victorious, on him We shall bestow a vast reward?"*

F.   In defense of **The Quran**

Lest the reader thinks that the writer is totally negative about Islam and **The Quran**, let it be recorded here and now that it is not quite so.

1. Muhammad unified the Arabic language of the various tribes into the clearest and most eloquent of the day. It is believed that the Quraish Arabic was the most classical in Arabia during the seventh century. It was articulate, eloquent and contained an enormous amount of vocabulary. Imagine that 1400 years later the Quraish Arabic survives in **The Quran**. Despite the fact of its archaic and difficult vocabulary, Arabic authors, poets and orators consult it for accuracy of their classical speech every day.

2. Muhammad proclaimed the oneness of God to a pagan world around him and preached it forcefully. Although there are many links to Biblical tradition in that concept of monotheism, according to Christian theology, many theologians agree that it was a tremendous improvement over the paganism of that day.

3. Historians have been enormously mystified at the ability of Muhammad to solidify the Arab tribes into such a fighting machine as to motivate Muslim's armies to conquer most of the world within one hundred years after his death. However, to be very clear on this point, when one studies carefully the doctrine of Jihad, that tremendous sweep in warfare and colonization becomes clearly no mystery at all. Holy war over infidels is the secret of their success, neither the beauty of the Quranic Arabic nor the new doctrines of Muhammad.

In reality **The Quran** is a book of sermons by a preacher of the seventh century Arabia who used his poetic messages to ignite a revolution and bring reform to the backward and pagan people of Arabia. But the motivation is purely selfish, because he wanted to be the emperor of Arabia and used the so-called revelations to promote his ideology and fulfill his dreams within a mere twenty-three year epoch.

G. Early advances of Islam by the sword—623-732

1. The incentives of plunder and conquest were powerful enough to excite the Bedouins to follow

Muhammad in his early raiding parties and eventually in conquering the world. Of course, the attraction of 50 percent of the spoils of the war for the warrior was too much for anybody to disregard. In addition, the "Jizyah" tribute which was exacted from the conquered people, who had to pay as high as 29 percent of their annual income to keep their religious faith, was a remarkable ploy to help Islam multiply rapidly. How is that? Most people at that time in history could not afford the tax, so they became Muslims. Although Muslim authorities called this tax protection tribute, it really was unfair to make non-Muslims pay it while at the same time having to live as second-class citizens.

2. The desert, the camel and the horse gave Muslims a great advantage over their opponents. The sure-footed Arabian horse, whose flaring nostrils can take in large quantities of air, was a grand fighting machine. The one-humped camel, which can drink twenty-five gallons of water in ten minutes and survive for days on a diet of thorny bushes and dried grass, was used for endurance. The camel's nickname in Arabic is "the ship of the desert!" The camel's two-toed soft feet served the same purpose as balloon tires on a dune buggy and can run faster than any other animal on the desert sands. Then the newly invented camel saddle allowed the warrior to fight from atop the camel with greater agility.

3. The expectation of religious merit through Jihad was extremely alluring. To fight for Muhammad with earthly rewards and eternal promises was the greatest thing that had ever happened to Arabia's backward

people in the history of the world. Now it is the discovery of oil in the twentieth century.

4. The spiritual vacuum which was created by a lukewarm Christianity, lack of missionary zeal and zero interest in evangelism paved the way for Islam to multiply rapidly.

5. No one can deny that with 360 local idols the people were confused and tired of too many gods, rules and regulations. To worship one god simplified Muhammad's religion and presented his teachings as imaginative, logical and attractive to a backward, illiterate and simple people.

H. Later advances of Islam

1. The frequently repeated statement that "Islam is the fastest growing religion in the world" is both factual and fallacious. Statistically, Christianity is the fastest-growing religion, but one can easily determine that the major reason for the growth of Islam now is mainly biological. Children born into a Muslim family are automatically Muslims. They have no choice whether in childhood or adulthood. Islam becomes a prison with no exit. It is not difficult to recognize that when a Muslim man is allowed four wives, and when Muslims, by and large, have convinced themselves that the blessing of Allah is in having many children, five or more per family, one realizes why the growth. Furthermore, converts to Christianity far outnumber converts to Islam every year. Africa's population in 1900 had only 4 ½ percent Christians. A hundred years later it was 46

percent! Yet Africa boasts more Muslim countries than any other continent.

2. Besides the population explosion in Muslim countries, the oil riches, particularly since the 1950's, have been used to build mosques, Muslim centers and propagate Islam in every imaginable way. It is the conviction of this writer, that without the oil the Arab world would have still languished behind the civilized world by at least a hundred years.

3. Throughout the poorer countries of the world, Muslims are welcomed and people are turning to Islam because it guarantees financial aid from petro-dollars for the country itself and individuals who espouse Islam.

In countries like Egypt with only 10 percent of the population of seventy million claiming Christianity, tens of thousands change their Christian names to Muslim names in order to procure job opportunities because of religious discrimination. Although the approximately fifty thousand who do that annually are considered converts to Islam, the fact is most of them never go to a mosque, pray to Allah or read **The Quran**. At heart they are still loyal Christians. Historically, it is a fact that about 50 percent of the population of Egypt was Christian before Islam conquered Egypt! Additionally, some Western business people who are eager to do business in Saudi Arabia turn to Islam as a form of persuasion to forge partnership with Muslim business people because of the nature of laws and regulations.

4. The fanatical desire to conquer the world is another serious point for the advances of Islam. In 732 A.D. Charles Martel, at the Battle of Tours in France, stopped the one hundred year march of Islamic armies. Thirteen hundred years later Muslims once again are attempting to conquer the world through terrorism and intimidation and the velvet glove of immigration. A number of evangelical scholars began calling London, at the beginning of the twenty-first century, the "European capital of Islam." I remember very clearly that while visiting London in 1985, Muslims were declaring, "If we can take London for Islam, we can take the world." It is no longer just some Middle Eastern countries becoming Islamic republics, like Iran, Sudan, Libya and Somalia, but also Nigeria and Pakistan, as well as other countries, who are enforcing the Islamic Sharia. It seems that hardly a week passes by without the media telling us of some Islamic terrorist group blowing up buildings, kidnapping people or terrorizing innocent civilians with suicide or car bombings.

"And slay them wherever ye catch them, and turn them out from where they have turned you out; for persecution and oppression are worse than slaughter; but fight them not at the Sacred Mosque, unless they (first) fight you there; but if they fight you, slay them. Such is the reward of those who suppress faith. (surah 2:191)

"And fight them on until there is no more persecution or oppression, and the religion becomes Allah's. . ." (surah 2:193)

5. Unfortunately, Christians, particularly in the southern part of the U.S.A. have given a cause to the African-Americans to join Islam because of discrimination and prejudice. Although the race relations have improved considerably in the past fifty years, still the memories of injustices and the today's practice of some prejudice in various forms pushes the blacks toward Islam. This tragic state of affairs is markedly obvious on Sunday morning when black and white Christians attend their own churches, with few integrated congregations. Southern white Christians believe that many blacks prefer to worship with all-black congregations. Of course, this is a cultural problem more than a Biblical problem, because Messiah Jesus made it very clear, "My house is a house of prayer to all peoples." True Christianity has no room for any kind of prejudice whatsoever.

6. Due to the fact that a large number of Muslims have been immigrating to America and Europe from around the world, the numbers of Muslims have increased in the U.S.A. In other words, the continuous increase of Muslims in the world, especially in the U.S. and Europe is not due to native-born citizens turning to Islam, but to immigration and biological growth.

7. It has been mentioned throughout the book that in America between eight to ten thousand American women each year marry Muslim men. Whether they like it or not, they are considered Muslims and for certain their children will automatically be Muslims, thus inflating the number of Muslims in America. Yet, research has revealed that the number of

Muslims is falling throughout the world because of the advance of the Gospel and the turning of multitudes of Muslims to Messiah Jesus. According to an Al-Jazeera T.V. news program on 12/12/2000, sixteen-thousand Muslims, in Africa alone, leave Islam every day. The report added that throughout the world nearly six million Muslins leave Islam annually to join the Christian faith! Millions of born-again believers in Messiah Jesus are convinced that He is the Hope of the world's people who seek salvation, security and spirituality, as well as the Hope of Muslims for time and eternity.

There was never a time in history where evil was substituted for good, warfare considered peace, hatred accepted as love, pillage as virtue, except in the law of Satan, the lawless one and his vile followers.

Virtue has its messengers. Evil too has its messengers. Each of the messengers produces his own ideologies. It is unlikely that virtue and vileness are equated in the balance. Consequently, there is no comparison between the godly and the ungodly. (The True Furqan "The Conspirators" 39:10-11)

IV

WHO ARE THE BLACK MUSLIMS

A. Early Islam in America

efore we delve into the subject matter of this chapter, it is of great significance to mention the following facts. First, the popularized opinion today, that the majority of the African slaves who were brought to America were Muslims, is erroneous. It is believed that perhaps 20 percent or less was such, and that was between the eighteenth to the nineteenth centuries. George W. Braswell, Jr. states in **Islam Its Prophet, Peoples, Politics and Power**, published by Broadman & Holman Publishers, Nashville, TN: 1996, on page 210, that most of the slaves who were brought at that time were converted to Christianity.

Secondly, Islam in America has grown mainly among the black population—2 million in the last twenty-five years. The various reasons for the growth in the Western countries generally and America specifically will be discussed later in great detail.

Thirdly, it is an increasingly intriguing phenomenon that the white population has not responded positively to Islam in any significant numbers, except among white women who wed Muslim men.

Historically, several Muslims came to the United States to help introduce camels into the Southwest in the 1850's. When the project failed, Hajj Ali stayed and became a prospector in California. The first known convert to Islam was Alexander Russel Webb, who in 1887 encountered Islam in the Philippines while he served as a Consul and became a Muslim. Furthermore, Syrian and Lebanese immigrants started migrating to the United States in 1875 when the Ottoman Empire was beginning to crumble.

According to Haddad's "A Century of Islam in America," published in the "Muslim World Today," 1986, there have been four waves of immigration by Muslims. The first happened before World War I. The second wave came after World War I, primarily from countries in the Middle East. They settled in Detroit and Dearborn, Michigan, because they could work in the automobile factories where extensive knowledge of English was not required. This immigration was halted by World War II. The third wave began after that war and lasted until the mid-sixty's. Again, most of them came from the Middle East, but for the first time a good number immigrated from Eastern Europe. The fourth wave began in 1967, when President Lyndon Johnson introduced new liberal immigration laws, never before entertained by the most populated Christian nation in the world.

Moreover, developing Muslim countries, because of the newly-developed oil wealth, began to send their youth to American colleges and universities for higher education and better training. It is estimated that there were over one hundred thousand Muslim students in the United States among the immigrant population in the 1960's. The latest figures for the year 2000 indicate that foreign students number as high as seven hundred fifty thousand, with at least 20 percent being from Muslim nations.

B. Black Islam is an American phenomenon

1. Timothy Drew

Born in rural North Carolina in 1866, Timothy Drew, who changed his name to Noble Drew Ali, founded the Moorish Science Temple of America in 1913 in Newark, New Jersey. Apparently, he traveled much in the Middle East and was given the name Ali when he visited Mecca. Upon his return he became a street-corner preacher in Newark. Drew taught that blacks were not of Ethiopian origin, but Arab Moors, with Islam as their original religion. He claimed that they were descendants of the Moabites of Canaan with their ancestral homeland being Morocco. Additionally, he stated that the blacks were free before the American Revolution and that the Continental Congress put them into slavery. He asked President Woodrow Wilson to return their red Moorish flag, which he claimed had flown in Independence Hall and had been kept there since 1776.

Somehow, the movement grew and Drew opened temples in Detroit, Chicago, Harlem, and Pittsburg. It is believed that by the time of his death there were nearly thirty thousand followers. The name "Moorish Temple of Science" was changed in 1928 to "The Moorish Science Temple of America," as if it made any difference culturally or religiously! Gordon Melton mentions that Drew published **The Holy Quran** in 1927, which is a sixty-page document of Moorish Scientist beliefs. (Religious Leaders of America, Detroit: Gale Research, Inc., 1991, page 138)

It is mystifying, indeed, to note that Drew Ali taught that his followers were to honor all the divine prophets, especially Jesus, Muhammad, Buddha and Confucius. Upon his death the movement split into several factions. Friday is their regular congregational gathering for worship, and much like any other Muslims, they pray five times a day, facing Mecca.

2. Ahmadiyya

It is surprising to discover that the history of the Black Muslims in America includes the Ahmadiyya community of North America, which was begun by Dr. Mufti Muhammad Sadaq in 1921. By 1940, membership in this group approached ten thousand. However, the Muslim World League considers this Ahmadiyya world movement apostate because the Ahmadiyya group claims that Qadiani, their founder, is a prophet like Muhammad, and declares that Jihad is un-Islamic. They aggressively seek converts and have their own version of **The Holy Quran**. They claim that there are five-thousand followers in America as of the mid-ninety's.

3. Ansaru Allah

Another group began with Isa Muhammad in 1970, with headquarters in Brooklyn, NY, who named it "Ansaru Allah," which means in Arabic, "supporters of Allah." Although he retired in 1988, he came out of retirement to write an intriguing book, **360 Questions to ask the Orthodox Sunni Muslims**. His pseudonym, as the writer, is Rev. Dwight York. He sent this author one of the first copies of the book as a gift. The group was very impressed with our book, **Islam Revealed**, ordered 500 copies and marketed them in New York subways. In his book, York interrogated the Sunnis, especially those of Saudi Arabia, as to the falsehood and hypocrisy of their faith and practice.

4. The Nubian Islamic Hebrews

In 1970, a Sudanese named Muhammad Ahmad Ibn Abdullah founded, in New York City, the "Nubian Islamic Hebrews." He claimed to be the expected successor of the prophet Muhammad. The American Nubians considered themselves Hebrews with a theology that is a mixture of Jewish, Christian and Muslim beliefs.

5. The Hanafis

In 1958, Hamas Abdul Khaalis founded the Hanafi movement, which adhered to the basic tenets of Sunni Islam. The movement was based in Washington, D.C. Tragically, five members of his family, along with two others of his followers, were murdered by five members of the Nation of Islam in 1973. Five years later, his group attempted to stop the screening of the movie, "Muhammad, Messenger of God," in Washington, D.C. They seized the District Building, the Islamic Center, and the B'nai B'rith buildings in Washington, D.C. Only one hostage was killed out of the one hundred who were found in the buildings and the crisis was over in two days. Eventually, Khaalis was sentenced to a prison term of twenty-one to one hundred twenty years and the Hanifis came into disrepute and disintegration.

6. Islamic Party of North America

The Islamic Party of North America was begun in 1972 in Washington, D.C. The group's stated purpose is to propagate Islam through commitment and study.

7. United Submitters International

Rashad Khalifa was born in Egypt in 1935 and immigrated to the United States in 1959. He earned a doctorate in Bio-chemistry at the University of California at Riverside. He published a wonderful translation of **The Quran** into English, which rivals any other English translation. However, Mr. Khalifa got into serious trouble with militant Muslims because he published a revolutionary book, **The Miracle of the Quran**. It promoted a mysterious Quranic code using the number nineteen as Allah's guarantee of the authenticity of **The Quran**. The worldwide Islamic excitement faded like the falling of autumn leaves when   Rashad's claims of scientific computer analysis was found to be groundless. The so-called scientific proof of the **Quran's** divine inspiration turned out to be a hoax. Furthermore, he tantalized his readers and followers with the claim that he could tell the end of the world, identifying some Quranic verses as satanic in origin, and included an all out assault on the Arab Muslims for idolatry because they follow **The Hadith** and the **Sunna**.

Even Mr. Deedat, of South Africa, my opponent in the international world-class debates, produced a booklet and a video to expound on that theory. When this author confronted Deedat at the National Exhibition Centre, Birmingham, England in 1988, he retracted and withdrew the booklet and the video from the marketplace. To the Muslims, the worst blasphemy Khalifah committed was his claim that he was Allah's messenger in the line of Abraham and Muhammad. The reader is urged to find more information in **Mission to America** by Yvonne Y. Haddad and James Smith, Gainesville: University Press of Florida, 1993. On January 31, 1990, Khalifah was stabbed to death in the Tucson, Arizona mosque where he had presided for eleven years. The murder was never solved. His followers call themselves "United Submitters International."

C. The Nation of Islam and Elijah Muhammad

On the streets of Detroit, on July 1930, Farrad Muhammad appeared selling silk. Some believe that he was of Arabic background, and claimed to be the supreme leader of the universe. Farrad taught that God was black and the black race was the superior race, while the white man was the devil incarnate. The movement was called "The Lost-Found Nation of Islam." As the movement grew the name was changed to "The Nation of Islam." Some reports indicate that he was jailed in Detroit on moral accusations in 1932, then again in Chicago, and because of a power struggle he disappeared without a trace.

Only one month after Farrad began his movement in Detroit, Elijah Muhammad met him and began to follow his teachings. His original name was Elijah Poole and he was born in Georgia in 1907. His move to Detroit in 1923 was to find a job in the factories. He established a temple in 1932 in Chicago, which he made his headquarters. Because Elijah Muhammad claimed that Farrad had appeared and disappeared mysteriously, he proclaimed that Farrad was the incarnation of Allah. Therefore, Elijah became the messenger of this new prophet of Allah, Farrad Muhammad. With the deification, Farrad's birthday was declared as an annual holiday and called "The Savior's Day Convention."

Elijah built his Nation of Islam on Farrad's teachings that humanity was originally black, their religion was Islam and they had founded Mecca. A special tribe of blacks was created, called Shabazz, which became the ancestor of the Negroes in America. Six thousand six hundred years ago, the god was called Yacoub, and being black, he created a new race of white people, who actually were a race of devils. The white race was made the world's rulers. In his own time God was to appear, destroy the white race and restore the black race to its rightful position of leadership. Subsequently, God appeared as the man, Farrad Muhammad. During the civil rights movement of the 1950's, the Nation of Islam grew in numbers among the uneducated African Americans and various institutions were established. The headquarters remain in Chicago and the number of mosques and their members vary, according to who is giving the estimates.

D. Malcolm X and his journey of discovery

On May 19, 1925, Malcolm Little was born in Omaha, NE, into a black Baptist minister's family. The Ku Klux Klan harassed his family and very likely was responsible for burning his home when he was four. When he became an orphan at thirteen, he traveled to Boston to live with his sister. In 1942 he moved to Harlem where he got mixed up with drugs and other vile activities. He moved back to Boston, and because he was caught burglarizing homes, he served six years in prison. Somehow, while at Norfolk Prison Colony he became a Muslim in 1948. Once released from prison in 1952 he traveled to Detroit where he found work and changed his name to Malcolm X. His first opportunity was to be assistant minister at Temple No. 1 in Detroit during the summer of 1953. Elijah Muhammad spotted his capabilities and appointed him minister of the prestigious Harlem Temple No. 7 in June, 1954. He became instrumental in establishing temples in Boston, Philadelphia, Atlanta and Los Angeles. Malcolm founded the weekly newspaper, *Muhammad Speaks*, in 1957. He married Betty X in 1958, and they had four daughters.

Despite the fact that the press called Malcolm X "the angriest negro in America" in 1950, he was to experience much change. As a loyal and devoted follower of Elijah Muhammad, he proclaimed that Elijah was a prophet. The following were the main points of what the Nation of Islam believed, and it appeared in the weekly newspaper *Muhammad Speaks*:

1. One God—Allah

2. **The Quran** and the scriptures of all the prophets of God

3. The truth of the Bible, though it is now corrupted, must be reinterpreted

4. Allah's prophets and their scriptures

5. Mental resurrection

6. Judgment, which will take place first in America

7. Immediate separation of Negroes and white Americans

8. Justice, whether under God or not (respect U.S. laws)

9. Integration is hypocritical and deceptive

10. Muslims should not fight, especially for the United States

11. Muslim women should be respected and protected as others

12. Allah appeared in the Person of Master W. Farrad Muhammad in July 1930

13. Farrad was the Christian Messiah and the Muslim Mahdi

In addition to their above declaration, the following list of demands was printed:

1. Freedom
2. Justice
3. Equality of opportunity
4. Separate state/territory
5. Release of all Muslims from prisons
6. An end to brutality and mob attacks against Negroes in the U.S.
7. Equal employment opportunities
8. Tax exemption for Negroes

9. Equal education (separate schools for boys to age sixteen and for girls to age eighteen, with girls guaranteed a college education)
10. No race mixing

An ideology of racial superiority and separatism was mixed with Islamic terminology and practice. The white race, because of its association with Christianity, is considered evil because whites enslaved the black race. Although the white slave traders were assisted by black Africans, who sold their brethren into slavery, this is a fact rarely admitted by militant blacks. The emphasis on hygiene and moral standards are very positive. Moreover, the Nation of Islam encouraged its members to open businesses and trade with each other. Some farm land and apartment buildings were also bought in Georgia, Florida and other states.

Malcolm was a handsome, tall, red-haired and light-skinned black man who enjoyed speaking to the masses. However, when in 1963 Elijah named him the national minister of the organization, tensions began to rise. The power struggle was among other leaders as well as between Elijah's family and Malcolm himself. When the weekly *Muhammad Speaks* paper started giving him less press and decreased the promotion of his rallies, Malcolm visited Elijah's son, Wallace to discuss the problem. Having heard for years of Elijah's affairs with women, and even his adultery, Malcolm chose not to believe any of it. But Wallace did, and became estranged from his father as a result of the moral code of his father.

When two former secretaries implicated Elijah Muhammad in paternity suits, Malcolm counseled the young women in a very compassionate manner and learned from them that Elijah feared him, considering him a dangerous threat. When Malcolm faced Elijah with the charges of the women, Elijah claimed that what happened to King David, Lot and his daughters, in **The Bible**, had happened to him. Malcolm became at odds with Elijah because of the above-mentioned matters and because he did not obey Elijah's specific instructions of not commenting on President Kennedy's assassination. Malcolm's statement that "the assassination was a case of the chickens coming home to roost" was the final straw for Elijah, who suspended him from all his duties. Consequently, Malcolm's world, which revolved around Elijah Muhammad, came crashing down with speed and fury.

Therefore, in early 1964 Malcolm left the Nation of Islam and formed the Muslim Mosque, Inc. When he traveled to the Middle East, visiting Muslim people, and making the pilgrimage to Mecca, he changed his name to El-Hajj Malik El Shabazz. Upon returning to America he began speaking of the brotherhood of the races—that the white man is a product of racist society, but not inherently evil. He even criticized the moderate approach of Martin Luther King. Late that year he formed the organization of Afro-American Unity. He believed that blacks of all faiths should unite and then black and white coalition can take place.

Some believe that Malcolm X was a true revolutionary, but the Nation of Islam, in their weekly newspaper *Muhammad Speaks* called him a hypocrite, traitor, cowardly and the chief hypocrite of all hypocrites. In other issues of the same paper, Elijah was called by extraordinary titles such as "the word of God made flesh and blood, the Elijah of Malachi and the Jesus of Saint John."

Malcolm experienced numerous threats on his life and family. An official at Temple No. 7 in Harlem was ordered to kill him. The man refused and instead joined Malcolm and his movement. Malcolm's home was fire-bombed on February 14, 1965. A week later, while he was addressing nearly four hundred members of the Afro-American Unity in Harlem, on February 21, 1965, three assassins murdered him in a gruesome and grotesque plot. They were all former members of the Nation of Islam. His autobiography was turned into a motion picture. The true motives for his murder were never established at their trial.

However, this writer believes wholeheartedly that, first of all, Malcolm X was killed when he began to turn to Christ, because he became disenchanted with the false doctrines of Islam. Secondly, he was murdered because of his grave disappointment in the infidelity and depravity of his hero, Elijah Muhammad. A third reason for his murder was the extreme jealousy that developed between him and Louis Farrakhan.

It was rumored that Louis Farrakhan declared, in one of his speeches, that anyone who denounced Elijah Muhammad, like Malcolm had done, should be shot. The widow of Malcolm X, now called Mrs. Malik El Shabazz, expressed her conviction that Louis Farrakhan was the cause of her husband's murder, even to the extent of attempting to kill him in retaliation. Eventually Farrakhan sought and found reconciliation with the widow to unify his followers.

E. Louis Farrakhan—control of the Black Muslims

Louis Farrakhan was named by Elijah Muhammad as the national representative after Malcolm X's murder. Farrakhan also became the minister of the prestigious Temple No. 7 in Harlem. The man was born in Guyana, South America, and grew up in a godly Presbyterian family. His mother immigrated with him to America and he demonstrated musical skills, which eventually made him a successful calypso singer and an accomplished violinist. It is very ironic to note that Malcolm X himself mentored Farakhan.

Elijah Muhammad died on February 25, 1975, after ruling over the Nation of Islam for forty-one years. The Muslim world did not give him any recognition, but condemned him, considering his movement as a grotesque heresy. Many believe that the so-called teachings and practices of Islam were just a cover-up for his racial ideology. His son, Wallace Deen Muhammad, was to be the new leader, who must overcome a legacy of deception, corruption and financial chaos. Records show that at the death of Elijah, the Nation of Islam had acquired huge holdings in Michigan, Alabama and Georgia and was worth seventy-five million dollars—it was a financial empire for sure!

Louis and Wallace Deen worked together for a while as Wallace attempted to change the nation and bring it in line with world-wide orthodox Islam. By late 1976, the name was changed to "World Community of Islam in the

West." The financial situation was becoming very dubious. Major financial surgeries were necessary. Therefore, old businesses were sold, and temple ministers were placed on a fixed monthly salary. Astonishingly enough, Wallace was able to save the financial state of the Nation of Islam from total collapse by these measures.

In 1978, Farrakhan left the WCIW to rebuild the former Nation of Islam upon the teachings of Elijah Muhammad. In the same year the titles of the ministers were changed to Imams (as regular Muslims call their mosques' leaders) and the Council of Imams was formed. He also changed the fasting month from December to the mainstream of Muslim's lunar month of Ramadan. Temples were renamed mosques, and chairs were removed so that members sat on the covered floors. Furthermore, Arabic was used for prayer and the entire group became more in line with Islamic theology and practice. "The Fruit of Islam," which was basically a security-functioning group, was disbanded, and Farrakhan waved an American flag in the services for the first time in 1977.

By the early 1980's, Wallace had Americanized the movement whereby the children in the mosque's schools recited the pledge to the American flag each day. Their main newspaper became known as *World Muslim News* and then changed to *American Muslim Journal*. It is interesting to note that many leadership problems erupted because of the numerous changes of titles, names, practices and celebrations. Wallace changed his name also in 1980 to Warith, which in Arabic means "inheritor." He acquired the names of Imam and President. He even equated himself with Jesus, which

Louis Farrakhan imitated in his sermons. Warith thought of himself as combining the best of his father, Elijah, and Martin Luther King.

Mr. Farrakhan later claimed to be the leader of an American Islamic group known as the Black Muslims. The calypso singer actually dreamed of becoming God. His movement poses a real threat to America domestically because of constant criticism of national and international policies. The group is also a threat internationally, because it is becoming a subversive force on American soil. Black Muslims create discord among the races constantly. February 18, 2002, while watching television in Nashville, TN, this writer came across a program in which Farrakhan was the guest speaker in some church. It was hard to believe that he announced, *"You ask me about Muhammad? The name in Arabic means 'praised one.' Jesus is the praised one, of course. So Muhammad is Jesus and Jesus is Muhammad."*

Unfortunately, the illiterates, the uninformed and the alienated in Black America seem to believe such misleading pronouncements as fact by this most powerful African-American leader.

Farrakhan was seen as fomenting trouble within the organization. So Warith attacked Farrakhan in one of his speeches as coming to the organization for money, good homes and friendship with people in high places. The final break came when the money which was collected by Elijah Muhammad over the years was to be given to his estate or the organization. Elijah did not leave a will. Therefore, the inheritance laws gave the children, who were born outside of legal marriage, as much right as the legitimate children from the inheritance of the estate. The American Muslim Mission (AMM), as an organization, was brought to court and millions of dollars were awarded to illegitimate family members of the deceased leader.

At the AMM national convention, held in Georgia, with twelve thousand in attendance, Warith set the stage for the disintegration of the AMM and called the members simply as Muslims. In 1985, the movement was officially integrated into the general Muslim community in the United States. Warith moved to California and began to speak and lecture at universities, churches and synagogues. Surprisingly enough, on February 5, 1992, he addressed military leaders at the Pentagon and gave the invocation the next day on the floor of the U. S. Senate.

Farrakhan was convinced that he was supposed to succeed his mentors, Elijah Muhammad and Malcolm X, however, Wallace assumed the mantel for the Nation of Islam. In March of 1978, Farrakhan announced plans to rebuild the Nation of Islam in line with the doctrines of the late Elijah Muhammad. Between 1979 and 1983, the friction between Wallace and Farrakhan increased tremendously and Farrakhan in early 1983 had an article in the AMM journal presenting his objections against Wallace and the AMM:

1. Confusion
2. All work in the way of self-independence has ceased
3. The feet that walk after the Law of God are nailed to the acceptance of the sport of this world

4. The movement represents death and that the old Nation of Islam had to die so that Farrakhan could resurrect it
5. There was no honor given to Elijah Muhammad in his own house
6. Elijah Muhammad was relegated to appear as a weak, immoral man, a trickster misrepresenting himself, God and the Truth
7. That Imam Wallace Muhammad hates his father

Farrakhan, therefore, set out to rebuild the Nation of Islam on the foundation of his original mentor, Elijah Muhammad. The newspaper, which began in 1933 by Elijah, *The Final Call*, was resurrected. Now Farrakhan's followers are estimated at one-hundred thousand and he remains a popular speaker among African-Americans, especially students and church goers. There are over eighty mosques associated with Farrakhan with the show-piece mosque being the one in Chicago, which he refurbished as his headquarters. He calls it "Maryam Mosque" after the mother of Jesus.

Farrakhan took the Muslim world by surprise when he appointed Sister Ava Muhammad, a New York attorney, to be a minister in the Nation of Islam, a move that no Muslim had ever dared make. His clean-up campaigns in black neighborhoods and the use of the security guards, Fruit of Islam, to patrol drug-infested areas, has won him high marks. His recent book, **A Torchlight for America**, and his weekly addresses, which are printed in *The Final Call*, depict his teachings.   On February 28, 1994, Farrakhan appeared on the cover of *Time* magazine, which included two cover stories. Some referred to him as "the calypso-singer who would be God."

F. The ramifications of the One-Million Man March on Washington

Louis Farrakhan made a national call for a million black men to assemble in Washington, D.C., October 16, 1995. The announced purpose of the march was to inspire a moral and spiritual rebirth among African-American men. Interestingly enough, Benjamin Chavis, a former N.A.A.C.P. executive director, who was stripped of his title in 1994 for alleged misuse of funds and sexual harassment, became his fellow organizer.

"Whoever will let him come," was stressed by Farrakhan, because he was not asking anyone to march under the banner of Islam. One of his staff members declared that the march was also to gauge Farrakhan's popularity in America. The number of participants was estimated from four hundred thousand to over eight hundred thousand. The platform speakers included Jesse Jackson and Benjamin Chavis. Farrakhan himself spoke for over two hours, asking the marchers to pledge themselves to self reliance and respect for women. He also promised to launch a nation-wide voter registration drive to make African-Americans into a third political power, according to *Time* magazine, October 30, 1995.

The Million Man March was the vision of Louis Farrakhan, who was the chief organizer. He gained major exposure in the mass media with articles featuring his picture in newspapers and magazines. T.V. and radio talk shows interviewed him on their programs. When he was asked as to why he calls Jews "bloodsuckers", he responded by explaining that he was referring to the function of a leech. A leech takes, but it never gives anything to what it takes. He went on to say that in the 40's and 50's some of the merchants who were Jewish owned the tenant buildings, the businesses, the pawn shops and they drew the blood from the black community. Arab merchants, Vietnamese and Koreans replaced them. Such people generally take from the community, but don't give back. He stated that even some blacks do the same. He added that some call him a "nightmare" and others a "dream come true." (*Newsweek*, October 30, 1995, page 36)

Three events in 1995 thrust Farrakhan into the national spot-light. The first was the arrest of Malcolm's daughter, who plotted to kill him because of his role in her father's assassination. The second was the use of the Fruit of Islam to provide security for the attorneys of O. J. Simpson in Los Angeles. The third was the Million Man March.

Despite a serious bout with cancer, Farrakhan is still the most visible leader of the Black Muslims in America. However, Warith Muhammad has gained national and international respectability. He received the Walter Reuther Humanities Award and the Four Freedoms Award. He is considered by the governments of Qatar, Abu Dabi and Saudi Arabia as the only trustee to distribute funds to all Muslim organizations in America and Canada.

G. Muslim organizations in America

There are numerous organizations which seek to meet community needs of Muslims and some voluntary national organizations:
1. The American Muslim Council was formed in June 1990.
2. The Council of the Masaajid operates with offices in New York City promoting cooperation among mosques.
3. The Islamic Society of North America was established in 1982 to meet the needs of Muslim American citizens and students.
4. The Muslim Student Association was established with the aid of Saudi Arabia in 1963 to counter the Arab Student Organization which was supported by Nasser's regime of Egypt. This is the largest and most active group, producing a monthly journal, "Islamic Horizons."
5. The Muslim World League began in Mecca in 1962 and as an international organization has offices in New York City. It distributes Islamic materials and financial assistance to mosques, Muslims and Muslim prisoners.
6. The Federation of Islamic Associations began in 1954 by Lebanese Americans to promote Islam and publishes "Muslim Star."

Inasmuch as the lure of America attracts people from everywhere, especially from the Middle East, many Muslim students settled in America. Consequently, we have the Islamic Medical Association, the Association of

Muslim Social-Scientists and the Association of Muslim Scientists and Engineers.

With the Democratic political system in America and the vast religious freedom provided through the Constitution, not only is Islam growing, but other religions and sects also. Nevertheless, this writer believes that the challenge is before the Christian citizens of America to first live lives of high moral standards, demonstrate love for fellow believers and compassion towards American neighbors, whether natives or immigrants, which can definitely attract others to the Christian faith. Furthermore, it is his personal conviction that since we cannot go to some of the countries which need the Gospel, many people from these same countries are here in America as students and immigrants. The Holy Spirit can lead us to reach them with the Gospel freely and effectively. The hope of the world is not Islam, Communism, Atheism, Socialism, Scientism, or any other religion or ideology—but Messiah Jesus and his Good News. It is not reformation of one's religion or the following of any religion that changes humanity, but it is the inward change of heart and mind which takes place when one confesses his sins, repents and turns his life to Jesus, the Messiah.

H. What attracts people to Islam?

The most accurate records, by the outstanding book, <u>Mission Handbook 2004-2006</u>, published by EMIS, Wheaton, IL, lists that over 900,000 affiliates of other religions become converts to Islam annually. Subsequently, one must ask what is the attraction to an archaic system of laws and by-laws, doctrines and practices which seem attractive to bring in such large numbers?

Islam's theology—many are willing to accept a simple unity of God and brotherhood of man in contradistinction to the complicated ideologies of other religions.

Superiority of Islam as taught by the Quran and Muslims gives a boost to people who join Islam. This appeals to African-Americans tremendously.

Lofty morality is symbolized by the separation of the sexes, pro-life stance, prohibition of drinking liquor and adherence to the Mosaic commandments.

Attributes of God which number ninety-nine give the convert a new concept of this mighty Allah and his many capabilities as the supreme being. Worshipping him five times a day in a simple routine manner is a draw also.

Muslim brotherhood is demonstrated in the mosque as everyone sits on the same level on the carpeted floor. The annual "haj" is where rich and poor dress the same and participate in the same ceremony in Mecca. The fasting during Ramadan makes the convert feel a part of a really great host of sincere and devoted people.

When Time Magazine published a major essay in 2003 on the subject "Should Christians Convert Muslims" two things were not dealt with realistically. First, the question should have been "Should Christians Evangelize Muslims." We do not convert anybody. According to the Bible, the Holy Spirit is charged with that awesome responsibility. The other question should have been "Should Muslims Convert Christians." Surah 15:125 states, ". . .call men to the path of your Lord." Our "Great Commission" is not too different from their aggressive "dawah", which is Arabic for "invitation."

When statistics show that nearly 2 million American Blacks have converted to Islam in twenty-five year or so, these reasons emerge—self-respect, discipline, moral standards, deliverance from drug culture and alcohol, as well as family values and a new identity are the basic reasons for the African-American to join Islam. Others add chastity and modesty, which are emphasized more than in Christianity. Still others feel Christian discrimination forced them to abandon the faith and join Islam.

It is very significant to state that Muslims are increasing at the rate of 2.5 percent a year in America and 85 percent of these are African-Americans. Additionally, up until 2002, 100,000 Muslim immigrants swelled the numbers. However, because of 9/11 that number of immigrants has been drastically reduced. Nevertheless, I must warn every Muslim convert of the damnable destiny that awaits him if he later decides to leave Islam. "Anyone who changes his religion of Islam, kill him." (Al-Bukhari vol. 9, page 45, and Quran 9:11-12)

I. Theoretical questions

Some theoretical questions may help us telescope the outcome of an Islamic-American republic as we observe similar cases in the past few years.

1. What happened to the government of Iran after deposing the Shah of Iran? Neither the citizens of Iran nor the neighbors around the country, not even the distant nations of the world have seen any progress politically, economically or technologically, so far. Some experts on the Iranian affairs have indicated

that less freedom has resulted, instead of more. Greater numbers of people have been in prison or executed than in the days of the Shah. Restrictions of human rights have erupted everywhere. But the worse has been the involvement of the Islamic government in terrorist activities worldwide and the clandestine building of an atomic reactor.

2. The Taliban government of Afghanistan applied strict Islamic law and what happened to the country as a result? The nation plunged into primitive living standards, women were not allowed to go to school or work, television and music were outlawed and freedom of expression and the press disappeared.

3. Although Muhammad is the most common name in the world, can anyone find such a name on any important invention which has benefited the human race over the past hundreds of years? Many Middle Eastern countries have become extremely rich because of petroleum. Yet, they are very poor in providing inventors. They can threaten the world with oil embargos, but where are the inventors.

4. Is it possible that a rich Muslim is so involved in a harem and many concubines that he becomes too exhausted to invent anything? If he is poor, he covets the harem of his neighbor and becomes a victim of self pity over his poor state, with no time left for inventions. Additionally, the fundamentalist and the fanatic dream of killing other infidels and non-Muslims in order to achieve in Paradise what he cannot acquire on earth—seventy-two virgins plus untold riches.

Then we ask what does he do with his time? It is obvious to the peoples of the world, who watch television, hear the news or read the papers, that such a person spends his time inventing new methods of destruction and terrorism.

Therefore, one has to conclude that since the end of World War II the faithful, fanatic and fundamentalist Muslim has contributed two things to the world. The high price of oil is one, while the other is world-wide terror and destruction.

The fourteen year civil war which destroyed the democracy of Lebanon, the disintegration of civil law in Somalia, the ruthless conflicts of several Eastern European countries, Iran's regression to Mullahcracy and the bloody mess in Iraq are a clear demonstration of the above facts.

Some observers are convinced that a majority of militant Muslims seem to live in a tightly-closed shell which does not allow their brains to function rationally or intelligently, for lack of oxygen.

It is fundamentally necessary to emphasize that "Islam" does not mean "peace." That word for peace in Arabic is "Salaam." Islam really means "to make peace by laying down your arms in surrender and submission." In other words, Allah wants humans to become his slaves while Jehovah God, the true living creator God wants humans to become his adopted children by repentance from sin and faith in the sacrificial work of Messiah Jesus on Calvary.

We must be optimistic Christians as to the eventual outcome of the clash of civilizations. Three times as many people join the Christian faith from other religions, including Islam, every year. Whereas 950,000 join Islam, 2,950,000 join Christianity every year since 1991. Furthermore, Christians must learn how to handle Muslim misconceptions about the Trinity of God and Divinity of Jesus by studying Surah 3:55; 4:157; and 19:15.

Muslims are taught that Allah loves only the righteous. (Surah 3:76, 4:107) The Heavenly Father in contrast loves the sinner and is willing to forgive and save all who repent. (II Peter 3:9) The true roadmap to peace" in the world is through Jerusalem's Calvary hill and the cross of Jesus Christ. (Romans 5:1) "We have peace with God through our Lord Jesus Christ." The Jesus film has been viewed by over 3 billion people. The new film, "The Passion of the Christ" has become a historic success since it was released in April 2004 and is having an impact worldwide, even in Muslim countries.

Assuredly, they did crucify Jesus the Messiah, the physical son of Mary, as a physical and real human being, and killed Him for certain as a substitute for sinful humanity

Human spirits are created by us and they eventually return to us. As for the earthly bodies, they are from dust and return to dust except the body of Our Word, the Messiah, who ascended into Heaven and someday shall return. For it is through Him salvation and redemption are offered to the entire world. (The True Furqan "The Crucifixion" 9:10-11)

V.

SEPTEMBER 11ᵀᴴ 2001 AND THE AFTERMATH

A. America's false sense of security

The following excerpt of a longer version, mentioned in chapter seven, should be helpful in elucidating this point.

1. *"America is being invaded, yet Americans do not seem to realize it. What has been taking place over the past three decades in Iraq, Iran, Indonesia, Nigeria, Pakistan, Somalia and Afghanistan should be a clear signal of warning to America. But Americans are too busy following the T.V. show, 'Who wants to be a millionaire', wondering who is the new golf hero, or boxing champion, or football or baseball star and what basketball team will achieve the national championship and curiously enough, who won the lottery lately! In other words, Americans seem unaware of the brewing attack on its way of life."*

The previous paragraph opened up a major press release by the author, prepared only one week before the attack on America, September 11, 2001. An unbelievable coincidence took place when the U.S. postal service issued a stamp to commemorate Islam and recognize Muslims the very same month of September 2001! One wonders why Saudi Arabia, the historical and religious heart of Islam, does not recognize the presence of 900,000 non-Muslims on their soil, by permitting them freedom to worship and to share their faith. Are Muslims fearful because their religious foundation is very shaky historically and theologically?

Consider also the spectacle a few years ago of Iran and Iraq declaring "Jihad" (holy war) on each other which lasted eight years. Untold suffering and the death of one million fellow Muslims finally overwhelmed everyone and they stopped fighting, with no winners. The Iraqi regime called America "The Great Satan" during the short Gulf War of 1991. The Islamic god Allah, however, was no match for "The Great Satan."

2. Muslim countries are not democratic

How many people in the world have ever heard that Afghanistan's Muslim government, on a Sunday morning in 1980, sent bulldozers and completely demolished the recently built international church in Kabul, the capital. In 1999, Afghanistan's militant regime once again demonstrated an intolerant attitude towards culture, archeology, art and history, when they dynamited the historic monuments of Buddha.

Subsequently, a year later the religious police, who like their counterparts, "the mutawe-en" in Saudi Arabia, are above the law, arrested twenty-four western and national Christian aid-workers. The accusation was that some of them "were caught red-handed with **Afghan-language Bibles** and videos of "Jesus of Nazareth." In short, freedom of religion is practiced and available in most Muslim countries only to Muslim citizens! It is obvious that throughout history, democracy and Islam cannot co-exist!

There are over a billion Muslims in the world today! Yet, out of the thirty-nine majority Muslim countries and thirty others with large minorities of Muslims, only Turkey, Jordan and Kuwait have any semblance of democracy! As if that is not obvious, lately the clamor to declare "Sharia," (Islamic law), as the law of the land in Iran, Nigeria, Indonesia, Somalia, Pakistan, etc., demonstrates something that no one is eager to discuss. On the one hand, many of the poorer countries of Africa are wanting the Islamic law because it guarantees them petro-dollar contributions from the Islamic oil-producing countries. On the other hand, there is an astonishing amount of terror which is gripping the Muslim world due to two extraordinary reasons.

3. Reasons for Muslim's Fears

First, Muslims are losing ground theologically, numerically and religiously because of the invasion of the "Truth Revolution." Neither **The Quran** nor Islam can stand the acid test and probing eyes of higher criticism of archeology, philosophy, language, grammar, logic or history. Higher criticism that has been focused on **The Bible** for so long, for the first time in 1400 years, is being focused on **The Quran**. The myth that the "prophet of Arabia" was illiterate, therefore, he could not have written **The Quran** (but God himself did) is now disproved. In **Islam Revealed**, which has been printed eight times by the end of 2002, six reasons for Muhammad's literacy are mentioned on pages 52-53.

The other devastating reason for their fear is the discovery of the Yemenite documents in 1972. Anyone can consult *The Atlantic Monthly* magazine of January, 1999, under the title "What is **The Quran**?" The article details the accidental discovery of caskets full of ancient manuscripts of **The Quran** by laborers during the restoration of the great mosque at Sanaa, the capital. The painstaking and laborious effort of ten years provided 32,000 photos demonstrating irreconcilable differences between the Quranic Arabic manuscripts which were written in the eighth and fourteenth centuries and today's **Quran**. The documents demonstrated clearly that **The Quran** developed over the centuries with numerous adaptations.

Second, the Dead Sea scrolls substantiate Biblical accuracy. However, the 32,000 photographs of the Yemenite documents of the Quran, dating from the eighth to the fourteenth centuries, reveal the fact that **The Quran** has been polluted by changes in its text over the years. Subsequently, scholars can declare very forcefully, that **The Quran** developed over the years and in no way can its text be accepted, as it is now, as the final revelation of God to humanity. In fact, the contents of **The Quran** do not reveal any new information, inspiration, or instructions which had not already been known to the Jews and Christians for hundreds of years.

One still shudders when he remembers the little paradise country of Lebanon and the tragedy of twelve years of civil war. History records the fact that at the conclusion of World War I in 1918, the triumphant governments of the western world decided to help the Arab Christian minority of the Middle East. Therefore, in the ocean of Muslim countries which occupy the entire Middle East, an island was established for the Christian Arabs who had no recognized geographical identity. (As of the year 2000, Arab Christians of all denominations throughout the world number over sixteen million.) To assuage the Muslim potentates and governments who assisted in winning the war against the Axis and the Turkish Empire, the constitution for Lebanon concluded that the President of this new democracy of Lebanon would always be a Christian, but the Prime Minister would be a Muslim. The remarkable success of Lebanon's economy, society, education and democratic system greatly disturbed the fundamental Islamists.

As a result of the six-day war between Israel and its neighbors in which Israel was victorious in 1967, tens of thousands of Palestinians fled into Lebanon, entering it legally and illegally. Because the majority of those refugees were Muslims, within a few years they were able to offset the numerical balance between Muslim and Christian, thus creating a larger Muslim population than the Christian. Although they were refugees, still they demanded a voice in the government. According to the constitution of Lebanon, that was not feasible. Consequently, the onslaught of a twelve-year protracted civil war caused the killing of one hundred forty thousand people, the displacement of a million others, the injury of over half a million more, and resulted in the destruction of Lebanon's infrastructure. When former American President Reagan ordered some marines to be peacekeepers, the same ungodly, violent people had a suicide truck-bomber explode his truck, himself, and two hundred eighty of the American marines as they lay sleeping early Sunday morning in 1986.

The U.S. was more successful in intervening in Bosnia by siding with Muslim rebels and squashing the Christian army. While in New Bern, NC, very recently a teary-eyed Bosnian Christian lady inquired, *"Why did America side with the Muslims?"* This writer explained that America has always supported the weak and down-trodden and felt Muslims were such. So President Clinton's administration sided with the Muslims as a political policy, not a religious disposition.

The peaceful mission to starving Somalis and the horrible treatment American servicemen received in return, once again demonstrated to the world the raw evil of militant Islam. The recent dramatic film of *Black Hawk Down* immortalized the brutal and barbaric event.

As for the whole tragedy in Lebanon, the world opinion backed the Lebanese Christian administration, prompting Israel's Defense Forces to enter Lebanon and force the eviction of the Palestinian Liberation Organization leadership and followers to Morocco. The PLO was the one who spearheaded the entire tragic affair of slaughter, mayhem and destruction of Lebanon for so long. Of course, Syria's military forces were more eager than the Israeli forces to occupy the entire country, subjugate its people, and control the economy of what was the banking center of the Middle East. It will take fifty years for Lebanon to recover its previous glory and overcome the ravages of the nasty civil war.

Is that what militant Palestinian Muslims are trying to do to Israel right now in 2003? It is the only Jewish State in the world with 5,500,000 people out of their 15,000,000 worldwide. Arabs control 98.5 percent of the lands of the Middle East, comprising over 5,000,000 square miles and twenty-two countries! One is bound to wonder why the Arabs of the Middle East refuse to share some of their Middle Eastern hospitality by letting their cousins and half brothers have a mere one-tenth of one percent of their land mass. Is there some sinister demonic spirit roaming in the Arab World, which keeps them from demonstrating mercy, reconciliation and love toward their Jewish relatives?

4. The state of some Muslim countries

What then can the world believe about modern **Saudi Arabia's** administration? They consistently jail

Christian expatriates, torture some, force the expulsion of the white-skinned, but execute the brown and black-skinned workers when they are caught in worship or witnessing to Muslims.

Now an unprecedented class-action suit is being prepared against the government of Saudi Arabia, by the survivors of the attack on America, demanding one trillion dollars because fifteen out of the nineteen hijackers were Saudi citizens.

For the past eleven years the Sudanese militant Islamic administration has terrorized, marginalized, ostracized and slaughtered its own citizens in the southern regions. Many concerned world citizens have been hearing about that lately because of the outcry of organizations which are dedicated to exposing religious, economic, political and cultural persecution. There are authentic documents which demonstrate that over two million people have been killed so far because they are not Muslims, but are Christians and animists. The ancient inhumane practice of slavery is going on right now in Sudan, which is the largest geographical country in Africa. Their administration has vowed to make Sudan the most Islamic country in the world. The reason why we have not been hearing much about Sudan is due to the recent discovery of oil. Western national interest in the oil business keeps critical mouths shut so as not to antagonize the dictators of such despicable, brutal and inhumane regimes in order to keep cheap oil flowing.

5. Who is the creator God?

Many wonder if the "Allah" of **The Quran** is the creator God of **The Bible**. Out of the so-called ninety-nine excellent names for the Muslim "Allah," surprisingly enough, none refers to him as a "Heavenly Father," or "God is love," not even "God is spirit." "Allah" is seldom loved, but always feared. He is called "the proud," (**Quran** 59:23) the "most deceiving," (3:54) the "plotter" (8:30) a "torturer," (9:14) and a "murderer" (8:17). Few Arabic-speaking Muslims comprehend at all the famous words "Allahu Akbar" which they loudly declare when delighted or depressed. They are indoctrinated to believe that the phrase means "god is greater." Consequently, one must ask the question, "greater than what, or whom?" Because Islam grew in the midst of pagan Mecca with three hundred sixty-two idols and goddesses, Muhammad was claiming that his god is "akbar," GREATER than all the others. The word "akbar" in Arabic did not only mean "greater," but was also the name of the moon god!

It is therefore noteworthy that the Muslim house of worship is surmounted by the crescent, the moon god. In contradistinction, the Christian's house of worship is surmounted by the cross, a symbol of God's love. Furthermore, the star surmounts Jewish Synagogues because they were commissioned by Yahweh God to be a light to the nations. The six-pointed star of David, which is also on the flag of Israel, is a reminder that Yahweh created the entire universe in six days! Islam even follows an archaic lunar calendar, not the more accurate solar one. All

Muhammad did was to embellish "akbar" with Biblical characteristics of the Creator God to attract the illiterate Bedouins to his new religion. Whenever anyone researches Islam's development, ceremonial activities, festivals, traditions and beliefs, he will be quite convinced that Islam is the Arab's interpretation of Judaism!

Six million people are involved in the American correctional institutions, out of two hundred eighty-six million population. There are two million supervisors, two million on parole and two million are incarcerated. Tragically enough in the crowded prison system, Muslims are growing in number, faster than any other religious group. Why? Islam is a violent religion and violence attracts violence. Therefore, criminals find an affinity in becoming Muslims. Moreover, upon becoming a Muslim, an inmate is given a new name. When he is released, there will be no record to track down his previous crimes. Additionally, prisoners are told that Muhammad was a black man and an African to attract the African-American inmates, since 75 percent of prisoners are black. Arabs are descendents of Shem, not Ham, thus they are white, not black-skinned. Even **The Hadith** tells, in several stories, how others knew Muhammad was a white man. Furthermore, Arabia is in Asia, not Africa. To add insult to injury, the Arabic word for slave and black is the same, "abd."

6. Questionable Ethical Instructions

What about the matter of beating one's wife, as a divine right sanctioned by Allah to Muslim husbands, according to **Quran** 4:34? Furthermore, not many realize that **The Quran** states in 2:228 that a man is superior to a woman. It is well known that Kuwait's Prince has twenty-nine wives. The original and first king of Saudi Arabia was King Abdul Aziz Al-Saud, who crowned himself king and called Arabia "Saudi Arabia" after his tribe's name, at the end of World War I. The Allies had promised him and other Arab leaders that if they took their side in the First World War, each of them would be recognized as a potentate of a geographical location of his choice. Not surprisingly, the first royal act of the crowned king was a marriage ceremony to 350 women. His offspring today comprise the royal family which is now close to 30,000. They alone enjoy freedom and liberty in the oppressive and regressive society. No one else in the entire country has that freedom. While millions wish to immigrate to America, very few want to go to Arabia to live, only to get a well-paying job.

Read the new incredible book, the first of its kind in 1400 years, which exposes all of these facts and more. Amazon.com lists it as **The True Furqan**, meaning the "true recitation." But the title is automatically intended to affirm that the Quran is actually a false one. Whenever one reads **The True Furqan** he is intrigued. Another is **Islam Revealed**, an eye opener on the subject. A brand new video entitled "Islam: A Threat or a Challenge" is a must-see, produced by the Anis Shorrosh Evangelistic Association.

When any intelligent individual contrasts **The Bible** with **The Quran** he is truly overwhelmed by the Biblical plagiarism. How can the One True Living God send humanity two books which claim to be His revelation and yet contradict each other? God is not a God of confusion, but of order. Is it at all possible that He sent us His greatest and most up-to-date revelation called **The Quran** in the most difficult language, out of 12,000, rather than the easiest language? If Allah is the same God as the Jewish and Christian God, why would He order the killing of His human beings, as Muslims have done over the centuries, led by their poet, general and prophet Muhammad? If any particular religious group does not practice worshiping Him exactly like other God-worshipers, He will judge them, not the Sword of Islam.

While in New Zealand in 1995 this writer heard the rumor, from a cell of Muslim converts from Iran, that:

"If the government of Iran would allow the same freedom of religion as in the West, fifty percent or more of the Iranian people would turn to Christ overnight."

Furthermore, in 1999-2001 over five hundred Muslims in Israel alone were converted to Christ and followed through with baptism. Approximately a thousand did the same during the following twelve months, according to a retired missionary who served among the Arab Muslims in Israel for thirty-seven years. Entire villages in Africa and the Middle East are discovering that Islam's human right's record disqualifies Islam from surviving as a viable twenty-first century religion and are turning to Christianity.

It is not at all shocking to learn that fear from reprisals keeps most Muslims from coming to Christ. Islam is the only religion which instructs the followers in **The Hadith** 9:50, by divine right, to kill a family member, friend or relative, if the new convert does not recant in sixty days. So one must wonder why is "Allah" always angry and hungry for blood like the ancient pagan deities. Why do Muslim militants demonstrate brutal and outrageous violence throughout the world? Abu Sayyaf's group operates in the Philippines. Hamas terrorizes Israeli and Palestinians alike. Osama Bin Laden, the most wanted terrorist in the world, has operatives in over sixty countries. Hizb Allah is supported by Iran's militant regime and is dedicated to the destruction of anyone or any country which disagrees with their agenda. Millions are convinced that fanatic, fundamental Islam, if not checked soon, will soon precipitate World War III.

Prophetically **The Bible** declares again and again that the portion of land, call it Palestine, Israel, Land of Canaan, or whatever, was given by God to Abraham and his descendants. (Genesis 17:8; Isaiah 11:11-12; Jeremiah 32:37; Zechariah 8:7-8) If we can convince the Israeli Jews and the Palestinian Arabs of this fact, that both are descendants of Abraham and are to inherit the land and should co-exist, maybe we can stop the bloodletting and exchange understanding for hate and forgiveness for bitterness. If indeed, the Arab Muslims (there are sixteen million Arab Christians who have no quarrel with Israel) decide to declare a Holy War against Israel, the consequences would be catastrophic. The conflict can become an atomic war because Israel has two atomic reactors and approximately four hundred atomic and hydrogen weapons ready to use in self defense. To pray for the peace of Jerusalem is a Biblical instruction. Yet, one must also consider praying for the fall of Islam which has brought to humanity more problems than blessings throughout its 1400 year history. And today, because of the tragedies of September 11, 2001, in New York, Washington, Pennsylvania, as well as throughout the world, we must tirelessly and earnestly labor in convincing the human race into rejecting Islam as a viable religion for the 21st century. Thereafter, we must turn to the Prince of Peace, who proclaimed,

"If the Son has made you free you are free indeed." (John 8:36) "This is my commandment that you love one another." (John 15:17) "It has been said of old love your neighbor and hate your enemy. But I say unto you, love your enemies, bless them who curse you and pray for them who abuse you!" (Matthew 5:44)

B. Seven causes for the Attack on America on 9/11/2001

The following seven points are the result of observation, analysis and probing research into the mindset of militant Muslims and terrorists:

1. The attack was fundamentally retaliation and reaction against the extraordinary success of the Christian "Jihad" for the heart and soul of Muslims. Whereas

Muslims historically have spread their religion by the "Iron Sword," Christians, by and large, have spread their faith by the Sword of the Spirit. Hospitals, schools, colleges, clinics, agricultural programs, correspondent courses, videos, radio, T.V. programs and faithful missionaries have spread the Gospel throughout the world so effectively that Muslims were losing out on the battle for the minds. To stop or hinder these efforts by terror and intimidation was the only choice left for Muslims to fight back.

2. Fear of modernity, democracy and scientific progress, caused millions of Muslims to long for the simplicity of the ancient days of Muhammad and revert to the culture of the Middle Ages! The well-known statement "Clash of Cultures" is a fact of life all over the world.

3. "Losing face" is one of the most powerful cultural quirks in the world of the Middle East. The Arab world has been extremely embarrassed because tiny Israel has prevailed against them in their wars of fifty-four years. Therefore, they want to show the world that they can fight, even if not in a conventional warfare.

4. Envy of America's success and progress economically, politically, scientifically and militarily causes a sense of jealousy. Muslim governments are corrupt and their culture is backward so they lash out at America.

5. "The Great Satan" idea is due to the fact that Hollywood has degraded women, pornography has polluted the airwaves through videos, the internet and magazines, abortion in western society has relegated human life to lower than animals, and greed controls America's economy. Militant Muslims think that to

destroy such corrupt, sensual, selfish culture would be best for humanity.

6. Personally, this 70-year old author is convinced beyond any doubt that the Attack on America, September 11, 2001, is also "an emergency call from God." The most powerful nation on the planet and the most Christianized country in the world has gotten away from its Biblical and Christian foundation and must return to its spiritual roots to survive.

7. The goal of Islamists, militants and fundamentalists is to conquer the world for Islam. Therefore, if America, the richest, youngest, most powerful nation, can be won to Islam the rest of the world will follow suit. The Doctrine of Dar Al-Harb (the House of War) and Dar Al-Salaam (the House of Peace) is engrained in Islamic history. Muslims are instructed to fight any country that is non-Muslim whenever they become strong enough militarily, in order to bring it under Allah and **The Quran**.

C. Who was involved in the demonic and diabolical terrorist plot?

1. Al-Qaeda, led by Osama Bin Laden, was established by the militant Saudi millionaire with headquarters, first in Yemen, then in Sudan and finally in Afghanistan. It is estimated that the operatives, numbering 50,000 are scattered in at least sixty countries. Their goal is to destabilize the governments of moderate Islamic countries and every western nation.

2. The beginning of this phenomenon in our modern times began with Sayyid Qutb, an Egyptian, who is called by Islamists the "Martin Luther" of the modern

Jihad movement. His book **Signs Along the Road** became the heartbeat of the radical Islamic movements of today. Qutb became the philosopher and spiritual leader of today's Islamic terrorist groups. **(Islam and Terrorism**, Mark A. Gabriel, PhD, p. 113-118, Charisma House 2002)

3. The philosophy of Mr. Qutb is followed to the letter by Osama Bin Laden and all other Muslim terrorist groups:

Demolish all governments and organizations that are established by man. Eliminate human racism that exalts one over the other. The return of God's kingdom can only be established by a movement of power and the sword. (Ibid, page 119)

4. The individuals and groups who are terrorizing people, governments, institutions, airlines and societies around the world come from varied nationalities, but have a common denominator of allegiance to the Doctrine of Islamic Jihad and the goal of taking over the world for Islam.

5. Although fifteen out of the nineteen hijackers of 9/11 were citizens of Saudi Arabia, the United States government took a conciliatory attitude toward Saudi Arabia because we want cheap oil to continue flowing to America. Forty-one percent of American's oil comes from the Middle East.

The war against international terrorism is different from any previous war in history. It is a religious war, despite the denials by the media and western governments. The capabilities of the terrorist groups are limited because of technological advances which can track their communication systems, freeze their financial assets, and thwart their physical movements. In short, these organizations and individuals are being decimated and destroyed very successfully, and the entire world is sick of such brutal and outrageous activities on its citizens in this global village of the 21st century. The unified voices of the majority of the 6 billion people of the 219 nations are proclaiming much like Mr. Reagan, the former president of the United States, declared, *"You can run but you cannot hide."* Winning the war on terrorism is assured, although it may take longer than the six-day war in the Middle East of 1967, or the Gulf War with Iraq of 1991, or the Afghanistan conflict of 2001-2002. Victory over terrorism is grounded in the fact that mankind desires to live in peace and will do whatever is necessary to achieve that. Most people agree with what President George W. Bush proclaimed in his address to the American people after the attack of 9/11:

> *"We will not waver*
> *We will not tire*
> *We will not fail*
> *Peace and freedom will prevail."*

D. The political invasion of America by Muslims

As to the political, so far, Muslims have succeeded in having one of the Imams open the Congress in prayer and another Imam do the same in the Senate. The F.B.I. found one of them aiding terrorists recently, but he fled the country. The ambassador of Saudi Arabia has time and again appeared on television, trumpeted on radio and the printed news as the Arabian prince-charming. He doles out sums of money to individuals and organizations throughout the U.S. to paint a positive picture of Saudi Arabia, a ruthless dictatorship.

It is ironic that out of the nineteen murderers, hijackers or suicide bombers of 9/11 fifteen were Saudi Arabian citizens! It does not seem to penetrate the brains of some of our political leaders that Saudi Arabia is no friend of America, but a cunning and cantankerous enemy of the United States. How come not many remember their catastrophic oil embargo of 1973?

One of the most obvious points of view is how Abdel Waleed, a grandson of the first king of Arabia, Abid el Aziz Al Saud, offered the mayor of New York soon after Black Tuesday ten million dollars to help with the recovery of the attack on the Twin Towers. Abdel Waleed was turned down because he inferred that America's favorable foreign policy towards Israel was one major cause for the attack on America by the fanatic Muslims.

Afterwards Abdel Waleed went back to his desolate sand-swept country and spearheaded a telethon to help the "suffering families of the Palestinian suicide bombers" to the tune of one hundred eighty-six million dollars. If that is not a slap in the face of America, what would you call it? Furthermore, the amount he offered Mr. Guiliani (the mayor of New York at that time and now a global hero) to express compassion for the families of the victims was a drop in the bucket. First of all, the benevolent prince owns "kingdom holdings," with estimated value of fourteen billion dollars! Yet, that is not the point of contention with this Saudi Arabian playboy billionaire. It is the fact that the nearly three thousand victims involved in the attack on America were innocents, whereas the suicide bombers were murderers of the innocents. It does not take a rocket scientist to see through this facial mask of religiosity, false compassion and crocodile tears.

Remember, please, there were far more casualties because of the attack on 9/11 than with the Palestinians in the three years of their uprising, in which they initiated the attack on Israel's innocent citizens and military forces. Furthermore, the defensive Prince Charming, the Saudi Arabian Ambassador, told the world on international T.V. that the telethon was to provide desperately needed funds for the families of the suicide bombers because their bread winners had died. Does this talking-head think that Americans are really that stupid? Out of the nearly 165 Palestinian suicide bombers, three were crazy females who caused their families to forever lose the joy of having grandchildren. Then we have only a dozen who were married. The others were single, brain-washed men between fourteen and thirty-four years of age. Why no Christian bombers?

Tragically, as of October 2003, more than 800 Israelis and nearly 2,500 Palestinians have lost their lives in the uprising. Can we not say that the Telethon was supporting terrorism just as much as Saddam Hussein's so-called "compensation" of $25,000 to each family of the suicide bombers? Many remember the delightful movie *The Thief of Baghdad*. My nickname for Saddam is "The Butcher of Baghdad."

As of 2002 there are 5,750,000 Muslims in America. They have been able to use some of their eloquent, influential and wealthy leaders to penetrate the White

House. It began with former President and Mrs. Clinton and continues during President George W. Bush's administration also. Muslim leaders are entertained and serenaded at the White House time and again, while the Christian Arabs in America, who number over two million, are totally ignored. Why? Arab Muslims control much of the "black gold." Money talks and oil politics has clout.

It is alarming, to say the least, that Muslims in America, who are mainly immigrants and not native-born, have managed to become the number one ethnic minority in the history of the United States, whose voting record supercedes every other group! Inasmuch as we are a pure democracy, it will be somewhere between ten to twenty years (if they keep growing as they are biologically and politically),that they will elect Senators and Congressmen of their own choosing to go to Washington and very likely greatly influence who sits in the Oval Office.

The clock is ticking away. Remember, that of all the destructive things that could happen to America is for a future American president to credit his election victory to Muslim's block-voting. Never forget that no Muslim country, in the seventy-nine nations which claim either a majority or a large minority of Muslim populations, is a democratic government at all, with the exception of Turkey. What would become of America, democracy, freedom, human rights, your family and mine, your children and mine, your grandchildren and mine? Somehow, people forget that the Dark Ages began with the Muslim hordes fighting the nations of the world for the first one hundred years of Islam. Then, they subjugated them for one thousand more years. Have we forgotten that they burned the greatest library in the world at that time in Alexandria, Egypt, and destroyed houses of worship by the thousands in the march to North Africa, Spain, Portugal, France, Austria, Albania, India and China? Even the Holy Sepulcher Church in Jerusalem was not spared in the 1200's. Finally, history cannot give us a positive hope if America buckles under the terror, religion and political system of Islam.

Even in the sleepy three-hundred year old marvelous city of Mobile, AL, whose international involvements are quite limited, the influence of political correctness is obvious. Numerous articles, which were saved for posterity, extol the virtues of Islam and in fact one major presentation going beyond the normal was given by the religion editor that promotes Islam rather than explain it. Our press releases which were sent to the paper in response to the barrage of articles did not even get a response, much less get printed in the paper. Did Muslims buy the paper?

Despite the previous twenty-year plan, the points are brief and several ideas must be added. When the U.S.A. removed some restrictions, which were placed on the rules and regulations of immigration to America, the Muslims were the first to take advantage of that. Since 1961, Muslim immigrants have come from every Muslim country to America. They seek greater freedom than they find in their own countries, educational opportunities as well as a greater economical improvement of their status. Yet the overriding purpose, as one observes, since 1961, is to increase the number of Muslims in America by intermarriage and by having as many babies as possible, since they cannot conquer it militarily!

In a survey of American-born women who have chosen Islam, conducted by Carol L. Anway and released under the title, **Daughters of Another Path**, published by Lee's Summit, MO: Yawna Publications, 1996, one can learn much of the ramifications of the subject. Although Carol admits that, of three hundred-fifty surveyed women, only fifty-three responded, or 15 percent. To me that poor response proves that the interest is minimal in answering such strategic questions as to why they became Muslim. Be that as it may, the majority turned to Islam from Christian backgrounds through fellow college students who influenced them or husbands who more or less pressured them to become Muslims for a more peaceful existence in the home. A sizeable number lost total communication with their own parents. Yet, Carol admits that she could detect that the fifty three who answered her questions were mainly the ones who thought of Islam as a positive move and made a difference in their lives. Consequently, one has to conclude from logic, if nothing else, that the largest number of those whom she sought must have had some trepidation and negative response to Islam.

The reader should be interested in discovering the religious identity of the fifty-three people who responded. Actually, this survey should be totally disregarded because there is no scientific method in the world that will accept a 15 percent response to a survey as valid to make any type of judgment, conclusion or determination of facts. Here are the interesting backgrounds:

Atheist-2, Baptists (Southern)-5, Christian-2, Christians with no denominational identification-14, Catholics-12, Greek Orthodox-2, Holy Rollers-1, Episcopal-2, Jehovah

Witnesses-2, Latter Day Saints-2, Lutheran-1, Methodists-2, Presbyterian-1, Seventh Day Adventist-1, World-Wide Church of God-1.

An outrageous thing is how quickly the media grabs any flimsy proof that Islam is growing in America by leaps and bounds. The oft repeated statement that "Islam is the fastest growing religion in America" is unsubstantiated. There has never been a complete statistical proof of this claim. Just like the above mentioned paragraphs denote the very weak foundation on which Carol Amway built her fractured structure of "American women turning to Islam," so is the statement that "Islam is the fastest growing religion in America and the world." One more point is necessary and it is the fact that Christians become Christians by conviction whereas people become Muslims by and large through being born into a Muslim family, by marrying a Muslim, or accepting Islam as a religion of convenience.

At any rate, this writer was approached by the President of the American and Canadian Student Islamic Association at the University of Kansas concerning a positive debate with Dr. Badawi. At that specific time, in 1990, most were unaware that he was the leading voice for Islam and Muslims in North America. The Egyptian national had earned a PhD in economics and was teaching that subject at St. Mary's Catholic University in Halifax, Nova Scotia, Canada. He later related that he had prepared one hundred-fifty radio and television programs promoting Islam entitled, "Islam in Focus." He was the best in the world, not just in North America, and was found to be articulate, suave, intelligent, personable, cunning and unfortunately, very deceptive. Incidentally, our informative website is www.islam-in-focus.com.

During the weekend the first topic covered was "**The Quran**: Word of God or Muhammad's." It eventually caused an uproar with Muslims, even as far away as South Africa, because the title of the debate had never been discussed publicly in 1400 years. A year later it was learned that Dr. Badawi was chased out of a lecture hall in South Africa because fanatic Muslims were upset with him for suggesting such a subject when he debated me. It is amusing, if not amazing, that the writer's victorious result at that debate culminated in the Muslim's change of the title of the debate on their videos from "**The Quran**: Word of God or Muhammad's" to "**The Quran**: Word of God or Man's." However, it was too late because the poster behind the podium is obvious on the videotape.

The second outcome was the refusal of the president of the American-Canadian-student association to send us a fresh copy of the video when ours became worn out, declaring they could not find a copy! However, a credible copy was found in England, which had been taken on a previous journey, and it was reproduced in an acceptable fashion.

Not surprisingly, the worst outcome was experienced by this writer in 1990 during his first visit to South Africa. The assassination plot was hatched in Capetown because the Muslims had viewed the tape of the debate "**The Quran**: Word of God or Muhammad's" and felt that I had insulted their prophet and their **Quran**. God intervened by sending 31-year old Chris Thaver to throw his muscular body over me when the dagger flashed. It did not penetrate his skull. Praise God! Yet, his gushing blood covered me. Miraculously, both of us survived. So far, as of June 2004, I have counted eleven attempts on my life. Can anyone, after these facts, be persuaded that "Islam is a peaceful religion?" The video of that unforgettable and horrible evening was secretly sent to me six months later by one of Mr. Deedat's staff. Originally a copy was sent to Durban, South Africa. The video encouraged the youth and adults to shoot me when I would come to their town three days later. The intercessory prayers of God's people preserved my life that scary evening in August of 1990.

They even fabricated lies declaring that We have hoodwinked Our worshipers formidably, devoured them fiercely, taken revenge on them forcefully, put them down flamboyantly, victimized them frequently, put them to utter shame fatefully, decimated them fanatically, made a joke out of them festively, destroyed them fully, tormented them frantically, cursed them factually and planned for them a terrible punishment finally.

Far be it from Us ever to punish Our worshipers without first giving them an opportunity to repent. The charlatans have fabricated such proclamations as Our Own instructions. Such is but the designs of Satan, the rejected one, in whose inner being poisons of blasphemy boil continuously. Therefore, he deceptively and ingeniously enunciated such declarations through the mouths of his devotees. In turn, they spewed them out into the ears of their adherents. Wherefore the adherents turned away from the

True Path angrily. (The True Furqan "The Illiterates" 40:9-10)

VI

AL QAEDA'S HISTORY AND GOALS

s early as ten years before the Attack on America, King Hussein of Jordan warned our American officials of Osama Bin Laden's dangerous network. ("Time", November 26, 2001, p. 21) The Saudi terrorist, whose millions were used to support growing Islamic militant terror organizations, began to organize a massive force scattered around the globe to do his bidding. Al Qaeda means in Arabic, "the headquarters." Because of 9/11 and other terrorist attacks, before and after that tragic date, everybody now knows about Al Qaeda.

A. Osama Bin Laden

During the Russian invasion of Afghanistan, the young Osama was recruited to fight with the Mujahadeen against the Russian invaders by the CIA. Once the victory was won through America's military support with weapons and training, Osama went back to his own country, Saudi Arabia. However, because of his extremism and seeming terrorist inclinations, the government stripped him of his citizenship, and he fled to

Sudan. Osama recruited Muslim fanatics from different countries to train them for terrorist activities. When the United States initiated a move against Al Qaeda and Bin Laden, he fled to his ancestral home, Yemen. From there he went on to Somalia and finally built his organization in war-torn Afghanistan. His terrorism and their extremism were a perfect marriage.

The three basic motivations for Bin Laden's anger and ruthless attitude toward the West were these:

1. His fury against America and American interests stems from its stalwart support of Israel. It was his conviction that the land of Palestine belongs to the Arabs and the Israelis are foreigners from Europe occupying the land. Osama believed that Israel does not have any right to have control of the Islamic Dome of the Rock and the Aqsa Mosque in the ancient walled city of Jerusalem. Furthermore, to him and other Islamic militants, they should not bargain with it, and it must be destroyed. The Oslo Peace Process or any peace process to achieve co-existence between Israel and its neighbors is unacceptable to him. Osama disregarded Israel's legitimacy by the U.N. organization. America supports Israel politically at the United Nations and elsewhere. It is abhorrent to him that eight hundred forty million dollars in economic aid is given to Israel annually, plus three billion more is given in military support. To the majority of Arabs, Israel is an oppressor of Arab's rights. Because Israel uses American fighter planes and weapons to control the Palestinian population, America is also guilty by association.

2. The presence of U.S. troops in his former country of Saudi Arabia, from the build-up in 1990 which led to the Gulf War in 1991, was a major concern. Of course, he overlooks the fact that Saddam Hussein's invasion of Kuwait precipitated the presence of the troops to evict the Iraqi invaders from Kuwait. One must not forget that the U.S. servicemen, numbering 10,000, were there at the invitation of the Saudi Arabian government. Not surprisingly, he and many Arab nationals strongly believe that the Saudi royals are not only corrupt but also are stooges of the U.S. It is ironic that many Americans are convinced that the American foreign policy is always favorable toward the Saudi government, because we deeply desire to keep the oil flowing cheaply, thus the role is reversed!

3. There is a strong belief, especially from the days of Ayatallah Khomeini, that America is the "Great Satan." Osama propagated that idea more than any other militant Muslim in modern history. Worse than that is the conviction by him and his followers, which are estimated at up to fifty thousand in over fifty countries of the world, that America is an infidel country which must be conquered. Any student of that Quranic doctrine will realize that the Holy War idea (Jihad) is fundamentally what placed Islam on the horizon of history, and it has never been revoked. Although most Muslims try to live at peace with their neighbors, the fact remains that the verses which urge Muslims to participate in "Jihad" have never been revoked. (surah 9:29; 4:74, 84; 5:33) In other words, Islam is supposed to take over the world, if not by teaching and preaching, then by force. ("Time", October 1, 2001, p. 45-46)

Some of you will say: "not so fast." What about the declaration of Jesus in Matthew 10:34, "Do not think that I came to bring peace on earth. I did not come to bring peace but a sword?" This is actually a classic sample of taking a quotation out of context. Once one reads the rest of the passage, then the discovery is made that Jesus was expounding the eventuality of the clash between right and wrong, righteousness and evil. They are opposite and cannot exist in one's life.

The other outstanding passage is ,
". . .But now. . .he who has no sword, let him sell his garment and buy one. So they said, 'Lord, look, here are two swords'. And He said to them; 'It is enough.'" (Luke 22:36,38)

Let it be emphasized first and foremost that there is not a single verse where Messiah Jesus, the Apostle Paul, or the Apostle Peter gave any instructions to the Christians of that century to promote their faith by force. It is to the eternal glory of the Christian communities of the world that the followers of Jesus have been willing to die for their faith in promoting it, rather than kill to win converts. Lately, many articles have been written to express utter shock at the discovery that in the last 100 years alone, as many as fifty million Christians have given their lives for their faith throughout the world. Somehow, we are reminded, in one way or another, every single year of the horrors of the Holocaust of the Nazi's. Can anyone ever imagine that such an incredible number of believers sacrificed their lives for Messiah Jesus?

Moreover, the tragedy of the Crusades has been a whipping boy by Muslims and non-Muslims alike. Yet, historically, it was never a truly Christian Jihad. It was actually an attempt by the European Christian countries to take back the Holy Land from the Muslims. Although they marched through many countries, the Crusaders never subjugated them, nor ruled them. Furthermore, it lasted less than 200 years, whereas the Muslim Jihad continues unabated for 1400 years now.

Thirdly, whereas Christian leaders from throughout the world began a journey of reconciliation, which took twelve months that started from the first geographical location of the Crusades all the way to Jerusalem. Along the way they stopped at each village and city and expressed sorrow for what happened because of the Crusades and publicly asked forgiveness from the town's leadership and people in the public square. Have the Muslims ever expressed such an attitude of reconciliation and love to the peoples they conquered?

It is necessary to underscore the fact that the peaceful purpose for Jesus' coming is recognized by what he said to Peter, when Peter struck the ear of Malchus, the captain of the temple guard of Jerusalem,

> *But Jesus said to him, 'Put your sword in its place, for all who take the sword will perish by the sword. Or do you think that I cannot now pray to My Father, and He will provide Me with more than twelve legions of angels?* (Matthew 26:52-53)

Osama Bin Laden found a very fertile ground for his type of terrorism in Afghanistan, and through his wealth and militant Arab Muslim fighters recruited from the backward Arab countries, he was able to forge a powerful coalition with the Taliban. Taliban means "students." After the eviction of the Russian forces, the Taliban movement emerged as the powerful force in Afghanistan's leadership. Basically, it started as a student movement to bring in fresh ideas and revival of Islam. The initial activities were very commendable in a land that has experienced the horrors and ravages of wars for twenty years. Whether it was Bin Laden's system of Islam which turned the Taliban into oppressors of their own people, or the Mullahs of Afghanistan is not very clear. Be that as it may, the world began to hear from the few reporters who could get into the country, that many schools were closed, women's rights were taken away, television sets and music were forbidden. Rules of worship, dress codes and who was allowed to attend schools were enforced upon the people.

It is important to mention that Ayman Al-Zawahiri, an Egyptian physician, became the closest ally and adviser to Ben Laden. The Taliban supreme leader, Mullah Omar, became Ben Laden's closest friend. Al-Zawahiri is considered the mastermind behind the assassination of President Anwar Sadat of Egypt along with Shiekh Abd El Rahman, the blind Egyptian cleric. The doctor spent three years in prison and after his release decided that it was safer to do terrorism from outside his native land of Egypt. However, not many have ever heard of Bin Laden's deputy, Mohammed Atef, the reputed architect of the September 11 attacks. ("Time", November 26, 2001, p. 42)

Many experts of the war in Afghanistan believe that Atef was killed in the Tora Bora region near Jalalabad when the American forces plastered that area with bombing raids. The devastation of that area by high-flying B-52's and Maverick laser-guided missiles and 5,000-lb. bunker busters may have buried Osama and Ayman as well. Mullah Omar's whereabouts are unknown, maybe he is dead too.

Although the terrorists of Al Qaeda may be using advanced technology and modern weaponry, their ideology is bankrupt and will, for certain, bring about their demise. Very few people on planet earth want to go back in time to the culture of Muhammadanism of seventh century Arabia. It is not practical in most countries of the twenty-first century to practice the way of life which characterized the Bedouins of fourteen hundred years ago. Civilization moves forward—not backward. We believe that just as the Taliban's rule failed miserably in persuading the people of Afghanistan to live that way, so eventually the Iranian rulers will experience the same thing. Progress is a part and parcel of human history. The advancement in every field of endeavor is sought by any thinking individual, whether he lives in the East or the West. The dawn of the twenty-first century is providing us with an amazing march towards democracy and the heart-felt desire to eliminate despots, autocrats and especially dictatorships. Citizens of the world want to breathe freely and America is dedicated to helping any nation achieve this worthy dream at a great cost to American lives and our pocketbooks.

Therefore, it would seem that in spite of the catastrophic damage that we have already experienced, because of the Osama Bin Laden's, Iranian clerics, and Jihadists, their strategies and terrorism will not conquer us. This whole chapter of modern warfare which follows an out-of-date world view and an archaic philosophy of life will soon pass away with a whimper, if not with a bang.

B. Moderate Islamic governments targeted

If the current conflict between Islamists and the West is called a "clash of cultures" and a "clash of civilization," one wonders what the clash of Islamists with moderate Islamic governments should be called. Could we call it a "clash of Quranic interpretation" or a "clash of militancy against moderation in Islam?"

It is popular among Islamists to declare that Muslim terrorists do not represent Islam at its purer sense and Islam is a peaceful religion. Then when they are confronted with the practices of Islamic governments such as Saudi Arabia, Pakistan, Algiers, Iran, Syria, Somalia and Indonesia, etc., they quickly offer a disclaimer. One will have to ask, what then is an authentic Muslim country? It is truly distressing that in every country in the world, which has proclaimed itself an Islamic republic or nation, the ethnic minorities and non-Muslim citizens suffer ruthless persecution, very harsh oppression in unbelievable ways and human rights are disregarded.

Every few weeks one is dismayed at attacks by Muslim terrorists from the Sunni branch against the Shiites, as it happened in Karachi, Pakistan, February 22, 2003. In the same country, at the end of the previous year, hand grenades were thrown at worshipers in a Christian church in Islamabad. The horrible news, which we heard from Yemen on December 30, 2002, of the attack at a

Christian hospital in Jibla confirms that militant Muslims are oppressors. A terrible and tragic killing of four American civilians and the mutilation of the bodies April 1, 2004, was gruesome in Fallujah. One of the victims was hung on a bridge over the Euphrates River which demonstrates the continuing atrocities, whether in war-torn Iraq or peaceful Yemen.

Saudi Arabia continues to arrest and torture Muslim converts to Christianity. It executes some publicly by the sword, if they are men, but shoots them if they are women. In Nigeria hardly any month passes by without atrocities inflicted upon Christians in the largest black country in the world. On the opposite side of Africa, Sudan is still involved in a civil war of twelve years with two million known dead already, both Christians and animists.

One must wonder who will ever please the Islamic terrorists as true Islamic government leaders. It seems that the terrorists want to destabilize the moderate Islamic governments, such as Egypt, Jordan and Morocco, to install their own brand of militant Islam. It is doubtful that they will succeed in their efforts, because more and more of the citizens of these Muslim countries are resolved through information and education to elect their own governments by the people and for the people. The steady march towards democracy may be slowed down, but it will never be halted.

Iran has been under the Islamic religious clerics since 1979 and the country has fared worse than in the days of the Shah. There is a cry among the people which is getting louder and louder, demanding that the Mullahs return to their mosques and leave the government to the civilians. Iran is a case in point, of the ultimate terror when religion and politics are one and the same. Islamic history reveals that such marriage was practiced in the past. However, in the 21st century such ideology is neither practical nor desirable. With the advances in science, technology, industry, transportation and space exploration, the archaic and ancient Islamic philosophy of life is no longer attractive to the masses now as it was 1400 years ago!

When anyone probes the larger picture of the countries of the world, it does not take him long to realize that the democratic rule is the most plausible political system invented by man. It is not the most perfect but the best at this time in history. America, as the bastion of freedom, has demonstrated to the world that religion and politics can be separate, but not separated. The majority of the U.S. citizens belong to churches and other houses of worship. In America there are eighty-six million evangelicals, sixty million Catholics, six million Jews and as many Muslims. But that does not mean they cannot participate in the political process of the nation. As a matter of fact, most of those involved in the political leadership claim a religious conviction and practice their faith in their daily lives.

The major difficulty which Islam is facing right now is "how to separate religion from politics." At one time in history, the Christian faith struggled with the same. Briefly, the popes of Rome held as much authority as a king or an emperor. But that apparition has been relegated to history for a long time. For many centuries now, most of the Christian countries of the world are playing a different tune.

The determined march to democracy by the nations of the world is unstoppable. The dynamic freedoms Americans enjoy are the envy of the world. With much physical, political and even bloody struggle many countries, especially after WWII, have achieved freedom from fear, want, speech and religion. Confidently we can say that the days of the dictators are numbered. We do not wish to see the people of the world looking at our system longingly. But we want to help them achieve their dreams and visions of liberated societies and stable governments "of the people, by the people and for the people," as the great Abraham Lincoln declared.

Moderate Islamic governments should be encouraged by the United States to pursue stability and progress with America's support. It is commendable that such governments have joined the U.S.A. in its war on terror with manpower, exchange of intelligence and opening their airports and seaports for American forces to utilize in their efforts against terrorists. Egypt enjoys 2.7 billion dollars of aid annually for its 68 million people. The U.S. views President Mubarak as a moderate and astute leader in the most populated Arab country in the world. His regime, although authoritarian, plays an important role in the stability of the region.

Jordan and its King Abdullah II is another such country which receives 543 million dollars of aid a year. Of course, the significance of Jordan stems from its geographical proximity to Israel and its good relationship with most of its neighbors. It is very reassuring to note that the government of Jordan does not allow unlicensed sermons in the mosque. Jordanian authorities were able to arrest three Al Qaeda terrorists a few days before September 11, 2001, through an intercepted phone call. That arrest thwarted the bombing of two resort hotels in Jordan. In October 2 of the same year, Jordanian agents uncovered another plot to blow up the U.S., British and Jordanian embassies in Beirut. ("Time", October 1, 2001, p. 45) Not long after the assassination of Mr. Foley, the U.S. consular in Amman, the terrorists were arrested and brought to justice.

C. The U.S. a mortal enemy of the Islamists and Jihadists

For many years, America enjoyed a lofty status of integrity, honesty, opportunity and progress in the eyes of the world's people. The political system is envied by a great host of nations. In a short two hundred years of existence, America emerged as the super power of the world with every reason to support that position.

Surprisingly enough, the thought by some people that other countries hate America is not a true statement, nor does it represent the populace of any given country. As far as this writer is concerned, who has been to seventy-nine nations of the world, the greatest proof is the continued immigration of tens of thousands of people every month to American shores. How many of my readers have ever heard of anybody wanting to immigrate to Sudan, Somalia, Iraq, Algiers, Saudi Arabia, Pakistan, Indonesia, etc. etc. etc. No way! Peoples of the world dream and strive to immigrate to America, the land of the free and the home of the brave.

Islamists and Jihadists are envious of our system of government, industrial complex, educational system, military power, vast resources and technological advances. Hardly any Muslim country is as self-sufficient as the United States of America. Our dependence on Middle Eastern oil is decreasing daily.

As I have attempted to explain, in various ways throughout this book, America is the mortal enemy of Islamists, because we stand for freedom. Whereas every Muslim country continues to dream about this cherished and God-given right, Americans enjoy freedom and its marvelous fruits every day.

It is this writer's firm belief that, neither the U.S. military power, nor the economical success, not even the democratic political system, is the reason for the attack on America by the Islamists and Jihadists. Rather, it is our missionary endeavor, evangelistic zeal and dynamic effort which have been so successful in winning converts to the Christian faith throughout the Muslim world.

For the past several years Islamists have been greatly alarmed because Americans have been able to penetrate centuries of barriers in reaching Muslims with the Gospel. Whether it is hospitals, schools, aid programs, agricultural projects, exchange students, technological projects, T.V. and radio programs, the Western nations generally and America particularly have been in the forefront with voluntary contributions and manpower to win Muslims as they continue to follow the Galilean conqueror. It is apparent to any serious researcher that fanatic Muslims are terribly terrified at our success and attempt to intimidate Christians or totally stop their evangelistic efforts by such ruthless individual assassinations of missionaries, diabolical mass murders by suicide bombers, truck bombs and other terrorist activities in America, Europe, Western Asia and African countries who are American allies.

D. The ultimate goal of Muslims is world supremacy

Actually the average Westerner does not have the foggiest idea about this matter. Additionally, Western government leaders look with arrogance and disdain at such an idea because they think we are too powerful for such an insignificant bunch of holy warriors (50,000). Yet, one can quickly look into the political history of most nations and movements and rediscover that it was always the few who toppled governments, rebelled against authorities and led revolutions. History attests that consistently only a few visionaries or dedicated rebels took over Russia, Turkey, Iran, and Iraq and enforced their ideology upon their people. In 1947, Mao and his few followers were able to evict Chiang Kai-shek, his government and powerful army from China. Fifty million lives was the final price of making China communist controlled. Now, the new Chinese bureaucrats are copying America's economical and political system with extreme success! Hitler comes to mind as far as this historical fact is concerned when he tried to control the world during WWII—at a cost of thirty-two million lives. China did not turn to Communism overnight, neither did Russia, nor did Cuba.

When General Muhammad brandished the scimitar of steel in the year 623, he was determined first to subjugate his Arab tribes to Islam. Thereafter, he had a plan to evict

Christian Arabs and Hebrew Jews from Arabia. His third plan was to invade the other countries and control them whether they came to Islam or not. When people ask this writer, during the numerous seminars on Islam, "How do you explain the phenomenal growth of Islam in the first hundred years?" The answer is very simple and sensational—it is the sword. Again and again, I would like to remind any thinking individual throughout this world of six billion souls that "neither Muhammad's name, nor his fame, not even his religion would have ever made an impact on the world in any form or fashion, if it were not for the iron sword of Islam." **The Quran** is replete with verses supposedly inspired by Allah demanding killing and fighting to promote Islam.

> *Those who believe do battle for the cause of Allah. . . .* (surah 4:76) *O ye who believe! Fight those of the disbelievers who are near to you, and let them find harshness in you, and know that Allah is with those who keep their duty (unto Him).* (surah 9:123)

Whereas Christianity grew by the sword of the Spirit (which is the Word of God), Islam grew by the scimitar of steel. As to the matter of warfare in Christianity, Muslims can point to the unfortunate crusades. However, it was basically a serious effort by Christianized countries to reclaim their lands which the Muslims had colonized, in particular the Holy Land. The Crusades lasted less than two hundred years. But the Muslim Jihad, which began 1400 years ago, has continued to this day.

Furthermore, no one can find a single verse in the New Testament which instructs

Christians to fight non-believers or use the sword to make converts. Yet, nearly one hundred verses in **The Quran** promote Jihad—holy war.

Let everyone be very clear in his mind. The last instructions of Jesus the Messiah expostulate, *"Go therefore into all the world and make disciples. . ."* (Matthew 28:19) In contrast, Muhammad instructs his followers to go fight and kill to make Muslims.

> *Then, when the sacred months have passed, slay the idolaters wherever ye find them, and take them (captive), and besiege them, and prepare for them each ambush. But if they repent and establish worship and pay the poor-due, then leave their way free. Lo! Allah is Forgiving, Merciful. Fight against such of those who have been given the Scripture as believe not in Allah nor the Last Day, and forbid not that which Allah hath forbidden by His messenger, and follow not the Religion of Truth, until they pay the tribute readily, being brought low.* (surah 9:5,29)

Christians, individually and collectively, have apologized publicly and privately for the Crusades. Yet hardly any Muslims, privately or collectively have ever apologized for their Holy Wars against non-Muslims. The media continues to wait for any recognized Muslim leader, in America or anywhere in the Muslim World, to apologize publicly for the horrors of Black Tuesday of 9/11!

The conflict of the twenty-first has many faces. One is between the "haves" and the "have-nots." Another is between the free loving people and the dictators. Still another is between the believers of Christianity and the believers of Islam. As for communism, its memory is fading even as China's 1,200,000,000 are turning to capitalism, consumerism and free enterprise, just as the former Soviet Union did in 1991.

Before this chapter comes to an end, it is necessary to relate that a new breed of Islamic warriors is emerging. "The Wall Street Journal" released a fascinating report by Karby Leggett from Rabat, Morocco, Keith Johnson from Madrid and David Crawford from Berlin, March 29, 2004, page A16. It informed readers that Takfir Wal Hijra ideology, which was launched in Egypt in the 1970's, is using immigration as a weapon against the Western nations. Evidence from the Madrid, Spain, train attack of March 11, 2004, points to Takfir. Here are the basic facts:

1. Ahmad Mustafa Chawqui introduced the Takfiri ideology in the 1970's.
2. Secret members of the sect, who were also in the Egyptian military, assassinated President Anwar Sadat during a national armed forces parade in Cairo on October 6, 1981.
3. Egyptian members of the Takfiri sect traveled to Pakistan and Afghanistan to spread their ideology among the Jihad fighters.
4. The ideology spread from Afghanistan to Morocco, Tunisia, Algeria and the Sudan in the early 1990's.
5. In the late 90's the Takfiri sect was promulgated in Germany, Spain, France, Belgium and the United Kingdom.

6. Between 2001-2004 Abu Musab Zarqawi built terror organizations based on Takfiri ideology in Iraq and several European countries.

The leader of the Madrid bombing is a Moroccan by the name of Jamal Zougam, and he is a Takfir.

This ultra-fundamentalist group has a close cousin called "Salafists." Both they and the Takfir use women operatives, who adopt western life styles to keep a low profile. These and other Al Qaeda splinter groups adhere to a philosophy of all-out armed Jihad against the West as well as apostate fellow Muslims.

Some European investigators believe that Muhammad Ali, the leading hijacker of September 11, 2001, was a follower of the Takfiri creed, specifically because he led a typical clean-shaven life style in the West for years. With trained mujahedeen, holy warriors and the ultra-radical Takfiri strain, a deadly combination is emerging making the war on terror a world-wide problem, indeed.

Jonathan Schanzer, a terrorism specialist at the Washington Institute for Near East policy to these groups as "Al Qaeda 2.0."

Abu Basir, a Takfiri scholar urged his fellow Takfiris to recognize that immigration is a key to entend their radical ideas into Western Europe.

Jamal Zougam, the leading suspect in the Madrid bombing was greatly influenced by a Moroccan mullah, M. Al Fazizi, who encouraged Muslims youths to join the Jihad and kill all nonbelievers.

These new warriors pretend to lead a modern lifestyle, yet, deep inside they are committed to a strict medieval doctrine of Islam, according to Dr. Magnus Ranstorp, a German intelligence officer.

Nevertheless, we have a couple of incredible promises from Jesus himself,

". . . *And on this rock I will build my church and the gates of hell shall not   prevail against it.*" (Matthew 16:18)

Another declaration is embedded in Philippians 2:10-11,

At the name of Jesus every knee should bow, of those in heaven, and of those on earth, and of those under the earth, and that every tongue should confess that Jesus Christ is Lord, to the glory of God the Father.

It is very extraordinarily exciting and exhilarating to recognize that the forces of evil shall not conquer the bastions of goodwill, but the love of God shall woo us and His peace and justice shall prevail—soon and very soon. Will you, therefore, join me as part of the dynamic solution, not part of the dreadful problem, through earnest prayer, giving of your testimony, talent, time and treasure and leave the multitudes and ranks of the unfortunate, liturgical, and uncaring silent majority?

The followers of the imposter descended into a deep pit. They exchanged peace for warfare, benevolence for raiding, purity for fornication and faith for faithlessness. Subsequently, their trade vanished; their profit was none other than a terrible torment. (The True Furqan "The Evil One" 44:6)

VII

PRESS RELEASES OF
UTMOST INTEREST

A. The September 11, 2001, full press release on Exposing Islam, **The Quran** and Fanatic Muslims

In the crucible of history, one discovers sooner or later that history is a record of individuals or groups of individuals or movements which planned their future and their goals, then endeavored to fulfill them. Because man is a reasoning and a thinking being, very few things just happen. For instance, the pyramids of Egypt took forty years to build at the cost of ten thousand lives. The tremendous Temple of Solomon was completed in seven years. The Taj Mahal of India was accomplished in thirteen years. When one researches in the philosophical, religious, social, economical, political and scientific fields, one will observe that individuals or groups worked diligently and planned very wisely to achieve their set goals. It is true that in few instances, especially in the geographic and scientific fields, accidental discoveries took place, such as the discovery of America and of penicillin. Even in our days of the twenty-first century, we are uplifted in learning that certain medicines, which were to be used for a particular disease, ended up producing more positive results for other diseases. Nevertheless, my lifetime of study and research, especially in the last twenty years, prompted me on September 11, 2001, to distribute the following press release:

Exposing Islam, The Quran and Fanatic Muslims

(This article was prepared only one week before the horrific and dastardly destruction of the Twin Towers of New York. My wife and I were celebrating our forty-fourth anniversary in N.Y. and visited the Twin Towers.)

To All Patriotic Americans:

Blow the trumpet in America! Sound the alarm!

We are being invaded in America and do not seem to realize it. What has been taking place in Iraq, Iran, Indonesia and Afghanistan should be a clear signal of warning to America. But we are too busy following "Who wants to be a millionaire," who is the new golf hero, boxing champion, football or baseball front-runner for national championship or who won the lottery lately!

Our postal service has just issued a stamp to commemorate Islam and recognize Muslims. Since when did Saudi Arabia, the heart of Islam, even recognize the presence of nine hundred thousand Christian expatriates on their soil? Saudis do not allow a church building to be constructed on their one million square mile desert kingdom. You cannot get a passport unless you are a Muslim! We have allowed the Muslims to establish fifteen hundred mosques and centers in

America, mostly with petro-dollars. Yet, not a single church building is allowed in Saudi Arabia, a country where our own military offered their very life-blood to defend Saudis against another Muslim tyrant by the name of Saddam Hussein.

Incidentally, have you wondered about the spectacle of Iran and Iraq declaring Jihad on each other? Thereafter, Saudi Arabia and Iraq did the same. These people called us "The Great Satan" during the Gulf War. I chuckle at the fantastic result of the war when Allah was no match for "The Great Satan." Will Muslims find a bigger Allah to do battle for them or simply discover there is no such deity?

Mr. Farrakhan was born in Guyana, South America, immigrated to the United States and claimed to be the leader of an American Islamic Group known as the Black Muslims. Recently while watching television in Nashville, TN, I ran across a program in which he was the guest speaker in some church. To my unbelieving eyes and ears he announced, "You ask me about Muhammad. The name means praised one. Jesus is the praised one. So Muhammad is Jesus and Jesus is Muhammad." How ignorant can one be to believe such rubbish?

How many of you even remember that Afghanistan's Muslim government one Sunday morning sent bulldozers and completely destroyed the only church building in Kabul, the capital, in 1980? (That was before the Soviet invasion and its aftermath.) Afghanistan's militant regime has once again demonstrated an imbecilic attitude towards culture, archeology and history by showing in worldwide media how they dynamited the historic monuments of Buddha. Not many days ago the religious police, who, like their counterparts in

Saudi Arabia are above the law, arrested twenty-four Western and national personnel. The accusation was "they were caught red-handed with **Bibles** and videos of the movie "Jesus of Nazareth." In short, freedom of religion is practiced and available only to Muslims. Have you ever wondered why democracy and Islam do not co-exist?

There are over a billion Muslims in the world. Yet, out of the thirty-nine majority Muslim countries and thirty large minority Muslim countries, only Turkey has any semblance of democracy! As if that is not obvious, lately the clamor to declare Islamic law as the law of the land, in Nigeria, Indonesia, Somalia, Iran, Pakistan, etc., demonstrates something that no one wants to talk about. On the one hand, many of the poorer countries of Africa are wanting the Islamic law because it guarantees them petrol dollar contributions from the Islamic oil producing countries. On the other hand, there is an astonishing amount of terror which is gripping the Muslim world due to two things.

First, they are losing ground because of the invasion of the "Truth Revolution". Neither **The Quran** nor Islam can stand the acidic test and heat of higher criticism of archeology, philosophy, language, logic or history which has been focused on **The Bible** for so long and is now focused on **The Quran**. The fallacy that the so-called "prophet of Islam" was illiterate, therefore he could not have written **The Quran** (but God himself did) is now substantiated by the incredible find of the Yemenite documents in 1979 of **The Quran**. Please consult Atlantic Monthly issue of January 1999 under the title "What is **The Quran**."

Second, whereas the Dead Sea scrolls substantiate Biblical accuracy, the 32 thousand photographs of the discovered documents of **The Quran** dating from the eighth to the fourteenth century expose the fact that **The Quran** has been polluted by changes in its text over the centuries. Subsequently, we can say, very forcefully, that **The Quran** developed over the years and in no way can it be accepted as the final revelation of God to humanity. In fact, the contents of **The Quran** do not reveal any new information, inspiration, or instructions, which had not already been known to the Jews and Christians, and even to some heathen people.

Many of my readers still shudder when they think of Lebanon and the tragedy of fourteen years of civil war. Are you cognizant of the fact that at the conclusion of the First World War the triumphant governments of the world decided to help the Arab Christians of the Middle East? Therefore, in the ocean of the Muslim countries, which occupy the entire Middle East, an island was established for the Christian Arabs who had no recognized geographical identity. However, to assuage the Muslim potentates and governments who assisted in winning the war against the Axis and the Turkish Empire, the constitution for Lebanon included that the President of this new democracy would always be a Christian, but the Prime Minister a Muslim.

Nevertheless, as a result of the Six Day War of 1967, between Israel and its neighbors, in which Israel was victorious, thousands of Palestinians escaped into Lebanon, legally and illegally. Another escape to Lebanon took place when the Jordanian army and Palestinian commandoes fought fierce battles in September 1970 and forced them out. The majority were Muslims. Within two decades they were able to offset the numerical balance between Muslim and Christian, thus creating a larger Muslim population than the

Christian. Although they were refugees, it was unbelievable that they demanded a voice in the government. According to the constitution of Lebanon, that was not feasible. Consequently, the onslaught of a fourteen-year protracted civil war caused the killing of one hundred forty thousand people, the displacement of a million people, the injury of over half a million people and the destruction of Lebanon's infrastructure. When former President Reagan sent some marines in 1983 to be peacekeepers, the same ungodly, violent people had a suicide truck-bomber with twelve hundred pounds of explosives blow up his truck, himself, and 241 of our marines as they lay sleeping early one morning.

Lest we forget now about our peaceful mission to striking Somalis, the horrible treatment we received in return, once again demonstrated to the world the raw evil of militant Islam. Eventually, the whole tragedy ended up with the world opinion backing the Lebanese Christian administration. The eviction of the PLO, both leadership and followers took place because they were the ones who spearheaded the entire affair, slaughter, mayhem and destruction. Of course, Syria's military forces were more eager than the Israeli forces to occupy the entire country, subjugate its people, and control the economy of what was the banking center of the Middle East. It will take fifty years for Lebanon to recover its previous glory and overcome the ravages of wanton practices of mayhem, slaughter and meaningless destruction. Is that what they're trying to do to Israel right now? It is the only Jewish State in the world. Arabs control 99.9 percent of the Middle East, five million square miles. Why can't they share some of their Middle Eastern hospitality by letting their cousins and half brothers have a mere one-tenth of their square miles? Is there some sinister demonic spirit roaming in the Arab World, which keeps them from demonstrating mercy, reconciliation and love?

What then do you believe about modern Saudi Arabia's administration? They consistently jail Christian expatriates, torture some, force the expulsion of the white-skinned, but execute the brown and black skinned workers.

For the past eleven years the Sudanese militant Islamic administration has terrorized, marginalized, ostracized and slaughtered its own citizens in the southern regions. We have been hearing about that lately because of the outcry of organizations which are dedicated to exposing religious, economic, political and cultural persecution. We have documents which demonstrate that over two million people have been killed so far because they are not Muslims, but are Christians and animists. The ancient miserable practice of slavery is going on right now in that land, which is the largest in Africa, by an administration that has vowed to make Sudan the most Islamic country in the world. The reason why we have been hearing about them lately is also due to the discovery of oil under the sandy valleys and hills.

Have you seen the movie "Not Without My Daughter" with Sally Fields, "The Siege" with Densel Washington or the French movie, "The Death of a Princess"? Get the documentary of Mr. Steven Emerson's "Jihad in America" and let your eyes be opened wide. Remember that millions saw it on PBS five years ago. Visit the so-called Salaam (Peace) Mosque where blind cleric, Abd El Rahman (who falsified his documents and acquired an entry visa into America illegally) instigated his followers to bomb our World Trade Center in 1993. Tragically, they succeeded today in destroying both Towers which inflicted on us more terror than Pearl Harbor.

Mrs. Hillary Clinton was the first occupant of our White House to celebrate the Feast of Ramadan with sixty-four Muslim leaders in America. A number of journalists discovered that she had done that more than once. Guess who paid for that feast—your and my tax dollars! Have you wondered how Muslims have succeeded in ingratiating themselves to the Clintons?   Money and more money! Journalists have dared to expose the China connection but none have so far demonstrated courage or honesty to expose the Muslim connection. Besides, Chelsea, their one and only daughter, dated the son of Saudi Arabia's ambassador to Washington, which entailed expensive gifts and extraordinary favors. Can you recall how the news media quoted Mrs. Clinton as saying that Chelsea had given her so much valuable insight on Islam as they were traveling throughout some African countries three years ago? How many of you realize that our chaplains have allowed Muslim clerics to open the Senate as well as the Congress in prayer? Muslims express an image of dedicated citizenry and peaceful coexistence while they are a minority. However, as soon as the number grows, look out for catastrophe. There will not be democracy or human rights. Religious freedom will disappear, and forget about your political rights or individual freedoms.

The Allah of **The Quran** is not the God of **The Bible**. Out of the so-called ninety-nine excellent names for Allah, none is a "Heavenly Father", neither "God is love", nor "God is spirit." In fact, the Holy Spirit is believed by all true Muslims to be the angel Gabriel? But in **The Quran**, Allah is called "the proud", the "destroyer" and the "vengeful."

Few Arabic-speaking Muslims comprehend at all the famous words "Allahu Akbar" which they loudly declare when delighted or depressed. They are indoctrinated to believe it means "god is greater."

Consequently, we ask the question, greater than what, or whom? Because Islam grew in the midst of pagan Mecca with 360 idols, gods and goddesses, Muhammad was claiming that his god is GREATER than all the others. Yet, few know that the word "Akbar" did not only mean greater, but was also the name of the moon god. Therefore, one is not astonished at all to observe that the Muslims' house of worship is surmounted by a crescent. The Christian's symbol of their faith is the cross—a reminder of God's great love for humans. The star surmounts Jewish synagogues because they were commissioned by Yahweh God to be a light to the nations. Islam even follows an archaic lunar calendar, not the more accurate solar one. Why? Because they are trying to please their god! All Muhammad did was to embellish "Akbar" with Biblical characteristics of Yahweh to attract his people to his new religion. Once one researches Islam's development, ceremonial oblations, festivals, traditions and beliefs, he will be quite convinced that Islam is the Arab's interpretation of Judaism!

In our crowded prison system, Muslims are growing faster than any religious group. Why? Islam is a violent religion. Violence attracts violence, therefore criminals find an affinity in becoming Muslims. Upon becoming a Muslim, inmates are given new names. When they are released there will be no record to track down their previous crimes. Additionally, prisoners are told that Muhammad was a black man and an African. Arabs are descendents of Shem, not Ham. Even

The Hadith tells, in several stories, how others knew he was a white man. Furthermore, Arabia is in Asia, not Africa.

There is not a single, solitary Muslim in the entire world who can claim that he knows whether his sins are forgiven or not. Muslims have neither a sacrifice for sin nor assurance of salvation from sin. Only a born-again Christian can know. As far as their doctrine is concerned, only Allah knows your eternal destination!

What about the matter of beating your wife, as a divine right sanctioned by Allah? Then, adding three more wives and as many concubines as you can afford? Have you heard that Kuwait's Prince has twenty-nine wives? Women only count in court as one-half of a witness. Therefore, if a man is testifying one has to have two women to counter his testimony. The first king of Saudi Arabia, King Abdul Aziz, was crowned by the British at the end of World War I. The Allies had promised him and other Arab leaders that if they take their side in the warfare, each of them would be recognized as a potentate of a geographical location of his choice. Surprisingly enough, the first royal act of the king was a marriage ceremony with 350 women. His offspring today comprise the royal family in excess of thirty thousand, who alone enjoy freedom and liberty. No one else in the entire country has much freedom.

Read the incredible new book that exposes all of these facts and more. Amazon.com lists it as **The True Furqan**, meaning **The Quran** is the false one. Judge for yourself! Another is **Islam Revealed**, an eye opener, on the subject. A brand new video entitled, "Islam: A Threat or a Challenge" is a must see, produced by our organization.

When any intelligent individual contrasts **The Bible** to **The Quran** he is truly overwhelmed by the Biblical plagiarism. How can the one true and living God send us two revelations which contradict each other? God is not a God of confusion, but of order. Is it at all possible that He sent us His greatest and most up-to-date revelation called **The Quran** in the most difficult language, out of twelve thousand, rather than the easiest language? Why in the world of logic would God, if He is the same God, order the killing of His human beings because they did not practice worshiping him exactly like another group. Some of you may inquire, what about Mormonism? Isn't it similar to Islam? In my opinion, Mormonism is actually Islam in America, but that is another story.

Have you heard the rumor that, "If the government of Iran would allow the same freedom of religion as in the West, 50 percent or more of their people would turn to Christ overnight." Furthermore, in the past two years over 500 Muslims in Israel have trusted Christ and followed through with baptism. Entire villages in Africa and the Middle East are discovering that Islam's human rights record disqualifies it from support as a viable Twenty-first Century religion. Fear from reprisals keeps most Muslims from coming to Christ. Islam is the only religion which instructs the followers by divine right to kill their family members, friends and relatives, if the new convert does not recant in sixty days. So one must wonder why "Allah" is always angry and hungry for blood like the ancient pagan deities. Why do his militant followers demonstrate brutal violence throughout the world? Abu Sayyaf's group (in the Philippines), Laskar terrorists in Indonesia, Hamas (of Palestine and Israel), Osamah Bin Laden (the Saudi millionaire terrorist) and thirty thousand Al Qaeda operatives in sixty countries, and Hizb

Allah (of Lebanon) are dedicated to the destruction of anyone or any country which disagrees with their agenda. Fanatic, fundamental Islam, if not checked soon, will precipitate WWIII.

We come to the conclusion with what is perhaps the most important issue in this press release, which is the conflict between the Arabs and the Jews. First of all, the fifty-three-year conflict with modern Israel began in the tent of Abraham and Sarah. Hagar's introduction to a monogamous marriage, by Sarah's obedience to cultural practices at her former home in Chaldea, initiated the conflict. Marriage vows included a promise by the wife that she would provide her husband with another woman if she could not deliver any children for him. Although God fulfilled his promise in providing Abraham and Sarah with Isaac, the competition had already begun between Ishmael and Isaac. Therefore, the four thousand-year old family feud which is fueled by a demonic spirit of hate, revenge, bitterness and bloody warfare is a family feud.

Second, if the Palestinian Arabs and the Palestinian Jews had been left alone in 1948 to take care of themselves, the entire exercise in futility, bloodshed, heartache and enormous waste of billions of dollars of armament would have been avoided.

Third, few people ever blame Jordan for annexing the Palestinian area which the United Nations assigned to the Palestinian Arabs. Imagine how unjust it was for Jordan to annex the area, call it the West Bank, claim it for its own, then because of world opinion and the Palestinian uprising, give it up in 1986.

Fourth, **The Bible** emphatically declares again and again that that piece of land, call it Palestine, Israel, Land of Canaan, or whatever, was given by God to Abraham and his descendants. If we can convince the Israeli Jews and the Palestinian Arabs of this fact, which is that both have the right to the land and should coexist, maybe we can stop the bloodletting and exchange understanding for hate. If indeed the Arab Muslims (there are sixteen million Arab Christians who have no quarrel with Israel) decide on a Holy War with Israel, the consequences are catastrophic and could become an atomic war because Israel has two reactors and approximately 400 atomic and hydrogen weapons ready to defend itself. Let us pray for the peace of Jerusalem and the fall of fanatic Islam which has brought to humanity more curses than blessings throughout its 1400 year history. And today, because of the tragedies in New York and Washington, we must pray earnestly that the Lord will propel the entire world into rejecting Islam as a viable religion for the twenty-first century and turn to the Prince of Peace, rather than the prince of darkness who devised **The Quran** and enslaved Muslims.

B. Can a devout Muslim be an American patriot and loyal citizen?

PRESS RELEASE

Can a Devout Muslim be an American Patriot and Loyal Citizen?

1. Theologically, no. Because his allegiance is to Allah, the moon god of Arabia.

2. Scripturally, no. Because his allegiance is to the five pillars of Islam and **The Quran**.

3. Geographically, no. Because his allegiance is to Mecca for he turns toward it in prayer five times a day.

4. Socially, no. Because his allegiance to Islam demands that he make no friends of Christians and Jews. (**Quran** 5:51)

5. Politically, no. Because he must submit to the mullah who teaches annihilation of Israel and destruction of America, the great Satan.

6. Domestically, no. Because he is instructed to marry four women and beat and scourge his wife when she disobeys him. (**Quran** 4:34)

7. Religiously, no. Because no other religion is accepted by his Allah except Islam—intolerance. (**Quran** 2:256)

8. Intellectually, no. Because he cannot accept the American constitution since it is established on Biblical principles, because he believes the Bible is corrupted.

9. Philosophically, no. Because Islam, Muhammad and **The Quran** do not allow freedom of religion and expression. Democracy and Islam cannot co-exist. Every Muslim government is dictatorial or autocratic except Turkey.

10. Spiritually, no. Because when we declare "one nation under God" the Christian's God is a Triune God while the Muslim's is one entity called "Allah", who is never a Heavenly Father, nor is he ever called "Love" in the ninety-nine excellent names.

We are urged by the media and pluralists to avoid intolerance and yield to religious pluralism. If we do it, it will destroy us. If Christ Jesus is not the only Way, the Truth and the Life, then the Gospel is not really good news to the peoples of the world. We are under orders from our great Commander in Chief, Christ Jesus of Nazareth, through the Great Commission to go into all the world and make disciples of all nations. Our commission is irreversible, irrepressible, irresistible and incredible. We do it or die.

C. What can Muslims do to demonstrate their loyalty to America?

We are not exaggerating when we declare that Islamic organizations in America have failed miserably in convincing the American public of the outrage that they claim most Muslim Americans felt over the horrors of 9/11. No unified statement ever came condemning the terror to this date. Individuals, yes. But no national voice, yet!

1. The numerous Muslim organizations along with Muslim intellectuals, doctors and business men should sign a statement condemning terrorism in the harshest terms and proclaim it through the media for at least thirty days. Furthermore, they should write the Embassies of their countries of origin asking their

governments to stop all persecution of non-Muslims, especially Christians.

2. Muslims should establish a taskforce which can provide the Federal government information and assistance which will help prevent further attacks, or help the arresting of anyone participating in future attacks.

3. Muslims should raise funds to help the sufferers of 9/11 as well as to assist the government in the war against terrorism. When India was in a war with their neighbors, a number of years ago, loyal Indians gave of their silver and golden jewelry to support the war effort. A recent survey revealed that the average Muslim in the U.S. makes $50,000 a year.

4. Muslims should join the armed forces to fight in the war on terrorism, thus giving visible evidence they are loyal citizens and not by-standers.

5. Muslims should organize a massive demonstration to march to ground zero, in New York to publicly repudiate Islamic terrorism. Each marcher could deposit a postcard or a flower at the site of the murders. A recognized Muslim leader could read a poem dedicated to the memories of the nearly 3 thousand victims, then everyone sing "America the Beautiful" and the National Anthem.

6. Muslim organizations should send a letter of condolence and apologies to the families of each victim. They should explain clearly that terrorists do not speak for them and the one hundred Quranic verses which teach killing are not applicable to the twenty-first century as they were to seventh and eighth centuries.

7. If they are truly sincere, Muslim organizations and mosques may print and distribute bumper stickers to

their people which declare, "Muslims for America and against Islamic terrorism."

D. Twenty-year plan for USA—Islam targets America

On immigrating from Jerusalem, Jordan, in January, 1967, this writer could not have imagined that Islam would become center-stage in world news. As sincere interest in the growth of Islam in America intensified, it was discussed, dialogued, and then debated with Muslim leaders throughout the world from an Arab Christian's view of Islam. So far, this author has had the privilege of participating in over twenty debates and discussions on every continent plus television and radio. **Islam Revealed** was released in 1988 and is now in its eighth printing. **The True Furqan** in now in its third printing in the three years it has been published. It is the only book which challenges the Quran in substance, style, language and contents. **The True Furqan** can be located on www.answers-to-islam.net or www.islam-exposed.org.

The following is my analysis of Islamic invasion of America, the agenda of Islamists and visible methods to take over America by the year 2020! Will my fellow Americans continue to sleep through this determined invasion as we did when we were attacked on 9/11?

1. Terminate America's freedom of speech by replacing it with hate crime bills, state-wide and nation-wide, thus silencing the opposition.
2. Wage a war of words using black leaders like Louis Farrakhan, Rev. Jesse Jackson and other visible religious personalities to promote Islam as the original African-American's religion while Christianity is for the whites! Strange enough, no one

tells our African-Americans that it was the Arab Muslims who captured them and sold them as slaves, neither the fact that in Arabic the word for black and slave is the same, "Abed."

3. Engage the American public in dialogues, discussions, debates in colleges, universities, public libraries, radio, T.V., churches and mosques on the virtues of Islam. Proclaim how it is historically another monotheistic religion like Judaism and Christianity.

4. Nominate Muslim sympathizers to political office for favorable legislation to Islam and support potential sympathizers by block voting.

5. Take control of as much of Hollywood, the press, T.V. radio and the internet as possible, by buying the corporations or a controlling stock with petro-dollars.

6. Yield to the fear of imminent cut-off of the lifeblood of America—the "black gold." America's economy depends on oil, (one thousand products are derived from oil), so does its private and public transportation—41 percent comes from the Middle East.

7. Yell, "foul, out-of-context, personal interpretation, hate crime, Zionist, un-American, inaccurate interpretation of **The Quran**" anytime Islam is criticized or **The Quran** is analyzed in the public arena.

8. Encourage Muslims to penetrate the White House, specifically with Islamists who can articulate a marvelous and peaceful picture of Islam. Acquire government positions, get membership in local school boards. Train Muslims as medical doctors to dominate the medical field, research and pharmaceutical companies. Take over the computer industry.

Establish Middle Eastern restaurants throughout the U.S. to connect planners of Islamization in a discreet manner. (Ever notice how numerous Muslim doctors in America are, when their countries need them more desperately than America?)

9. Accelerate Islamic demographic growth via:
   a. Massive immigration (one hundred thousand annually since 1961)
   b. Biological, birthrate highest among ethnic groups
   c. Muslim men seek to marry American women and Islamize them (eight to ten thousand annually). They divorce them and remarry every five years. Because one cannot have the Muslim legal permission to marry four at one time, this practice is a legal solution in America.
   d. Convert angry, alienated black inmates and turn them into militant Muslims. (So far two thousand released inmates have joined Al Qaeda worldwide). Only a few have been captured in Afghanistan and Iraq. On American soil it is estimated that the sleeping cells number five thousand in the first level (living in America two-five years) and ten thousand in the second level (five-ten years).

10. Reading, writing, arithmetic and research through the American educational system, mosques and student centers (now fifteen hundred) should be sprinkled with dislike of Jews, evangelical Christians and democracy. There are 300 exclusively Muslim schools with loyalty to **The Quran**, not the U.S. Constitution.

11. Provide very sizeable monetary Muslim grants to colleges and universities in America to establish "Centers for Islamic studies" with Muslim directors

to promote the ideology of a peaceful Islam in our institutions of higher learning.

12. Convince the entire world through propaganda, speeches, seminars, local and national media that terrorists have hijacked Islam, not the truth: "Islam hijacked the terrorists." Surprisingly, in January of 2002, Saudi Arabia's Embassy in Washington had the audacity to mail forty-five hundred packets to America's high schools free, containing **The Quran** and videos promoting Islam. They would never allow us to reciprocate.

13. Appeal to the historically compassionate and sensitive Americans for sympathy and tolerance towards the Muslims in America who are portrayed as mainly poor immigrants from oppressed countries. (The average income for Muslims as of 2000 is $50,000.)

14. Nullify our sense of security by manipulating the intelligence community with misinformation. Periodically terrorize Americans of impending attacks on bridges, tunnels, water supplies, airports, apartment buildings and malls. (We have experienced this too often since 9/11.)

15. Foment riots and demonstrations in the prison system demanding Islamic law "Sharia" as the way of life, not our justice system.

16. Open numerous charities throughout the U.S. but use the funds to support anti-American terrorism with American dollars here and overseas.

17. Raise interest in Islam on America's campuses by insisting that freshmen take at least one introductory course on Islam. Be sure that the writer is a bona-fide American Christian, scholarly and able to cover up the violence in **The Quran** and express the peaceful, spiritual and religious aspect only.

18. Unify the numerous Muslim lobbies in Washington, mosques, Islamic student centers, educational organizations, magazines and papers by internet and an annual convention to coordinate plans, propagate the faith and engender news in the media of their visibility.

19. Send intimidating messages and messengers to the outspoken individuals who are critical of Islam and seek to eliminate them by hook or crook.

20. Applaud Muslims as loyal citizens of the U.S. by spotlighting their excellent voting record as the highest percentage of all minority and ethnic groups in America.

E. Additional revelations

When privileged to start a ministry in England in the early 1980's, this writer was startled to learn that Muslims had targeted England for Islamization. This was their slogan, "If we can take London for Islam we can take all of Europe." The massive number of the Commonwealth citizens who immigrated to England was the first move. The second was the enormous biological growth after coming to the U.K. The third was the intense effort in marrying British women and Islamizing them. Still another was establishing Islamic businesses such as restaurants, grocery stores, dry cleaning and laundry businesses, taking over small motels and hotels and the taxi trade. Then they moved into teaching positions all the way from grade school, through high school and university levels. Of course, it goes without saying that one of their greatest targets was to take over much of the medical field.

Now in the year 2003, it was no surprise to hear Evangelical Christian leaders calling London "the Islamic capital of Europe." Inasmuch as the U.K. geographically and population wise is much smaller than the U.S.A., it was an easy target. Furthermore, the tragic decline of Christianity, morality and spirituality in England facilitated the invasion of Islam into England. Moreover, the extremely friendly attitude of the Royals towards Islam (because of oil money in England's banks) has been a boon to Muslims, but a pain to British Christianity. England, the former leader of the Christian world and the "premier-sending missionary" leader in the world for 200 years, could be called a society of post-Christians since 1950. The nation has turned its back on the Bible truths and is now reaping the consequences.

F. Political and media penetration

Because this writer's interest in Islam has been life-long for seventy-one years, having been born in the city of Nazareth, which was evenly divided between Christian and Muslim population, he was able to draw on experiences as well as research. (Incidentally, Christians and Muslims in Nazareth have been fighting over building a mosque in front of the Church of Annunciation since 1999.) Of course, my travels into seventy-nine nations of the world has been an education in itself. It must be admitted, however, that the twenty-plus debates with Muslim leaders and Muslim groups on every continent have given this writer a wealth of information and much understanding about Muslims and Islam.

The move into the media by Muslims in America preceded the political move. The petro-dollars by the billions has allowed Muslims the incredible opportunity of purchasing media outlets such as Associated Press, radio and television stations, newspapers and magazines, not only in America, but around the world. The politically correct viewpoint is no longer to criticize Islam but blacklist Muslim individuals who are terrorists and militants, thereby exonerating Islam as a religion. Yet the root of the problem is **The Quran** itself.

In October of 2002, during a one-hour debate on "100 Huntley Street" program broadcast on Christian Television System in Toronto, Canada, the author was forcefully put down by the host, Mr. Michael Coren, when pointing out the weakness of the Islamic position in declaring that their religion is peaceful. Very politely, it was mentioned that there are nearly one hundred verses in **The Quran** which command Muhammad particularly and Muslims at large to fight and kill Christians, Jews and pagans. Mr. Coren abruptly shouted, "Dr. Shorrosh, if you will keep talking like this, I will never have you on my show again." Startled at the response of a so-called converted Jew to Christianity, my response was immediate and penetrating: "Sir, do you want me to sacrifice truth for tolerance?" Since there was no response to the question from the host of this popular television program in Canada, (much like "Larry King Live" in the U.S.) Mr. Coren announced a break.

Lately, the propaganda has reached a high level of success. Muslims are touted as gracious and generous people. The popular T.V. program every evening called "JAG" the second week of December 2002 depicted three Saudi Arabians visiting JAG's headquarters. They came upon a private at the headquarters who, because of the Christmas season could not find lodging for his wife anywhere. She had just delivered their first baby. Imagine how silly the scene must have been to the Christian viewers when each of three

Saudi's (remember the three wise men of Christmas?) offered a gift to the newborn baby and his parents. First, one of the two younger men gave a golden coin, while the other a plane ticket to anywhere for vacation. Not surprisingly, the older man gave them a condominium in his sixteen-floor apartment building "with a view." This was another propaganda ploy to ingratiate Saudi Arabians to hurting Americans!

But more importantly is to prove to you how "Hollywood" has become "Saudiwood." Movies have taken great pains to follow the same theme, which is the case of the outstanding mini-series of 1999, "Mary, Mother of Jesus." The Quranic record was presented alongside the Gospel by depicting Jesus as making birds out of clay. Then, clapping his hands and giving them life, they flew away. This is strictly an early Egyptian Christian's fairy-tale about Jesus but related in **The Quran** as a revelation from Allah by Gabriel. (**Quran** 4:31)

Having attempted to communicate with the editor of the Mobile Register in Mobile, Al, on several occasions, the letters went unanswered. This very day of January 1, 2003 there are serious questions. Where did the impoverished deep South paper ever come up with the millions of dollars to build a new state-of-the-art gigantic five-story building? Second, is it possible that Muslim finances now control this paper and thus the employees refuse to write anything negative about Islam? Here is a copy of a letter that was never published.

July 10, 2002

Letters to the Editor
P O Box 2488
Mobile, Al 36652-2488

Is Truth to be Sacrificed for Tolerance?

(This is a response to the letter "Let's learn how to embrace tolerance" July 10)

The Quran had 124 verses promoting tolerance. Then came verse 9:5, "Slay the unbelievers wherever you find them," thus canceling all the tolerance verses. Muslim scholars call this the "annulling doctrine"! (2:106) So much for historical Islamic tolerance! Why did the so-called prophet wage sixty-six battles in the last ten years of his life? Additionally, there are over one hundred verses where "Allah" commands killing others. If Islam is so great, why is it that every Muslim country is a dictatorship except Turkey? And why are most religious persecutions and human rights violations taking place in the thirty-nine Muslim countries?

As for the pastor's comments in St. Louis, MO, June 10th, no Muslim has ever denied that Muhammad married Ayisha, fourth out of fifteen, when he was over fifty and she was nine years old. That identifies him or anyone else in such a relationship as "a pedophile." Are the few Catholic priests the only ones to be charged with such a crime?

As for Muhammad, one must remember:

1. A true prophet talks to God and God talks to him. Muhammad never experienced that. It was always a supposedly "angel of light" calling himself Gabriel.
2. In II Corinthians 11:14 we are informed, "For Satan himself transforms himself into an angel of light." Since angels do not lie, one will have to conclude that the angel appearing to Muhammad was a counterfeit Gabriel, because he denied what the authentic angel

had announced six hundred years earlier, that Jesus was God incarnate (Matthew 3:17; Luke 1:30-35), that Jesus rose from the dead (Luke 24:1-12) and that Jesus is to save mankind from their sins. (Matthew 1:18-23)

3. According to Revelation 22:18-19, God Almighty warns against adding or taking away any of the Biblical scriptures. Muhammad did both, he removed and added.

4. If the God of Islam is the same God, why do we see a regression from the ethical standards of the Sermon on the Mount (Matthew 5-7) instead of progression? Example—"love your enemies" (Matthew 5:44) now becomes "When you meet the unbelievers, strike off their necks". (**Quran** 47:4)

5. As to an unchanged **Quran** for fourteen hundred years, one should become more informed by reading "What is **The Quran**" in Atlantic Monthly, January 1999. The Yeminite Quranic documents from the seventh to the fourteenth centuries prove that **The Quran** has developed over the centuries and has been changed by Othman first, then other Muslim Khaleefs. Besides, the Iranian Muslims have 115 chapters in their **Quran**, rather than 114.

Islam never grew beyond the forty-five followers in Mecca and the 175 in Medina during the first twelve years of Muhammad's work. Without the iron sword (jihad), no one would have ever heard of Muhammad or Islam. By the way "Islam" in Arabic is interpreted by Muslims to mean "submission to Allah." The Arabic language defines "islam" as a derivative from the root verb **"sal-lama"** which means "he submitted, or surrendered to his opponent in battle, he gave up, he declared defeat, subjugated."

The entire world is facing more than a **clash of civilizations**. Islam wants two things: First, to convert the people of our planet to Islam by hook or crook. If some would not, then the second method, overrun their countries by force, as Muslims did between 622-722 A.D. and enslave, colonize and subjugate them to archaic, nomadic and savage rules. This is their final solution to world problems of race, religion, politics and economics.

The greatest problem which is facing mankind today is the **crisis of credibility**. The people of the Soviet Union, after seventy-two years of communism, realized it is neither credible nor the answer for their longing for liberty, justice and the pursuit of happiness. A peaceful revolution eleven years ago resulted. Islam is founded on a sandy foundation of a mixture of fact and fiction. More Muslims are finding that out and fleeing Islam. (In 1900 there was only 3 percent Christian population in Africa, now 46 percent.) That is why more than 80 percent of Muslims in America are immigrants from their oppressive regimes! Among the other 20 percent are their offspring's, deceived followers of Louis Farrakhan, the beguiled American women who marry Muslims and the Islamized inmates in our prison system.

Have you ever heard of any Americans immigrating to a Muslim country because it offers liberty, justice and the pursuit of happiness as America does?

Finally, as to Muhammad himself, and his so-called miracle of **The Quran**, there are three problems. First, if

Allah inspired **The Quran**, how can Muslims boast that it a miracle of Muhammad? Secondly, can Muslims show any single verse in **The Quran** where Muhammad declared that he performed any miracles? Thirdly, there is a new **Quran** in Arabic and English, which was released three years ago challenging **The Quran** in substance and style. **The True Furqan (Furqan** and **Quran** are synonymous) and is available on Amazon.com. Once Muslims discover that **The Quran** is a counterfeit Bible in the Arabic language, they will want to seriously consider **The Christian Bible** because it is in fact the only authentic, historical, logical and viable revelation to mankind by God himself.

G. Honest and enlightening articles

1. Capetown, South Africa Tribune—July, 1991, by Brian King

A Palestinian evangelist who fled South Africa more than two years ago has been circulating evidence in America of a plot hatched to kill him in Durban.

Snippets of an inflammatory video made in South Africa showing an assault on Dr. Anis Shorrosh in Cape Town with flashed messages urging his death have been shown in prime time TV broadcasts in Arizona, Alabama and Tennessee. Pirated copies of the complete video are also on sale in the U.S.A.

The evangelist, who has appeared on TV in every US state, sparked an uproar among Muslims during his 1990 South African lecture tour entitled *The Bible or the Qur'an – Which is God's Word?* The Jihad (Holy War)

Movement of South Africa was formed on his account. His hosts, the Apostolic Faith Mission, had to ask him to leave the country because they could not guarantee his personal safety.

During the dramatic tour:

&. A fellow Christian, unknown to Dr. Shorrosh, by the name of Chris Thaver, was stabbed in Cape Town while trying to shield him from attack (Shorrosh was kicked in the ribs), and a window in the car in which he was making an escape was smashed;

&. About 100 riot policemen had to whisk him away from the Durban City Hall after being confronted by angry Muslims;

&. He had had repeated death threats and had to switch flights twice to escape "Jihad personnel" waiting for him at Johannesburg and Frankfurt airports, and in America he received a call from a man who said in a sardonic voice, "I am President of the South African Jihad wanting to congratulate Dr. Shorrosh on his safe arrival."

The video, which came to light in the wake of the aborted tour, describes the evangelist as "another Rushdie" and depicts how he should be gunned down in Durban, since the dagger attack in Capetown had failed, for "insults" about the prophet Muhammad.

Against the video footage of the Cape Town assault, a depicted shooting is superimposed with the flashed sub-titled messages: "They should have used this (a gun)" and "Allah help us kill this "Shitan" (devil).

A very angry Dr. Shorrosh told the Sunday Tribune it had taken him two years to come to terms with what had happened in South Africa – and was now hitting back at what he termed "international terrorism."

"To resort to violence is whoremongering; it's devilish. All that violence was certainly planned," he alleged.

Informers, who secretly sent a copy of the video to America, told Dr. Shorrosh it was made following the failed assassination attempt in Cape Town to inspire Muslims to succeed in Durban.

"Now I understand what happened to me in South Africa," he says. The Christian scholar has accused his long-standing Muslim debating rival, president of the Islamic Propagation center International, Ahmed Deedat, of being behind the attacks and making of the video – a claim which Mr. Deedat has strenuously denied.

Mr. Deedat, approached by the Sunday Tribune for comment on the issue, hit back: "I think the guy (Shorrosh) has gone off his rocker. He got a bashing in Cape Town. Where was I? How, suddenly, does he have to run for his life from 500 to 1000 people in Durban? I wasn't at any of his meetings. Did all these people (Muslims) see this video?"

2. Jerusalem Post—April 21, 1993

Evangelist Takes Off His Gloves to Fight Islam

Religious disputations did not go out with the Middle Ages. A Nazareth-born Baptist minister is a modern practitioner of the art. Dr. Anis Shorrosh, 60, has been involved in religious debates since he came into contact with Ahmed Deedat, a Moslem spokesman, while visiting England eight years ago—1985.

After hearing the Moslem speaker and questioning him from the audience, Shorrosh challenged Deedat to a debate in London's Royal Albert Hall. The two held a second debate in Birmingham, which Shorrosh described as a great success, resulting in "the salvation of many Moslems who attended the debate. . .and several attempts on my life." Since then, he has held public disputations with Moslems around the world. But last week, he took a break from debating. Shorrosh was in this country leading a group on what he says is his 30th pilgrimage.

In his debates, Shorrosh argues that the Koran is filled with contradictions and grammatical errors which, he says, could not be there if it was truly the word of God. For Shorrosh, the Allah of the Koran is not the same as the God of the Bible. But his objection to Islam is not just theological. For him Islam is not only a religion. "It is a political system. I challenge anyone to show me a Moslem government that is not a dictatorship. It is oppression by a religious system and political system. It is more oppressive than communism," he says.

Moslems, of course, reject such Christian beliefs as the divinity and resurrection of Jesus. Shorrosh says the debaters argue that the text of the Bible has been corrupted and that their religion is superior because it is the latest revelation and thus the "most modern." They also argue that no one needs salvation or a savior.

Shorrosh says he has been successful in his debates. After the Birmingham disputation, for example, several young people were converted to Christianity. His message has helped Christians deal with the growth of Islam in Europe, he adds. But his, in turn, has engendered retribution. "They cannot handle losing very well," he says, adding that he was "targeted for elimination three times in the same week in South Africa."

After his talk in Cape Town, he says, a group of Moslems surrounded him, beat him and stabbed a friend who was covering him with his body. Three days later Shorrosh was warned that a sniper was in a building where he was to speak, and the lecture was canceled. Later he recounts, he came into possession of a video produced by a group called Islamic Propagation Center International in which Shorrosh was described as "another Rushdie." It called for the "help of Allah in killing this satan."

Moslem violence is not new to him, he says. When he was a child; his father was thrown from a train by a Moslem mob and then spent 11 years in a psychiatric hospital due to the resulting concussion. His father was released at the outbreak of the War of Independence, only to step on a land mine and die while escaping Israel.

In Jordan, to which the remainder of the family had fled, young Shorrosh won a scholarship to study in the US. He returned to Jordan and served as the pastor of the East Jerusalem Baptist Church, but left before the Six

Days War. Now he is an author, film producer, and "international evangelist."

Regarding Israel, Shorrosh says the Arabs and Palestinians "made a mistake by not practicing our tradition of hospitality" and not accepting the UN partition plan in 1947. Today, he is a bitter foe of the PLO, which he says does not represent the Palestinians. "If anyone says that the PLO represents them, it is out of fear." Israel, he says, has "wittingly or unwittingly taken the first step towards recognizing Palestine by cordoning off the territories. I urge them to let their cousins control their destiny, without military force and without the PLO."

He says his fellow Christian ministers warned him that his participation in pro-Israel events – such as a prayer breakfast honoring Israel in Washington and a visit, in 1973 when he brought a church choir to Hadassah University Hospital to comfort the wounded, would jeopardize his relations with the Arab churches. But this has not been the case, he says. He still returns to the Nazareth Baptist Church, where the local Baptist school has benefited from his talents as a fund raiser.

Until now, he has avoided publicity in this country and participation in debates here. But he says he would be willing to debate any Moslem spokesman here, just as he is willing to do so anywhere in the world. His only requirements are that the debate be in English, in which he now feels more comfortable than Arabic, and that he be provided with "massive security protection."

Moses declared to his nation, "You are not to kill the soul of any human because God has intensely forbidden murder," although people did that in the past.

Moreover, Jesus proclaimed, "O, people everywhere, whosoever hurts another human being even with an abusive word, deserves the torments of the fiery pit."

Then you exclaimed, "Kill them wherever you find them. When you confront your opponents strike off their necks." With such a creed you regressed to the lifestyle of the days of ignorance and paganism–the principles of murder and vengeance. The True Furqan "The Scale" 74:1-3)

VIII

THE HEARTBREAKING ARAB-ISRAELI CONFLICT

Throughout the history of the human race, hardly any problem has baffled and bewildered the Wise Men of the East and West as much as the Arab-Israeli conflict. Neither political nor military solutions have provided a satisfactory answer. With the numerous resolutions of the United Nations General Assembly and the Security Council, the conflict continues to fester, hearts are filled with anxiety, homes of terrorists are destroyed systematically, while the blood of the innocents spills daily.

Authors by the hundreds, yea, even by the thousands, have produced enormous numbers of books presenting the prophetic, political, economic, social, geographical and philosophical opinions to solving the monstrous problem. Administration after administration of the powerful nations of the West, as well as the leaders of the Soviet Union, has attempted to negotiate a peaceful solution between the warring parties, to no avail. The Palestinians cry out, "How long must we wait for justice and languish in refugee camps?" The Israeli respond, "How long should we live under siege by angry Arab states who want to destroy us?"

This writer will attempt to shed some light on this problem of the century, which has had only negative responses to any human solution so far.

A. Ancient history of the land and Israel

The following chronological list will acquaint the student of history with precise and valuable information before we delve deeper into the matter.

2000 BC—Abraham, the Patriarch, moves into Canaan from Ur of Chaldea.

1900 BC—Jacob, the first person renamed Israel by God's angel (Genesis 32:28).

1785 BC—Jacob arrives in Egypt.

1440 BC—Exodus from Egypt.

1400 BC—Conquest of Canaan and Establishment of Israel.

1400-1010 BC—Judges and Prophets rule with frequent battles with neighbors.

1010 BC—King David captures Salem, renames it Jerusalem, Capital of Israel.

722 BC—Assyria conqueres the Northern Kingdom.

586 BC—Babylon overwhelmes Judah, the Southern Kingdom.

336-323 BC—Greeks overrun the Land through Alexander.

168 BC—Maccabian Revolt.

B. Roman occupation

27 BC-70 AD—Roman armies conquer the land Israel.
27 BC-4 AD—Herod the Great.
4 BC-33AD—The history-changing times of Jesus the Messiah.
135-320 AD—Hadrian renames Israel "Palestine" and Jerusalem "Aelia Capitolina."
320-637 AD—The Eastern Roman Empire rules from Constantinople.

C. Islamic invasion

637 AD—Arab Muslims occupy Palestine led by Omar Al-Khattab.
732-1099 AD—Islam overshadows the Middle East and Spain.
1099-1291 AD—The Crusader period.
1291-1517 AD—Egyptian Mamluks rule the land.
1517-1917 AD—Ottoman Turks take over the Middle East and parts of Europe.

D. Are the Palestinians descendants of the Philistines?

The Roots of the Philistines—Arab propaganda and Muslim's insistence that the Arab Palestinians are the offspring of the ancient Philistines can neither be substantiated historically nor biologically. Historically these people migrated from the island of Crete in the prehistoric period. Because they were seafarers they occupied the seashore of what is known today as the Gaza Strip.

1500-1000 BC—During the rule of the Judges and Prophets of Israel and even into the golden reign of David and Solomon, the Philistines were the fiercest enemies of Israel (Book of Judges, I and II Samuel).

1000-586 BC—Philistines are totally eradicated or incorporated into the main stream of Israel's society and disappear from history.

The historian Pliny, the Elder, mentions Palestine in the first century A.D. During the Greek and Roman periods Palestine appears as part of ancient Syria.

Today's Palestinians are descendents of Arab invaders from the seventh to the tenth century of Muslim occupation, plus many Armenians. Armenians escaped the slaughter of one million of their countrymen by the Muslim Turks in 1899 in Armenia. The author's own roots are from Arabia 400 years ago when they came to Nazareth. The town's people declared that this Bedouin has put down his roots here, thus was called "Shorrosh" in Arabic.

E. British mandate

1914-1918 AD—Arabs and Jews agree with the Allies to overthrow Turkish rulers.

1915—Sykes-Picot secret Agreement to split the Middle East signed.

1917—Balfour Declaration promotes a Jewish national home in Palestine.

1918—Laurence of Arabia captures Aqaba while Allenby conquers Jerusalem.

1929—Militant Muslims massacre Jews in Hebron and Safed.

1937—The Peel Commission advocates partition of Palestine.

1938—White Paper rejects partition idea and restricts immigration of Jews.

1941—The outspoken Palestinian leader, Haj Amin al-Husseini, sides with Hitler offering to help exterminate Jews.

1941-1945—The Holocaust death camps exterminate 6 million Jews by Nazis.

1946—President Truman Agrees to the Partition of Palestinian.

F. Modern history of the Israeli-Palestinian conflict

1948—U.N. General Assembly votes for the partition creating a Palestinian and a Jewish state side by side.

1948-49—First modern Arab-Israeli War is fought because Arabs reject partition.

1949-67—Jerusalem is a divided city between Jordan and Israel.

1950—Jordan's King Abdullah annexes the Palestinian Territory calling it the West Bank of Jordan and soon after is assassinated by a Palestinian Muslim militant at Al-Aqsa Mosque.

1955-56—Egyptians blockade the Gulf of Elat forcing Israel to retaliate by attacking Egypt and capturing the Sinai.

1957—Under pressure from the U.S., Israel withdraws from Sinai.

August 29, 1960—Jordanian prime minister and eleven others are killed by a bomb in the foreign ministry building, Amman, Jordan. Two of the bombers fled to safety and eleven others are sentenced to death for the attack.

1964—Yasser Arafat establishes the PLO (Palestinian Liberation Organization).

May 25, 1967—President Nasser of Egypt, along with Leaders of Syria, Iraq, Jordan and Saudi Arabia move troops to attack Israel.

June 5-10, 1967—The Six-Day War is fought with Israel as the victor, despite overwhelming odds.

June 5, 1968—American presidential candidate Robert Kennedy murdered by Jordanian terrorist, Sirhan Bishara Sirhan, in Los Angeles, CA. He was arrested and became the cause of further attacks, as Arab terrorist groups demanded his release.

July 22, 1968—Popular Front for the Liberation of Palestine carry out first ever aircraft hijacking, seizing an El Al Boeing 707 in Rome, Italy, and diverting it to Algeria. Thirty-two Jewish passengers are held hostages for five weeks.

December 26, 1968—One Israeli killed in Popular Front for the Liberation of Palestine machine gun attack on El Al aircraft at Athens airport, Greece. Two terrorists were captured but later released by the Greek government after a Greek aircraft was hijacked to Beirut. Three days after the Athens attack Israeli commandos raid Beirut airport, Lebanon and blow up thirteen Arab airliners worth $43 million.

1970-1973—The Union of Soviet Socialist Republics provides arms to Arab Countries of Egypt, Iraq and Syria to attack Israel again.

1970—Civil War in Jordan led by loyal Jordanian officers evicts PLO commandoes from Jordan on Black September.

1971—The Commando Units of PLO forced out of Jordan, and move to Syria and South Lebanon.

October 6, 1973—Egypt and Syria attack Israel in a surprise move on Yom Kipur.

October 2-24, 1973—Israel, almost overcome, recovers and returns the surprise.

1974—Arab leaders followed by U.N. General Assembly agree that the PLO should represent the Palestinian Arabs.

April 11, 1974—Popular Front for the Liberation of Palestine-General Command terrorists seize part of the Qirayt Shemona settlement in northern Israel. Eighteen Israelis are killed after the terrorists detonate explosives during a rescue attempt.

May 15, 1974—Ninety children are held hostage by Popular Front for the Liberation of Palestine terrorists in a school at Ma'alot, Israel. Twenty-one people are killed and seventy-eight wounded during a bungled rescue attempt by Israeli Special Forces troops.

November 23, 1974—British DC-10 airliner hijacked at Dubai, UAE, by Palestinian Rejectionist Front terrorists and eventually flown to Tunisia where a German passenger was killed.

January 19, 1975—Arab terrorists attack Orly airport, Paris, France, seizing ten hostages in a terminal bathroom. Eventually the French provided the terrorists with a plane to fly them to safety in Baghdad, Iraq.

December 21, 1975—Top international terrorist, Carlos "The Jackal" holds eleven oil ministers and fifty-nine civilians hostage during the OPEC meeting in Vienna, Austria. After flying to Algeria and taking delivery of several hundred million dollars in ransom money,

Carlos and his Popular Front for the Liberation of Palestine terrorists escape.

June 17, 1976—An Air France airliner is hijacked by a joint German Baader-Meinhof/Popular Front for the Liberation of Palestine terrorist group and its crew are forced to fly to Entebbe airport in Uganda. Some two hundred and fifty-eight passengers and crew are held hostage but all non-Israeli passengers are eventually released. On July 4th Israeli commandos fly to Uganda and rescue the remaining hostages. All the terrorists were killed in the rescue, as are three passengers and one commando.

August 11, 1976—Popular Front for the Liberation of Palestine and Japanese Red Army terrorists attack passenger terminal at Istanbul airport, Turkey, killing four civilians and injuring twenty.

1976-1984—Lebanese rebels, Muslim fighters and Palestinian commandoes launch a war against the Christian government, army and people of Lebanon

October 13, 1977—Four Palestinian terrorists hijack a German Lufthansa Boeing 737 and order it to fly around a number of Middle East destinations for four days. After the plane's pilot is killed by the terrorists, it is stormed by German GSG9 counter-terrorist troops, assisted by two British Army Special Air Service soldiers, when it puts down at Mogadishu, Somalia. All the ninety hostages are rescued and three terrorists killed.

1977—President Anwar Sadat makes his historic journey to Jerusalem for peace.

1978—South Lebanon is invaded by Israeli defense forces to destroy Palestinian commando bases which were launching constant attack on northern Israel.

1979—A peace-treaty between Egypt's President Sadat and Israel's Prime Minister Begin is signed in Washington, DC with President Carter's help.

October 3, 1980—Four Jews killed and twelve injured in a Palestinian bomb attack on synagogue in Paris, France.

April 16, 1981—Palestinian terrorist team attempt attack on Israel from Lebanon in hot air balloon. Israeli air defenses shoot down the balloon killing all the crew.

May 13, 1981—Pope John Paul II seriously wounded in assassination attempt in Rome, Italy, by Turkish "Grey Wolves" terrorist Mehmet Ali Agca. It was revealed that he was trained by a number of Middle Eastern terrorists groups and had links to the Soviet intelligence services.

October 6, 1981—Egyptian President Anwar Sadat shot dead by rebel troops who machine-gunned the reviewing stand at a military parade in Cairo, Egypt. Seven other people are killed and twenty-eight wounded. The assassins are later executed.

1982—An all-out offensive by Israeli defense forces reaches Beirut forcing the PLO to leave Lebanon for Tunisia.

June 3, 1982—The Israeli ambassador in London, England, Shloomo Argov, shot and seriously injured by terrorists from the Abu Nidal group. The attack is used to justify the Israeli invasion of Lebanon that started immediately after the attack.

September 16, 1982—Discovery of mass murders at refugee camps in Lebanon.

November 11, 1982—Israeli military headquarters in Tyre, Lebanon, destroyed by Islamic suicide bomber leaving seventy-five Israeli soldiers dead, along with fifteen Lebanese and Palestinian prisoners.

April 18, 1983—Sixty-three people, including the CIA's
Middle East Director, are killed and 120 injured in a
400 pound suicide- truck bomb attack on the US
Embassy in Beirut, Lebanon. The driver is killed.
Responsibility is claimed by Islamic Jihad.

October 23, 1983—Simultaneous suicide-truck bombs on
American and French compounds in Beirut, Lebanon.
A twelve thousand pound bomb destroyed a US
Marine Corps base killing 241 Americans, and 58
Frenchmen are killed when a four hundred pound
device destroyed one of their bases. Islamic Jihad
claims responsibility. U.S. and French aircraft strike
suspected terrorist bases in Lebanon's Baka'a valley
in retaliation.

November 4, 1983—Twenty-eight Israeli soldiers, and
thirty Palestinian and Lebanese civilians are killed in
a suicide-truck bomb attack on the Israeli military
headquarters in Tyre, in southern Lebanon.

December 12, 1983—US Embassy in Kuwait was
targeted by Iranian-backed Iraqi Shia terrorist who
attempted to destroy the building with a truck bomb.
The attack was foiled by guards and the device
exploded in the Embassy fore-court killing five
people.

March 8, 1984—Car bomb in Beirut, Lebanon, kills
eighty and wounds more than two hundred civilians,
in what is believed to have been an American CIA-
backed attempt to kill the leader of the Hezbollah
terrorist group.

March 16, 1984—CIA station chief in Beirut, Lebanon,
William Buckley, kidnapped by the Iranian-backed
Islamic Jihad who tortured, then executed him.

April 12, 1984—U.S. serviceman killed and eighty-three
people injured in bomb attack on restaurant near

USAF base in Torrejon, Spain. Responsibility claimed by Hezbollah as revenge for the March bombing in Beirut.

April 17, 1984—British security forces including Special Air Service counter-terrorist troops lay siege to Libyan People's Bureau (embassy) in London after a British policewomen is killed by small arms fire originating from inside the building. After threats were made to UK citizens living in Libya, the British government decided to respect the diplomatic immunity of the staff of the People's Bureau and allowed them to leave for Tripoli. No one was arrested for the murder.

April 22, 1984—Four Palestinian terrorist hijack bus carrying Israelis in Gaza, occupied territories. Israeli Special Forces storm the bus and kill two of the terrorists after they had been captured.

September 20, 1984—Suicide-bomb attack on U.S. Embassy in East Beirut kills twenty-three people and injured twenty-one others. The U.S. and British ambassadors were slightly injured in the explosion which was attributed to the Iranian-backed Hezbollah group.

March 16, 1985—U.S. journalist Terry Anderson is kidnapped in Beirut, Lebanon, by Iranian-backed Islamic radicals. He is finally released in December 1991.

April 5, 1985—Bomb explodes outside Hezbollah headquarters in Beirut killing eighty people. CIA-backed Christians are blamed.

June 6, 1985—A TWA Boeing 727 was hijacked en route to Rome, Italy, from Athens, Greece, by two Lebanese Hezbollah terrorists and forced to fly to Beirut, Lebanon. The eight crews and 145 passengers were then held for seventeen days, with only one American hostage murdered. After being flown twice to Algiers, on the aircraft's return to Beirut the hostages were released after the US Government pressured the Israelis to release 435 Lebanese and Palestinian prisoners. Incidentally, the persevering pilot died in 2003.

June 9, 1985—U.S. academic, Thomas Sutherland, at the American University, Beirut, kidnapped by Islamic terrorists and held until November 18, 1991.

September 25, 1985—Palestine Liberation Organization Force 17 commando squad kills three Israeli tourists aboard a yacht in Larnica Marina, Cyprus. The three-strong group, including Briton Ian Davidson, are imprisoned by the Cypriots.

September 30, 1985—Four Soviet diplomats kidnapped in Beirut, Lebanon, by Islamic Liberation Organization, which was thought to be a front for the Iranian-backed Hezbollah. One of the Russians was killed but the other three were released unharmed after a relative of the terrorist group's leaders was kidnapped and killed by the Soviet KGB.

October 7, 1985—Four Palestinian Liberation Front terrorists seize the Italian cruise liner, Achille Lauro, during a cruise in the eastern Mediterranean, taking more than seven hundred people hostage. One U.S. passenger was murdered before the Egyptian Government offered the terrorists safe haven in return for the hostages' freedom. U.S. Navy fighters intercepted the Egyptian aircraft flying the terrorists to safety in Tunis and forced it to land at the NATO airbase in Italy, where the terrorists were arrested. The Italian authorities, however, let two of the terrorists leaders escape on diplomatic passports.

November 23, 1985—Ninety-eight passengers and crew of an EgyptAir aircraft are held hostage by Palestinian terrorists at Luqa, Malta. Five passengers were shot by the terrorists and two died. An ill-planned assault by Egyptian Force 777 commandos resulted in some fifty-seven passengers being killed when the terrorists set off explosives in the aircraft.

December 27, 1985—Suicide grenade and gun attacks against passenger terminals at Rome and Vienna airports by the Abu Nidal terrorist group results in sixteen people being killed and more than one hundred civilians injured.

April 5, 1986—Two U.S. soldiers are killed and seventy-nine American servicemen are wounded in Libyan bomb attack on a night club in West Berlin, Germany. Then, days later, U.S. Air Force and Navy jets bomb targets in Libya in reprisal for the raids, hitting targets in Tripoli and Benghazi. One USAF F-111 is shot down in the raid killing its crew of two. Some ninety-three Libya civilians are killed in raids. Three British hostages held by Islamic groups in the Lebanon are killed in response to the raid.

April 17, 1986—British television journalist, John McCarthy, seized in Beirut by Iranian-backed terrorist and held hostage with a large group of other westerners until August 8, 1991.

September 5, 1986—Pan Am Boeing 747 seized by Arab terrorists in Pakistan. They kill seventeen hostages and wound 127 after panicking and thinking they were under attack. Security forces then storm aircraft and free the hostages.

September 12, 1986—U.S. academic at the American University in Beirut, Joseph Cicippio, seized in Beirut by Iranian-backed Islamic terrorists. He is eventually released on December 1, 1991.

September 17, 1986—A ten-month series of bomb attacks in France attributed to Lebanese and Armenian terrorists begins. One bomb in Paris kills five and injures fifty-two.

October 21, 1986—American businessman, Edward Tracy, kidnapped in the Lebanon by Islamic terrorists and held for almost five years until August 11, 1991.

1987—The first "Intifada" begins in Gaza and the West Bank wanting Israel out.

January 10, 1987—British church envoy, Terry Waite, disappears in Beirut, Lebanon, while on a mission to secure the release of other western hostages held in the city by Iranian-backed groups. Eventually released on November 18, 1991.

January 24, 1987—American citizens, Jesse Turner and Alann Steen, seized in Beirut by Islamic terrorists. Turner is held until October 22, 1991 and Steen is released on December 3, 1991.

November 25, 1987—Two hang gliders used by Palestinian terrorists to cross into Israel from Lebanon. Six Israeli soldiers are killed during an attack on an army camp and eight wounded.

1988—King Hussein tells the world that Jordan no longer controls West Bank.

February 5, 1988—U.S. Marine Corps Lieutenant Colonel W. Higgens, kidnapped and murdered by the Iranian-backed Hezbollah while serving with the United Nations Truce Supervisory Organization in southern Lebanon.

March 16, 1988—Four thousand Kurdish civilians killed during Iraqi nerve gas attack against Halabja in northern Iraq, after Iraqi dictator Saddam Hussein ordered the use of biological weapons to put down Kurdish revolt against rule from Baghdad.

April 5, 1988—One hundred and twenty-two people were held hostage after a Kuwaiti Boeing 747 was hijacked and diverted to Mashad, Iran, before flying on to Cyprus. The Kuwait Government refused requests by the Iranian-backed Shia hijackers to release seventeen convicted terrorists. After fifteen days the hijackers were granted asylum in Algeria and released their hostages unharmed.

December 21, 1988—Pan Am Boeing 747 blown up over Lockerbie, Scotland, by a bomb believed to have been placed on the aircraft at Frankfurt Airport, Germany. All 259 people on the aircraft were killed by the blast which has been attributed to a number of Middle Eastern terrorist groups. Two Libyan intelligence operatives are being tried in connection with this attack.

1989-1991—Soviet Jews migrate in great numbers from Russia.

May 12, 1989—British World War II veteran, Jackie Mann, seized by Iranian-backed terrorists in Beirut, Lebanon, and held until September 23, 1991. Four days latter German aid workers, Heinrich Struebig and Thomas Kemptner, were also kidnapped in Lebanon by Islamic terrorists and held until June, 1992. They were the last of some eighty westerners held hostage in Lebanon to be released.

September 19, 1989—One hundred and seventy people killed when French UTA airliner explodes in mid-air over Niger. The French government issued warrants for the arrest of four Libyans.

1990—The Iraqi army invades and takes over oil-rich Kuwait.

1991—The U.S. with its twenty-nine coalition forces attacks Iraq and liberates Kuwait.

March 17, 1992—Israeli Embassy in Buenos Aires, Argentina, devastated by bomb killing twenty and injuring scores more. Islamic terrorists suspected.

February 26, 1993—World Trade Center in New York, USA, badly damaged by a massive bomb planted by Islamic terrorists. The car bomb was planted in an underground garage and left six people dead and more than one thousand people injured.

1994—Israeli Labor Party leader, Yitzhak Rabin, and Yasser Arafat sign the Oslo Accords.

April 6, 1994—Hamas car bomb in Afula, Israel, kills eight and wounds forty-four.

April 13, 1994—Hamas bomb kills five and injures thirty in Hadera.

July 18, 1994—Forty civilians killed in bomb attack on Jewish social center in Buenos Aires, Argentina. Iranian diplomats in the city are expelled after being connected with the incident.

October 19, 1994—Hamas suicide-bomber kills twenty-three civilians and injures forty-seven on a bus in the center of Tel Aviv, Israel.

October 23, 1994—Two Spanish nuns murdered by Islamic GIA terrorists in Algeria.

November 11, 1994—Islamic Jihad militant sets off bomb near Netzarim settlement in Gaza, killing three officers.

1995—Dr. Baruch Goldstein, a Jewish Settler, shoots forty-five Palestinian Muslim worshipers at the historic 2000 year-old Abrahamic Mosque in Hebron.

1995—The Nobel Peace Prize is awarded jointly to Yasser Arafat, Shimon Peres and Yitzhak Rabin.

January 22, 1995—Two Islamic Jihad militants blow themselves up amid a group of soldiers near Netanya, killing twenty-one.

April 9, 1995—Islamic Jihad suicide bomber attacks military convoy in Gaza, killing seven soldiers and an American tourist.

May 5, 1995—Five foreign oil workers murdered by Islamic GIA terrorists in Algeria, as their campaign against military regime gathers pace.

June 26, 1995—Assassination attempt made against Egyptian President Honsi Mubarak in Addis Ababa by Islamic radicals who ambushed his motorcade.

July 24, 1995—Unidentified suicide-bomber kills six passengers and himself on a bus outside Tel Aviv.

July 25, 1995—Algerian GIC Islamic terrorists explode bomb in metro station in Paris, France, killing seven people and injuring eighty-four.

August 21, 1995—Bomb on a Jerusalem bus kills five and wounds 69.

November 2, 1995—Yitzhak Rabin is assassinated by nationalist militant Jew.

November 13, 1995—Seven foreigners, including a number of US servicemen, are killed in bomb attack on National Guard training center at Riyadh, Saudi Arabia.

November 19, 1995—Islamic radicals plant bomb in Egyptian embassy in Pakistan killing seventeen.

December 11, 1995—Car bombings in Algiers by Algerian GIA Islamic terrorists kill fifteen civilians and hundreds more injured.

February 11, 1995—Algerian GIA terrorists explode car bomb in Algiers killing seventeen. The following month, two more are killed in another GIA bomb in the Berroughi and ten are killed in a train ambush in western Algeria.

February 25, 1995—Hamas suicide bomber kills twenty-six Israeli civilians on a bus in the Palestinian town of Hebron. An hour later one Israeli is killed and thirty-five injured in Ashkelon, Israel, by another Hamas bomb.

February 26, 1995—A Palestinian rams a bus queue in Tel Aviv Israel, killing one and wounding twenty-three civilians.

March 3, 1995—Eighteen killed and ten wounded in Hamas suicide bomb attack on bus in Jerusalem.

March 4, 1995—Thirteen civilians are killed and scores wounded when another Hamas suicide bomber attacks a shopping mall in Dizengoff Street, Tel Aviv.

April 19, 1995—Eighteen Greek tourists were gunned down near the historic Pyramids in Egypt by Islamic terrorists aiming to destroy the country's tourist industry.

June 25, 1995—Islamic radical terrorist opposed to the western military presence in the gulf region, explode a truck bomb next to a USAF housing area at Dhahran, Saudi Arabia, killing nineteen American servicemen and injuring 385 more.

August 26, 1995—Six Iraqi dissidents hijack a Sudan Airways A310 Airbus airliner en route from Khartoom to Jordan and divert it to Stanstead, England. After 8 ½ hours negotiating with British authorities, the hijackers release all the thirteen crew and 180 passengers unharmed.

June 25, 1996—A truck bomb destroys the Khobar Towers in Dhahran, Saudi Arabia; 19 Americans are killed and 372 are injured.

January 7, 1997—Two Arab bombs in Tel Aviv, Israel, leaves thirteen injured.

March 31, 1997—Palestinian suicide bomber kills himself and three women at a Tel Aviv café.

July 30, 1997—Two Palestinian terrorists blow themselves up in the Mahane Yehuda market, killing themselves and sixteen shoppers.

September 4, 1997—Bomber kills a total of twenty Israelis. Palestinian extremists blamed.

1998—Benjamin Netanyahu and Yasser Arafat sign the Wye River agreement.

August 7, 1998—US Embassies in Nairobi, Kenya, and Dar-es-Salaam, Tanzania, heavily damaged by massive bomb attacks. In the Nairobi attack 247 people were killed, including twelve Americans, and four thousand injured. Ten people were killed and seventy-four injured in November 2, Tanzania incident. U.S. intelligence blames Islamic groups linked to Saudi dissident Osama Bin Laden.

August 27, 1998—Eighteen injured in Tel Aviv bombing.

November 6, 1998—A Palestinian terrorist car bomb at the Mahane Yehuda market kills two terrorist suicide-bombers from Islamic Jihad and wounds twenty-one Israelis.

2000—Israel defense forces leave Lebanon as Prime Minister Ehud Barak promised.

September 28, 2000—Ariel Sharon visits the Temple Mount and precipitates the "Al-Aqsa Intifada", the second Palestinian uprising.

2000-2003—Ariel Sharon elected Prime Minister and the fighting intensifies with suicide-bombings against military and civilian targets by various Palestinian terrorist organizations.

November 2, 2000—Two Israelis killed by a powerful Palestinian terrorist car bomb at central Jerusalem's Mahane Yehuda market, a frequent target of attacks. Islamic Jihad says it carried out the bombing.

November 22, 2000—Two Israelis killed and fifty-five wounded by a Palestinian terrorist car bomb that explodes during the rush-hour in northern town of Hadera.

December 28, 2000—At least one Palestinian terrorist bomb explodes on a bus near Tel Aviv, wounding thirteen Israelis.

January 1, 2001—Car bomb explodes in west Jerusalem. One woman injured.

February 8, 2001—Two car bomb explosions in the heart of the ultra-Orthodox area of west Jerusalem. No one is killed.

March 1, 2001—At least one person is killed and none injured in an explosion in northern Israel. A group calling itself The Battalions of Return says it is responsible.

March 4, 2001—A suicide bomber blows himself up in Netanya, killing three Israelis and injuring dozens more.

March 26, 2001—Shalhevet Paz, a ten-months old Israeli baby was killed by Arafat's sniper with telescopic rifle from a Abu Senna Palestinian window to a children's kindergarten in Hebron.

March 27, 2001—Thirty people are injured in two separate bomb attacks in Jerusalem. A bomber is killed in the explosion.

March 28, 2001—Three people are killed and several critically injured in a bomb explosion on the border between Israel and the West Bank. The Islamic militant group, Hamas, admits carrying out the attack.

July 2, 2001—Two separate bombs exploded in cars in the Tel Aviv suburb of Yehud. Six pedestrians were injured. The Popular Front for the Liberation of Palestine claimed responsibility.

July 9, 2001—A Palestinian suicide bomber was killed in a car-bombing attack near the Kissufim crossing point in the southern Gaza Strip. Disaster was averted as the bomb exploded without hitting any other vehicles. Hamas claimed responsibility for the attack.

September 11, 2001—The World Trade Center and Pentagon attacked by Arab Muslim terrorists with nearly three thousand lives lost and tens of thousands injured.

September 12, 2001—U.S.A., led by President George W. Bush initiates war on terrorism and the countries which harbor terrorists.

October 7, 2001—England and U.S.A. launch first strike against terrorist targets in Kabul, Afghanistan for harboring Osama Bin Laden and Al-Qaeda.

April 11, 2002—A suicide bombing with a gas truck at a historic Tunisian synagogue on the resort island of Djerba kills twenty-one people, mostly German tourists.

June 14, 2002—A suicide bomber blows up a truck at the U.S. consulate in Karachi, Pakistan, killing fourteen Pakistanis. Authorities say it is the work of Harkat-ul-Mujahedeen, linked to Al Qaeda.

September, 2002—The U.S. and its coalition forces prepare for war against Iraq to remove Saddam from the government and destroy weapons of mass destruction.

October 2, 2002—Suspected Abu Sayyaf guerrillas detonate a nail-laden bomb in a market in Zamboanga, Phillippines, killing four people, including an American Green Beret. Four more bomb attacks in October blamed on Abu Sayyaf, a group linked to Al Qaeda, killing sixteen people.

October 6, 2002—A small boat crashes into a French oil tanker off the coast of Yemen and explodes, killing one crewman.

October 12, 2002—Nearly 200 people, including seven Americans, are killed in bombings in a nightclub district of the Indonesian island of Bali. Authorities blame Jemaah Islamiyah.

November 28, 2002—Suicide bombers kill twelve people at an Israeli-owned beach hotel in Kenya and two missiles narrowly miss an airliner carrying Israelis.

December 30, 2002—A gunman kills three American missionaries at a Southern Baptist hospital in Yemen. Yemeni officials say the gunman, sentenced to death in May, belonged to an Al Qaeda cell.

May 11, 2003—A bomb explodes at a crowded market in a southern Phillippine city, killing at least nine people and wounding forty one. The military blames the Muslim separatist Moro Islamic Liberation Front.

May 12, 2003—Four explosions rock Riyadh, the Saudi capital, in an attack on compounds housing Americans, other Westerners and Saudis. Eight Americans are among those killed. In all, the attack kills thirty-five people, including nine attackers.

May 16, 2003—Bomb attacks in Morocco kill at least twenty-eight people and injure more than one hundred. The government blames "international terrorism," and local militant groups linked to Al Qaeda.

August 5, 2003—A suicide bomber kills twelve people and injures 150 at the J.W. Marriott in Jakarta,

Indonesia. Authorities blame Jemaah Islamiyah, a Southeast Asian group linked to Al Qaeda.

November 8, 2003—A suicide car bomb kills at least seventeen people and wounds 122 at an upscale compound for foreign workers in western Riyadh. Osama bin Laden's Al Qaeda Terror network is blamed.

November 12, 2003—A suicide bomber in Nasiriyah, Iraq, blew up a truck packed with explosives at an Italian paramilitary base and killing 27 people, wounding 79.

Throughout December 2003 until June 2004 numerous terrorist bombings, assassinations and hostage-takings occurred in Iraq, Israel, Indonesia, Spain, France and other Western nations.

On March 11, 2004, ten blasts on a commuter rail line in Madrid, Spain, kills 200 and injures thousands and Al Qaida operatives claimed responsibility.

G. Issues and answers

The above information certainly sheds some light on the long history of a land beloved by Jews, Christians and Muslims. Some theologians believe the conflict started in the tent of Abraham, because Hagar was introduced to a monogamous marriage, resulting not only in the birth of Ishmael, but also precipitating a very deep sense of jealousy between Sarah and Hagar. The Genesis record tells us that the harsh treatment of Hagar by Sarah forced the former to flee the household of Abraham. She returned at the behest of the angel of the Lord. However, fourteen years later, the conflict between the women had become overwhelming to the extent that Hagar and her son, Ishmael, were sent away to an uncertain future. Joktan, Lot, Esau and the six sons of Katura and Abraham, comprise the fathers of the Arabs. Ishmael stands out as the prominent and most visible of the forefathers of the Arab people. Is it possible that the continuous conflicts, the apparent jealousy and the raw hatred between these two peoples is due to the Arab's desire to take revenge upon the Jews, whose forefathers had mistreated Hagar and Ishmael?

The Prophethood, according to **The Quran** had been granted only to Abraham, Isaac and Jacob (surahs 6:89, 29:27, 45:16 and 57:26). Waraqah bin Nawfal announced that Muhammad had seen an angel, not a demon, at Hira caves. He promoted the idea that Muhammad, the first Arab prophet, had equal footing with the Hebrew prophets.

The commonality of Islam and Judaism is truly amazing when one studies the roots of both religions. When Muhammad began his career, he declared himself a warner and a preacher who has come to revive the religion of Abraham. That statement is the more interesting when one realizes that **The Quran** itself is by and large borrowed from the book of Genesis and other documents of the Old Testament.

Some Muslim scholars go so far as to declare that the similarities of Moses and Muhammad are undeniable. Once a person looks at their background, divine call, the deliverance of the Jews from bondage in Egypt, and the Arabs from the bondage of paganism, the similarity becomes more obvious. Yet, the most significant commonality is the belief in one God, the strict discipline of a moral law and the establishment of a theocratic society. One cannot deny the collection of what God revealed to Moses in the Pentateuch, and the Muslims claim that Muhammad received a similar revelation in the form of **The Quran**.

Although the majority of the 250 million Arabs are Muslims, still there are more than sixteen million Christian Arabs. Furthermore, the twenty-two Arab nations control 98.4 percent of the lands of the Middle East whereas Israel owns only one-tenth of one percent! Whenever one follows the history and the development of the conflict between the Arabs and the Jews to this day, realization is made that the Arabs' cultural tradition of saving face may be as important a problem as the entire history of the problem. In other words, the Arab nations, with overwhelming armies and populations have time and again waged wars with Israel, yet, end up defeated. Somehow, a solution to this dilemma must be found. The day may come when another set of leaders from Israel and the Arab side shake hands in friendship at the White House for the world to see as they determine to forgive each other and march toward peace and prosperity for which both have been longing for centuries.

Even as far back as 1991, this writer attempted to shed the light on the Israeli-Palestinian problem in the following article. It was sent to the leaders of the involved parties including the United Nations Secretary General. Some of these ideas were discussed at the Madrid, Spain, conference on the peace process. My wife happened to be watching the evening news. She remarked how amazing it was that some statements of the "Seven Points of Light" in the following article were mentioned. Actually, one does not have to be a rocket scientist, historian, capable politician or a Middle East expert to recognize that despite the complexity of the problems, one can say solutions are available if both sides are willing to communicate, compromise and forgive each other.

Seven Points of Light to Solve the Palestinian Tragedy

1. The U.N. should authorize the arrest of the P.L.O. leadership and charge them with war crimes. The only alternative is to allow them to manage the Palestinian affairs in Jordan, since 60 percent of Jordanians are Palestinians. The P.L.O. represents only 10 percent of the Palestinians and, by means of intimidation, the rest of the 4.5 million.

2. Give the Palestinians seven months to come up with new political leadership within the West Bank, by allowing those qualified to seek office in a primary election to a fifty-two-member parliament.

3. "Land for peace" worked when Israel returned the Sinai to Egypt in 1979. We do not want that for the Palestinians. Here is a better idea: Give them nothing. Why? They already own 80-90 percent of the land they live on and cultivate. Let them keep it. It is theirs and furthermore, the former West Bank areas which have a majority of Palestinian Arabs should be part of Palestine.

4. Israeli settlements constructed since 1967 can remain undisturbed within the new Palestinian territory. Settlers will be considered as welcomed Israeli citizens. Palestinians living and working in Israeli territory will also be welcomed as guests, yet remain citizens of Palestine.

5. Jerusalem is non-negotiable for Israel. However, let each religious group (Armenians, Christians, Jews, and Muslims) have complete control of their religious properties except for overall security.

6. The capital of Palestine should be Samaria, the ancient capital of Israel in Biblical days, known today as Nablus. The reason: It's the most populated Palestinian city, and has all the requirements for a capital—commercial, agricultural, and political leadership for the entire West Bank.

7. Finally, any Palestinian in the world can return to his former homeland by a new "Law of Return," provided:

a. He has never associated in terrorist activity.

b. He has relatives or property in either Israeli or Palestinian domain.

c. He can find employment within 180 days of his return, or else be deported to his former country of origin.

If a displaced Palestinian from the 1948, 1967, or 1973 war owned property in Israel which cannot be returned to him, for whatever reason, a comparable piece of property or equivalent monetary value can be granted him in its place—whether he wishes to live in the land or remain in the country of his domicile.

The P.L.O. henceforth will no longer be referred to as the "Palestinian Liberation Organization," but shall be referred to as "Palestinians Loving Others." Its President and members of Parliament shall be elected by the bona fide Palestinian citizens throughout the world at appointed U.N. voting centers. No Palestinian can become a candidate for any government position if he is a citizen of another country unless he renounces that citizenship. They shall have the right to organize their own police force, but no standing army. Furthermore, they will have the right to sign a peace treaty which will include Israel to the west, Jordan to the east, and Egypt to the south. Later on, Syria, Lebanon, and Iraq can be included in this general peace treaty. They will allow instant communications, open transportation and free travel by the citizens of all these countries.

From now on, terrorists of whatever nationality, who are captured, brought to justice and convicted, shall be executed within seventy days. Any nation on this planet harboring terrorists or encouraging such activity, in whatever shape or form, shall be ostracized by the United Nations, and an embargo will be placed on its commercial businesses, airlines, ships, autos, trucks—even bicycles—and shall be banned form entering any United Nations country. These sanctions shall be lifted once the culprits are handed over to a United Nations' tribunal, which will deal with them within the U.N. Charter and the laws of the country where they perpetrated their activities.

H. What is the second intifadah (the shaking)?

Mr. Ariel Sharon, as minister of housing, had received confirmed reports that Muslim Waqf, who oversees the function of the Temple Mount, was doing some illegal excavations. With one hundred police personnel he marched to that touchy area of Jerusalem. Jews, Christians and Muslims consider this area sacred because 4000 years ago God Almighty directed Abraham to offer Isaac on Mt. Moriah in a test of faith.

Now it came to pass after these things that God tested Abraham, and said to him, "Abraham!" And he said, "Here I am." And He said, "Take now your son, your only son Isaac, whom you love, and go to the land of Moriah, and offer him there as a burnt offering on one of the mountains of which I shall tell you." Genesis 22:1.

One thousand years later King David prepared all the necessary material for Solomon, his son, to build the temple on a grandiose scale. Christians believe that the renovated and expanded temple by Herod the Great between 4 B.C. and 37 A.D. was where Jesus preached and where the Holy Spirit first descended upon the disciples in a physical, visible public manner.

Muslims, however, take issue as to who was the son which Abraham offered. They claim it was Ishmael.

In the name of Allah, the Beneficent, the Merciful. Glorified be He Who carried His servant by night from the Inviolable Place of Worship to the Far Distant Place of Worship the neighbourhood whereof We have blessed, that We might show him of Our tokens! Lo! He, only He, is the Hearer, the Seer. Surah 17:1.

With few words we are told that Allah took Muhammad overnight from the Masjid Al-Haram to the distant mosque which is supposed to be Jerusalem. The city is not mentioned by name in **The Quran**. Furthermore, if the Quranic reference is to Solomon's Temple, it was destroyed by the Romans in 70 A.D.

In fact, the most plausible explanation and interpretation of this verse must be a reference to the Prophet of Arabia's escape from Mecca to Medina. Historically, at that specific time, in the Islamic chronology, there was only one mosque—the one at Mecca. Consequently, one must surmise that the verse refers to Allah's protection of his messenger when he escaped for his life from Mecca to Medina in 612. This makes much sense inasmuch as there was no other mosque in existence besides the one in Mecca, except the one in Medina. In other words, Allah was reminding Muhammad how he protected him when he fled for his life from the assassins and showed him his mercy by taking him to start a new life in Medina. It is remarkable that Muslim historians affirm that there were 175 believers in Medina in contradistinction to forty-five in Mecca. Thus the idea of his going to Jerusalem overnight on the flying horse, Buraq, is simply a fairy-tale. Muhammad never mentioned Jerusalem in **The Quran**, whether in reference to this verse, or anything else in his life.

At any rate, the rumors spread like wildfire that Ariel Sharon represented Jewish authority, which had come to take over the sacred Dome of the Rock and the Aqsa Mosque properties. The wild rioting, stone throwing and fist fights suddenly erupted like an active volcano because the Arabic radio egged on Muslims to descend on the Temple Mount to defend the sacred grounds from being taken over by the Israeli Zionists.

Thus, the second intifada was borne and with it the horrors of suicide bombers, kidnappings, school children and young people blown away at restaurants and coffee shops, homes destroyed, businesses going bankrupt, tourism a thing of the past and the entire economy in shambles. The worst calamity, of course, was the murder and killing of over 2000 Palestinians and over 600 Israelis. The entire process of peace, entitled "The Oslo's Ten Year Peace Plan" was washed down the drain!

To the credit of President George W. Bush and his administration, a crucial effort loomed large on the horizon full of hope and promise. Despite the serious wars in Afghanistan and Iraq, Mr. Bush was able to persuade King Fahid of Saudi Arabia, King Abdullah II of Jordan, Palestinian Prime Minister Abbas and Prime Minister Ariel Sharon of Israel to a summit meeting in June 2003 at Taba, Egypt, the renowned resort by the Red Sea. With pomp and circumstance the "road map" was agreed upon by all parties in an official ceremony covered by the world's leading media.

The euphoria was short-lived because the Palestinian Authority could not restrain the terrorist groups within their midst. Horrible bombings of buses, cars, clubs, shops and border checkpoints brought more bloodshed among Palestinians and Israeli alike. Despite a well-published Washington invitation for Abbas to strengthen his position, the new Palestinian Prime Minister resigned in frustration.

As of December, 2003, the new Prime Minister, Mr. Ahmed Qureia, appears more communicative with Arafat, as well as Sharon. He seems to have more clout, support and authority than Mr. Abbas.

I. The heartbreaking Arab-Israeli problem can be resolved

1. Palestinians and Israelis must admit to themselves and to each other that both have done wrong to each other

and it is time to act with a rational mind rather than a mindless spirit of vengeance and hate.

2. To keep rehashing the past injustices by one against the other is extremely counterproductive. The past is past and gone. We must live with hope for the future. Forgiveness is needed on both sides.

3. Terrorist groups have eroded trust and hope by both entities. The entire Arab world is now looked upon by the peoples of the world with disdain and disgust. They look upon Palestinians and Israelis with scorn and little sympathy. Terrorists must be stopped at any cost, whether they are Arabs, Jews or Muslims.

4. Israel can once again welcome the Palestinian labor force which propelled the building programs, skilled and unskilled workers, through Israel's economic success story, prior to the intifada.

5. The Arab nations as a whole should issue a clear announcement welcoming their cousins as a viable, vital and valuable nation under the sun and a real partner in the future of the entire Middle East. Fifty-five years of warfare is too much.

6. Arab countries must welcome Palestinian refugees as full citizens of the countries they have been residing in since 1948, 1967, 1973 or 1982.

7. Israel should allow a select group of displaced Palestinians between the ages of 40-60 only to return to Israel's own land. These people must provide solid evidence that they still have property within Israel's borders. If the properties have been confiscated or appropriated by the state or individuals, monetary remuneration should be offered or another piece of land given of equal value.

8. Jerusalem, being the most unsolved mystery of the ages throughout the Middle East history, must still

function as the capital of Israel. However, the Palestinian state can have the Muslim quarter of the old city as their symbolic capital while Ramallah continues to be the official headquarters of the new State of Palestine. In other words, ceremonially, old Jerusalem can be claimed as Palestine's capital while the overall security would still remain with Israel's police force, not Israel's Defense Forces (IDF).

9. To satisfy the longing of Orthodox Judaism, the Islamic Waqf, in a gesture of good will, should give the vacant five acres north of the Dome of the Rock where Jews can build a temple, even the size of King Solomon's. This action will create a closer relationship of the two peoples.

10. Strict security must be enforced for all who enter within the walls. No weapons whatsoever should be allowed, except with the guards at the gates of the city. Special ID cards for those living within the walls should be issued. Only tourists and relatives of those living within walled Jerusalem should be welcomed into Jerusalem's walled city at any given time.

11. Once every three years at Yom Kippur, at the end of Ramadan, then at Christmas, joint ceremonies should be conducted annually to promote goodwill throughout the land with musical programs, dramatic plays, folk festivals, dialogues, discussions and speeches.

12. Three mayors should be elected, with an Israeli, a Christian, and a Muslim rotating annually. A sincere commitment towards tolerance, reconciliation, forgiveness and love will bring about a new day of peace and prosperity. Then the traumatized, tired and totally hopeless souls of the young and the old

warring cousins, the Arabs and the Israelis will experience peace.

We cannot conclude this crucial chapter without a reference to pre-tribulation theories of most evangelical Americans.

Since Hal Lindsey popularized the subject of the second coming with his best-seller, **The Late Great Planet Earth**, in the seventies (75 million in print), hundreds of other similar titles have been added by other writers. The latest series by Tim LaHaye and Jim Jenkins, the **Left Behind** series, have sold nearly 100 million copies.

At any rate, the entire scenario can be summarized into:
1. Israelis return to Biblical Palestine—1948. (Zech. 8:7; Eze. 37:11-14)
2. Israelis return to Jerusalem—1967. (Zech. 8:8; Isaiah 11:11-12)
3. Israelis return to the Lord (?) through a series of conflicts with their neighbors (Zech. 13:11-12) concluded with the Battles of Armageddon (Eze. 38-39) which Messiah Jesus will interrupt and rapture the believers to glory. (I Thes. 5:1-11; Zech. 12:10)
4. After a tense, terrible and traumatic seven year tribulation Jesus will destroy the Antichrist and establish His Kingdom for a 1000 year reign, with Jerusalem as the international capital of the New World order. (Zech 14:4; II Thes. 2:1-17; II Peter 3:3-14; Jude 14-16 and Rev. 1:7-8)

Of course, such beliefs indicate that no matter who tries to bring peace to the City of Peace, they will fail. Only Jesus the Messiah can do that. Yet human beings who love God and have compassion for others can promote peace even if it is only temporary!

O, you who are hypocrites, yet still claim to belong among Our worshipers: We yearn to see you prosper. We do not wish you to be impoverished.

Moreover, We seek for you love, not hate; faithfulness, not faithlessness; trust, not mistrust; and reconciliation, not irreconciliation.

We furthermore wish for you security, not fear; peace, not war; and compassion, not aggression.

Additionally, We covet for you chastity, not promiscuity; respect, not disrespect; goodwill, not pillaging; and forgiveness, not taking revenge.

We also long to see you educated, not uneducated; charming, not backward; humble, not haughty; just, not unjust; dwelling in the Light, not dwelling in darkness.

Moreover, We desire for you wisdom, not ignorance; brotherly love, not hostility; and enlightenment, not confusion. Will you try to discern what We intend for you?

Subsequently, repent, be enlightened and pursue the virtuous pathway. It is preferable to the path which you have chosen in the past, a path of ignorance, sickness, poverty, terrorism and insecurity, which are by-products of complete infidelity. (The True Furqan "Prosperity" 59:1-7)

IX

IRAQ—YESTERDAY, TODAY, AND TOMORROW

This is an extraordinary day. The chapter begins on the day Saddam Hussein was captured at Adwar, near his hometown of Tikrit, December 13, 2003. This writer was in Tikrit two weeks earlier touring the famous city. One is impressed by its modern streets, beautiful buildings, massive presidential palace and burned military headquarters. The latter were hit by missile attacks nicknamed "shock and awe" when the war commenced on March 19, 2003. The news of the capture of one of the two most-wanted fugitives in modern history was welcomed by millions throughout the world and particularly the American military forces, who had been combing the countryside searching for him ever since they entered Baghdad. Osama Bin Laden has been and still is the other "most wanted."

Iraq is almost the same size as California, 169,240 square miles. The majority of its population is Shiites. Yet the 15 percent Sunnis have been in control for twenty-five years. Out of the 25,000,000, 94.4 percent are Muslims and 3.3 percent Christians. Unfortunately, only fifty percent of the population is literate. (Illiteracy is always a hotbed for dictators.) Despite the fact that Christians are a small minority, surprisingly they make up 37 percent of all doctors in Iraq. There is a serious need for national unity among the Arabs, Kurds, Turkomans, Persians, Iranians, Assyrians and other ethnic groups. Not only to survive, but also to become a viable modern society, Iraqis must have political unity by establishing a new government which respects as well as represents all of the cultural and religious members of the population. Men and women of wisdom, integrity and tolerance are greatly needed to lead Iraq into its brighter future.

A. Iraq's brilliant past

Few Christians, but more Jews, are aware that almost one-fourth of the Old Testament was written in ancient Iraq. Many believe that the Garden of Eden was in ancient Iraq. But I do not. I believe it was in the Holy Land. Here are some intriguing historical facts concerning Iraq:

1. Jehovah appeared to Abraham in Mesopotamia (Gen. 12:1-2, 6-7; 15:5).
2. The Garden of Eden, according to many archeologists, was in Iraq (Gen. 2:14).
3. Mesopotamia, which is now Iraq, was the home of Balaam (Deut. 23:4).
4. Noah built the ark in Iraq (Gen. 6-8).
5. Historically, the Tower of Babel was in Iraq (Gen. 11:1-9).
6. Abraham was from Ur, which is in Southern Iraq (Gen. 11:27-32).
7. Isaac's wife, Rebekah, was from Nahor, which was in Iraq (Gen. 24).

8. Jacob met Leah and Rachel in Iraq (Gen. 29-31).
9. Eleven of Jacob's thirteen children were born in Haran, Iraq (Gen. 29-30).
10. Jonah preached in Nineveh—which was in Iraq (Jonah 1-4).
11. Assyria, which was north Iraq, conquered the twelve tribes—722 B.C. (Jer. 52).
12. Tiglath Paliser III was the first Assyrian King listed in the Bible (I Chron. 5:26).
13. Amos cried out in Iraq (Amos 7:11; 9:4).
14. Babylon, founded by Nimrod, destroyed Jerusalem in 587 B.C. (Gen. 10:6-10).
15. Daniel was in the lion's den in Iraq (Dan. 6).
16. The three Hebrew children were in the fiery furnace in Iraq (Dan. 3:25).
17. Belshazzar, the King of Babylon, saw the "writing on the wall" in Iraq (Dan. 5).
18. Nebuchadnezzar took the Jews to Babylon (II Kings 24-25; Jer. 39,52).
19. Ezekiel proclaimed his messages in Iraq (Ezek. 1:1-25).
20. Ezra and Nehemiah were captives in Iraq (Books of Ezra and Neh.).
21. The drama of Esther took place in Iraq (Esther 1-10).
22. The Wisemen of the East were from Iraq (Matt. 2:1).
23. Peter preached in Babylon (I Peter 5:13).
24. The "Empire of Man" described in Revelation is called Babylon (Dan. 2:31).
25. Jesus was seen in the fiery furnace with the three Hebrews (Dan. 3:25).
26. Jesus referred to Nineveh, Iraq, in His preaching (Matt. 12:39-41).
27. Jews from Mesopotamia were in Jerusalem on Pentecost (Acts 2:1-9).

The ancient name was Mesopotamia, which means "the land in the midst of the rivers." Without the Tigris and Euphrates rivers, Iraq, much like Egypt without the Nile, would have been a desolation of millions of acres of dessert. The average temperature varies from 60 degrees in the winter to over 110 degrees in the summer.

Most people are involved in raising sheep, goats, donkeys, horses, camels and mules. In recent years, under Saddam's regime, the military forces have grown to about 1 million soldiers. The agricultural products are wheat, barley, rice and palm dates. Amazingly enough, the Iraqis produce 80 percent of the entire world's annual output of palm dates. Beginning with the 1930's, the chief industry became crude oil. As of November 2003, Iraq has been producing over 2,000,000 barrels a day. Most earthlings are unaware that Iraq's oil deposits are the richest in the world! Other materials which Iraq produces are textiles, bricks, cement, milling and tanning of leather products. Additionally, Iraq exports crude oil, cereals, dates, rice, wool, cotton, hides and skins. However, it imports iron, steel, tea, sugar, textiles, vehicles, lumber, paper, household appliances, machinery and satellite dishes.

It is well documented that ancient civilizations developed around great rivers. The Sumerian civilization developed during 4000 B.C. Babylonia, Assyria and Chaldea were conquered by the Accadians. In the fourth century B.C., Alexander the Great swept through these lands and died in Babylon on June 13, 323 B.C. at age thirty three. Next came the Parthians, the Romans, then, the Sassanides. In 633 it fell into the hands of the Arab Muslims.

From 750 A.D. to 1258 A.D., Baghdad became a world center of education where mathematics, philosophy, astronomy, geography and medicine were taught. Baghdad became the center of Islamic power and presence throughout the known world. Hulaqu the Mongol took control in 1258 A.D., for 400 years, and then the Ottoman Turkish army took Iraq over and ruled it from 1639-1918. The world-renowned story of "Ali Baba and the Forty Thieves" along with "Aladin and the Lamp" were supposed to have taken place in Baghdad.

The British won the mandate over Iraq after the end of WWI. Thereafter, from 1918-1933, Iraq was controlled by England. The British crowned Faisal I as King of Iraq in 1921 and Baghdad became the capital of Iraq. Although Iraq became independent in 1933, the British had to return in 1941-1945 because of a pro-Nazi coup de'etat in 1941.

King Faisal II was assassinated in 1958. General Kassem established a republic of which he became president. However, Kassem was killed in 1963 and Col. Arif took over. Then from 1966-1968 his brother ruled Iraq. General Hassan El Bakr engineered a coup in 1968 and became president of the republic until 1979.

B. Iraq's troubled times

The age of terror for Iraq began in 1979 when Saddam Hussein took over the presidency. Con Coughlin, executive editor of London's award-winning *Sunday Telegraph*, authored *Saddam Hussain, King of Terror*, published by Harper

Collins Publishers, New York, NY, 2002. It is a very rich resource for the life and times of Saddam and is an eye-opener on his evil empire. One wonders how an illegitimate child from Tikrit became the West's greatest adversary, even more than Osama Bin Laden! Furthermore, it is fascinating to learn that Saddam placed his troops on their highest military preparedness since the Gulf War of 1991—only two weeks before 9/11!

A long-standing border dispute with Iran, a standing army of one million, plus an eighty-billion dollar treasury, prompted Saddam to launch a war against Iran. Its newly formed mullahcracy of fundamentalist Muslims plus the vacuum in the Middle East for a singular Arab leader pushed Saddam Hussein to take such a risk for eight long and bloody years. With such a vast amount of money, reopened relations with the U.S. to supply weapons and a military force of one million, Saddam initiated the war against Iran. The end of the devastating conflict depleted his treasury, put him into a debt of seventy-five billion dollars and resulted in one million casualties plus two million injured Iraqis and Iranians.

Some conjecture that Hussein was aiming at liquidating a dangerous Islamic menace in Iran and give him a coveted standing with America. Iran is the largest Shiite Muslim country in the world and sits on the fifth largest oil reserves on earth. A victory over Iran would position Hussein as the supreme leader of the Arab World and the undisputed hero of the entire Middle East. President Gamal Abdel Naser of Egypt had enjoyed the designation and popularity of such an esteemed position. After Naser's death, the Shah of Iran tried to seize that title by using his oil income to purchase the most sophisticated arsenal from America. But he was deposed in 1979. Gaddafi of Libya also tried very hard and failed. The same happened to Egypt's President Anwar Sadat, who met an untimely death by assassination in 1981 by Muslim fundamentalists because he achieved peace with Israel.   Mubarak, who succeeded Sadat, became president of Egypt. He is popular, but lacks the charisma of Nasser and the diplomatic skills of Sadat. Saddam felt he could carry the mantle of leadership if he could conquer Iran. The war resulted in a stalemate.

With his financial resources drying up and the oil production not enough to cover his debts to Germany, France, Canada, the U.S. and USSR, he invaded Kuwait and annexed it in 1990. With Kuwait's rich treasury of billions of dollars along with their oil reserves, Saddam calculated that his move would help pay his debts, provide more oil revenue and make him the leader of the Arab world.

Prior to invading Kuwait, a mysterious plot was purported to have been hatched in Baghdad in the year of 1990. Saddam assured the Yemenites that if they were to unite their two countries, he would give them the southern territory of Saudi Arabia, which they had been claiming as their own for decades. And they united. King Hussein of Jordan was promised by Saddam to return him to his rightful position in Arabia as the Sherrif of Mecca and Medina. Muslims know that popular King Hussein was a descendent of Prophet Muhammad. Therefore, he had more right than the Saudi clan to rule the country. To Arafat, the Palestinian leader, Saddam promised the eviction of the Israelis from the entire country. He assured Arafat that even if an atomic weapon is needed, Saddam would have it ready to hurl against Israel.

President George H. Bush initiated "Desert Shield" in the fall of 1990 with the help of a multi-national force to liberate Kuwait. When the ultimatum was turned down by Iraq to withdraw from Kuwait, the "Desert Shield" became "Desert Storm." The Iraqis were forced out of Kuwait in a series of unprecedented battles by air, land and sea—February 1991.

Later that year, the world was shocked at the ruthless and barbaric methods Saddam used against the Kurdish dissidents who rose up against him. In one poisoned gas attack nearly five thousand men, women and children were put to death.

Over a period of ten years, with continued reports by fleeing Iraqis, electronic and human intelligence, American and British leadership were convinced that Hussein was developing WMDs (weapons of mass destruction), in addition to the brutality and mass murders of the opposition. But the U. N. was not totally convinced.

Nonetheless, on March 19, 2003, war began by coalition forces, largely led by England and the U.S.A. The stunning and swift victory had people scratching their heads everywhere. The Iraqi Army melted into the cities, hamlets and deserts of Iraq. The toppling of the huge statue of Saddam Hussein in central Baghdad near the university campus was a sight seen by millions around the globe on their T.V. screens, enforcing the fact that Saddam was defeated and Iraq was liberated. It is very significant to list the thirty-six nations which comprise the coalition forces. This will diffuse the critics who keep saying that the Iraqi war is an American war. The list appeared on page 31 of *Time* magazine's issue of May 3, 2004. Accordingly the US forces total 135,000, the British 11,000 and the other thirty-four nations have 16,648. It is shameful that Spain withdrew their 1,300 coalition forces as a result of their own 9/11 terrorist attack, intimidated by the terrible terrorists.

United States	135,000	Nicaragua	230
Britain	11,000	Singapore	200
Italy	2,700	Mongolia	180
Poland	2,400	Azerbaijan	151
Ukraine	1,700	Norway	150
Spain	1,300	Portugal	128
Netherlands	1,100	Latvia	121
Australia	850	Lithuania	105
South Korea	700	Slovakia	105
Romania	700	Philippines	96
Japan	560	Czech Republic	80
Denmark	496	Albania	70
Bulgaria	470	Georgia	70
Thailand	460	New Zealand	60
Honduras	370	Estonia	55
El Salvador	360	Kazakhstan	29
Hungary	300	Macedonia	28
Dominican Republic	300	Moldova	24

When this author was visiting Iraq in November 2003, like most visitors, the impression was "the media has not been giving the U. S. public, nor the rest of the world, a true picture of the situation." In other words, the incidents of bombings, explosions, killings and disruption of the activities of normal daily life, are exaggerated enormously. People seem to be carrying on with their daily lives in a very natural way, although some exceptions exist. First, there are periodic security forces checkups on any street, road or highway. Second, banks, post offices and telephones were not functional and there was intermittent power shut-off. Yet, one could utilize a satellite telephone. I bought a phone card for 250 minutes at a cost of only $6.00. Of course that entailed using the popular and ever present internet cafes. Among the surprises was that one American dollar could be exchanged for 2000 Iraqi dinars. However, in less than three months after my visit of November, 2003, the dinar's value had risen 30 percent. Now, one dollar would be exchanged for only 1300 dinars. Having observed the progress toward normalcy throughout Baghdad specifically and the rest of the country generally, it was obvious that the new dinar would rise quickly to a better exchange rate as the country becomes more stable and oil flows. Did I tell you that gasoline is sold for 25 cents a gallon?

I was in Lafayette, IN, December 13, 2003, lecturing at an international conference on Mid-Eastern affairs. The Sunday morning T.V. programming was interrupted. The breaking news informed the world that the "Butcher of Baghdad," better known as Saddam Hussein, had been captured. Adwar was the tiny village where the six hundred member American force discovered him hiding in a hole in the ground. His visage flashed around the world, displaying a hopeless, homeless, hapless soul.

The snow had fallen all around my host's lovely home, as if to proclaim itself as an omen for better days for Iraq. The ruthlessness, brutality, carnage, destruction, deception, thievery and chaos which this one man and his two sons, Uday and Qusay perpetrated, and the cruel administration which he ruled with an iron fist for twenty-five years had come to an end. But like a large serpent it kept wiggling trying to hurt everybody around it, despite the fact that the head and tail had been chopped off.

This is February 16, 2004. The Charlotte Observer, a North Carolina newspaper, printed that 537 American soldiers had died, 337 from hostile action and 164 from accidents since the war began March 19, 2003. One must not forget, however, that a sizable number of British, Spanish and other coalition troops have also been killed and injured. How about the 600 plus Iraqi policemen who have been killed since the war began until March 2004! The price of freedom has never been cheap. Look at this figure in perspective. In the year 2002 over 17,000 Americans were killed on our highways due to drinking drivers. In other words we kill in two weeks more people on our highways by drinking drivers than the entire casualties of the Iraqi War! Yet we do not hear media outrage at these statistics! Furthermore, USA Today printed on its front page 2/20/04 that 42,815 Americans were killed by vehicular crashes last year. One has to wonder how many of these were killed by drinking drivers because more than 26,000, who were killed, were drivers.

At times we are accused, as Americans, by other nations that we are trying to act as a world policeman. Our response is that since no nation is willing to carry this burden, and due to the fact that we are a compassionate people and hold the position of the only super power in the world, we say "Why not?" Additionally, no democracy has as many citizens within its borders as America except India. The Indians and the U.N. have almost always supported our efforts in trying to remove the despots and dictators of other countries, help the destitute and impoverished citizens and introduce democracy at a great cost to us in brain, brawn and billions of dollars.

On May 6th 2004 the Associated Press provided readers of daily newspapers a valuable list of war costs. It stated that the Congressional Research Service reported in October 2003 the following revealing statistics. Since 9/11, the U. S. has spent $165 billion on the Afghanistan and Iraqi War and anti-terrorism operations. World War I cost $558 billion; World War II $4.8 trillion; Korean War $408 billion; the Gulf War $82 billion. If freedom does not come cheap, neither do wars!

However, when we are not welcomed, as it happened in Lebanon in 1986 and in Somalia in 1999, we just fold our tent and depart. At times we have been guilty of supporting the regime instead of the populace. The reason is very simple. The regime serves the national interest more to our political liking rather than the other way around. That is the wrong philosophy for a nation such as America. But who in the universe is capable of always making the right decision, except God Almighty!

It is necessary to establish the fact that after our success in World War II American administrations were bewildered and befuddled as to what to do with all this enormous American power. President Reagan, after his landslide victory over dovish President Carter, rallied the nation toward a more assertive if not aggressive posture before the world. The USSR trembled, flinched and eventually disintegrated. His famous words, while standing at the Berlin Wall, "Mr. Gorbachev, tear down this wall!" will never be forgotten. Reagan gave the

USSR a new label by calling them "the Evil Empire." But Mikhail Sergeyevich Gorbachev did not tear the wall down. However, a short time later the Berliners themselves, on both sides of the wall, did tear it down in 1989, brick by brick, while the world watched on T.V. And Berlin, Germany, was united once again. Gorbachev was president of the USSR from 1988-1991 and presided over the dismantling of the "Evil Empire." That empire could not stand their people's will-power against the Communist tyranny and collapsed after seventy-two years of disastrous dictatorship! President Reagan passed into history on June 6, 2004, amidst a week of ceremonies, memorials and funerals befitting a great American president.

Grenada (in the Caribbean) was rescued from the grip of Communist's leaders just in time by the U.S.'s quick military action, through President Reagan's leadership. What shall we say of hitting Gaddafi of Libya and terrorizing him by letting him know "he could run but could not hide?" Finally, thirteen years after the tragedy of Lacarbie, Gaddafi agreed to pay each passenger's family who perished in the ghastly PanAm flight explosion, six million dollars each in January 2004. When we can make terrorists realize that their terrorism is very costly, they may begin to back-track as Muammar Gadhafi finally did. The June 21, 2004, issue of *Time Magazine* tells that Gadhafi was accused by the Saudi royals of ordering a hit on Crown Prince Abdullah and was called a liar aby them during an Arab summit last year!

Nonetheless, the sorry state of affairs which followed were eight years of reducing American military, cutting the American forces budget and emasculating our national and international security. Without a doubt, these unbelievable "Clintonics" contributed much to the catastrophe of 9/11/01. The reluctance of President Clinton to use American power effectively emboldened terrorists to attack us. It became more and more apparent to our enemies that "America is impotent" militarily.

American troops were dispatched to Lebanon, then to Somalia, but never did the job in either country, just like the tragedy of Vietnam. Nevertheless, there was a measure of success in Bosnia. Therefore America must decide that if we go to war, we should never call it quits until the enemy surrenders or is vanquished. Does any thinking American believe that terrorists would have attacked America on 9/11/01 if the U.S. government, led by President Bill Clinton, had executed the members of the terrorists group who attacked the Twin Towers in 1993, instead of giving them prison terms? Weakness was detected by the militant Muslims to attack us, our embassies and other American interests at will in Africa, Europe, the Middle East and anywhere else they liked!

Afghanistan was liberated from the horrors of the Taliban in the year 2002 and now Iraq. Once again the reader is reminded that ancient civilizations, such as Nimrod's, Hammurabi's and Nebuchadnezzar's, began in Mesopotamia. The oil, which is the life-blood of the industrial nations, flows from the Middle East and Iraq has more of it than any of these countries. The likelihood that the American public is appreciative of President Bush's effort in securing the oil wells of Iraq in the hands of the West, rather than modern Russia, or despots like Saddam, is not visible at this time. In other words, the appreciation will come later when the prices of oil elsewhere will rise drastically while they will remain steady in the USA. Great Britain, years ago, intervened in Iraq (1941-45) when a pro-Nazi coup de'etat was about to take control. The former Soviet Union salivated at moving into Iraq after their successful wooing of Egypt through the gigantic engineering feat of building the Aswan Dam in the seventies. The Cold War was not only fought over the supremacy of the world politically or militarily, but was also associated with who controlled the vast resources of oil in the Middle East.

According to an article which appeared in USA Today, December 16, 2003 on page 5A, one would be impressed with the following Status Update of 'Most Wanted' Iraqis. With the capture of Saddam Hussein, the top five of the 55 "most wanted" Iraqis are dead or in U.S. custody. They are:

Name	Former Position	Status
Saddam Hussein	President of Iraq, head of military	Captured Dec 13
Qusay Hussein	Saddam's son, military and security commander Saddam Fedayeen	Killed July 22
Uday Hussein	Saddam's son, commander of paramilitary	Killed July 22
Abid Hamid Mahmud al-Tikriti	Presidential secretary	Captured June 16

| Ali Hassan al-Majid | Presidential adviser, former southern regional commander | Captured August 21 |

Of the next 50, 36 have been taken into custody or have surrendered and 14 remain at large. They are:

Name	Former Position	Status
Izzat Ibrahim al-Douri	Vice chairman of Revolutionary Command Council; thought to be a leader of the Anti-U.S. insurgency	At large
Hani Abd al-Latif Tilfah al-Tikriti	Director of Special Security Organization provided Saddam plainclothes security	At large
Sayf al-Din Fulayyih Hasan Taha al-Rawi	Republican Guard Forces Chief of Staff	At large
Rafi Abd al-Latif Tilfah al-Tikriti	Director of Directorate of General Security which repressed political opposition	At large
Tahir Jalil Habboush	Director of Iraqi intelligence Service, which conducted counterespionage, interrogation	At large

Rukah Razuki Abd al-Ghafar Sulayman al-Majid	Chief of Tribal Affairs	At large
Sabawi ibrahim Hasan	Baath Party leader, Saddam's half brother	At large
Abdel Baqi Abdel Karim Abdallah al-Sadun	Baath Party regional command chairman	At large
Mohammed Zimam Abdul Razaq	Baath Party regional command chairman	At large
Yahya Abdellah al-Aboudi	Baath Party regional command chairman	At large
Nayef Shedakh	Baath Party regional command chairman	At large
Mushin Khadr al-Khafaji	Baath Party regional command chairman	At large
Rashid Taan Kazim	Baath Party regional command chairman	At large
Khamis Sirhan al-Muhammad	Baath Party regional command chairman	At large

Black Tuesday in U.S. history was the terrorist attack by Muslim militants on 9/11/2001.

Jerusalem, city of peace, one day will become trully so when Jesus returns.

Nazareth, where Jesus grew to manhood. Also the home of Dr. Shorrosh.

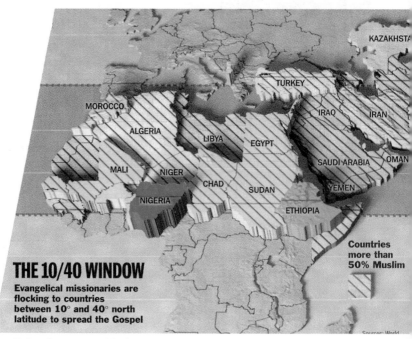

THE 10/40 WINDOW

Evangelical missionaries are flocking to countries between 10° and 40° north latitude to spread the Gospel

Countries more than 50% Muslim

Before Jesus returns Matthew quotes Him, "And this Gospel of the Kingdom must be preached into all nations as a witness to all people, then the end shall come." Matthew 24:14

Jesus changed Nazareth and the world forever by His love, death, resurrection and eternal teachings.

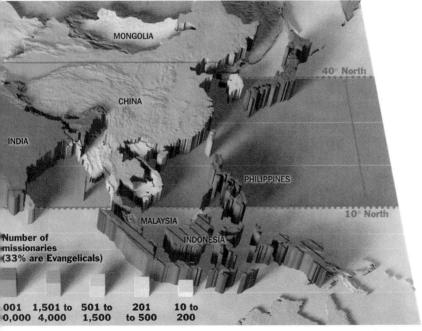

That is the reason for the aggressive missionary effort in Muslim nations. They have not heard the Gospel of Christ.

ANIS A. SHORROSH

Time magazine and many other intities missed the mark. We must ask "Should Muslims convert Christians?" then, "Should Christians evangelise Muslims?" Only the Holy Spirit can convert, not human agents.

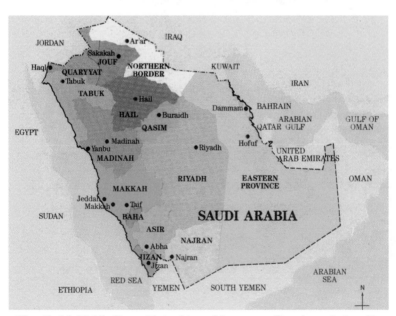

The oil-rich Middle East with Arabia and Iraq controlling the majority of it. 41% of U.S. oil comes from the strategic M.E.

Before this section is concluded it will be very helpful to present some informative details about some cities.

Babylon

The celebrated city of ancient history and Biblical lore has been restored. The streets have been paved, the walls rebuilt and the legendary palaces raised from the ashes of time. Saddam's purpose was to attract tourists and satisfy his longing for recognition as a world-class leader on par with King Nebuchadnezzar. It was this writer's good fortune to visit the ruins of the city on March 13, 2004 to observe the rebuilding progress which Saddam Hussein had undertaken. Unfortunately, the young Iraqi driver, Rev. Chambers and I were mistaken for terrorists by the Polish contingency. We were shot at twice to keep us from getting any closer to their position. Eventually, we were detained by the personnel of three armored vehicles, interrogated and delivered to the American contingency, who released us an hour and a half later.

Baghdad

The capital of Iraq was built by Caliph Mansour in 762 A.D. It is modern, growing and boasts one-fifth of the population. Baghdad means "founded by God," in Persian. Besides being the center of government, with road, air and rail transportation, it also has three sizeable universities and numerous other technical and specialized schools. The 1700-mile long Tigris River adds to the significance and beauty of it. One can actually navigate the first 1000 miles. The 1000-mile long Euphrates River does not flow through Baghdad but runs through Western Iraq and joins the Tigris only 100 miles north of the Arabian Gulf.

My second visit in March, 2004, which followed the visit in November, 2003, demonstrated the enormous progress of the economy. Piles of goods and appliances inside the stores and spilling out onto the sidewalks were a common sight! The streets looked cleaner and the cars more numerous. Still the awareness of the need for security throughout the city was apparent, because each hotel had barrels of cement and steel-spike barriers. The most unusual bit of information was that one-half of the Iraqi personnel, working for the Coalition Forces, had made a commitment to faith in Jesus, the Messiah, according to the civil coordinator for the Coalition Forces of Col. Nabeel Haj.

Basra
The one and a half million citizens make up the third largest city of Iraq. A strong Christian presence is growing in the midst of the Shiite Muslims. Its large Arabian-Persian Gulf port authority joins transportation of road and rail with Baghdad. Its strategic position and numerous oil fields have attracted many major and minor battles. As recent as March 21, 2004, several car bombs exploded at police stations and the military headquarters for the new Iraqi security forces killing and injuring many.

Kirkuk
The story of Kirkuk as a major energy supplier began in 1927 when the British discovered oil—the black gold. The city boasts five schools and twenty-six kindergartens, many of which are being rebuilt by Jordanian aid groups. It is located 155 miles north of Baghdad and has a strong Christian presence, as well as being the urban center for

the third largest ethnic group in Iraq, namely the Turkomans. On March 15, 2004, the opportunity in Baghdad's Presbyterian Church was to be followed immediately by a journey of three hours to Kirkuk. Due to mixed communication signals, it did not materialize. Sadly enough, a few days later, Baptist Aid workers, not far from Kirkuk, were ambushed. Five were shot and only one survived. Terrorists do not differentiate men from women, girls from boys, volunteers coming to help Iraqis from combatants.

Mosul (Ninevah)

The 1.7 million inhabitants make up the second largest city in Iraq and are mostly Kurds. Moreover, there are Turkoman and Assyrian minorities. Several universities are thriving along with the largest medical school in the country. From the days of Jonah until now, it continues as "that great city." (Jonah 4:1) The Turkomans are Turkish-speaking Muslims. Yet, 30,000 Christians are among this population. Originally the Turkomans migrated from Central Asia over a span of several hundred years.

C. Iraq's bright tomorrow

The most significant coming event on the horizon of the country of Iraq is the presentation of the new constitution on July, 2004. These lines are being formulated in May and the terrible insurgencies in several cities are seeking to thwart such an accomplishment. Over one hundred American soldiers have been killed in April alone, resulting in more deaths than in the initial war a year ago. At any rate, the new constitution must contain the compass by which to guide Iraqi citizens for years to come. The Iraqi ruling council must include in the new constitution a strong position on freedom of religion and implement it. Saddam did not only restrict and forbid the Christians to evangelize, he also imposed similar restrictions on Muslims! The American constitution has guided this society for over 200 years. So let us hope that something similar can be accomplished in Iraq. The resolve of President George W. Bush and America as a whole is to stay in Iraq until the people themselves are in charge and Iraq is stabilized by getting rid of violent elements.

A major undertaking in the country took place when the new currency was issued on the 15th of November, 2003, with the picture of Saddam Hussein removed from every denomination. Another change was the removal from the textbooks the belligerent references to the West, democracy, free enterprise, freedom of speech, freedom of expression, religion and the praises of Saddam and his regime. Instead of singing about Saddam in schools the children are being taught to sing about their country, its brilliant history and its bright future.

Fear is a powerful motivation for good or evil. The discovery of the numerous mass graves, after the collapse of Iraq, substantiated the justifiable sheer terror the Iraqi citizens lived under during the Saddam regime. Now, torture chambers have been destroyed. Sadly, thirty thousand bodies of missing Iraqis have also been uncovered in mass graves and thousands have been identified. The Baath party has been decimated and over 90 percent of the characters on the fifty-five deck of cards have been found, imprisoned or killed. Things are definitely looking much better today than ever before.

Yet fear is still experienced by the Coalition Forces and Iraqi citizens, especially the police. The diehard terrorist, remnants of Al Qaida operatives, Saddam's suicide bombers and foreign mercenaries are the cause of the fear and insecurity in Iraq.

Furthermore, throughout April a thirty-year old Muslim cleric has fanned the flames of insurgency by his militancy. But he is a wanted man by the Iraqi authorities for the murder of a fellow cleric who opposed him. Nevertheless, no one can be presumptuous to think that twenty-five years of terror, intimidation, oppression and persecution can be wiped out in a few months. This writer will always remember how some Christian leaders, on my first trip to Baghdad in November 2003, urged me privately to remember that they have just come out of the dark ages. Subsequently, they declared that I should not speak so boldly and freely in church services. Things are changing, but change takes time.

It is practically twelve months since military action against Iraq has taken place, and people are still being blown away by suicide bombers who are determined to destroy as many lives as possible, keep the sense of fear growing and the killing machine going. In April, 2004, in Fallujah, Mosul and Basra, hundreds of insurgents were killed, while the U.S. forces suffered a total equaling three times as many killed as when they conquered Iraq last year.

However, the voices of freedom, coexistence, peace and justice are becoming louder than ever. Furthermore, the briefcase of Saddam Hussein, which was found within his possession when he was captured in a hole in the ground in Adwar, a tiny village close to his village of Tikrit, contained a plethora of information about the key leaders of the squads who were bombing and causing havoc throughout the country. Additionally, American and Coalition Forces have become more acquainted with the terrain of the country, its culture and people. They are more agile in responding to threats and attacks, so as to quickly arrest or kill the perpetrators on the spot. I learned this when we went to Babylon, March 13th, and our car was forced by Polish officers to stop. They shot live ammunition warning us not to get any closer. Then they detained us for one hour until the American military police cleared us.

Tragically, more Iraqi's are being killed now because they are not as well protected in their local setting as the Coalition Forces are in their camps and armored vehicles. Soft targets, such as hotels, clubs, restaurants and aid workers' offices are still being targeted. The ruined remains of the Red Cross headquarters in Baghdad will forever be etched in my memory after viewing the terrible sight in November, 2003. My personal conviction is that even these atrocities will be forgotten before long and remembered as a nightmare along with the reign of terror of Saddam and Co.

Numerous schools have been opened, new school buildings have been erected, universities are back to normalcy and thousands of Iraqi expatriates are returning to Iraq to rebuild their wounded and bleeding country.

New businesses are being started and a huge number of vehicles are being shipped weekly, especially from Kuwait, to meet the demand for personal and family transportation. Even while this writer was there, one newspaper had an interesting story about ten thousand used vehicles being shipped from Kuwait that very weekend of November 24, 2003.

Nevertheless, the most startling discovery was that of observing an insatiable appetite for satellite dishes, T.V. sets, cars and trucks. Some shops had satellite dishes on the sidewalks, for lack of space inside the stores. One could purchase a home satellite dish costing as little as the equivalent of $25.00. The size of the dish and where it was manufactured determined its value. The most expensive foreign made dish would cost up to $500.00. On my second trip Dr. Crouch bought one for $110.00! Then he gave it away to a military chaplain March 12, 2004.

Having been privileged to appear several times on Trinity Broadcasting Network, from Los Angeles, CA, and Dallas, TX, this author was overjoyed to see the T.V. channel on Hot Bird number 6 and channel 153 in several homes. It is hoped that in a very short time, especially after July 1st, TBN will acquire a building in Baghdad which will be managed and operated by native Iraqi citizens to carry on the programming of TBN throughout Iraq. Satellite dishes have already been provided to the churches all over Iraq by TBN's generous president, Dr. Paul Crouch, in expression of Christian love for the people of Iraq. This generosity will cover a very small segment of Iraqi society. We still need a physical station which can cover the entire country.

To go into depth concerning the improvements in the political, educational, industrial, manufacturing and export business in Iraq will take another volume. Yet, the personal observation of this writer is that of a people who have been living in the dark ages and have suddenly come out into the light. It is of citizens who were oppressed, repressed and depressed, but are now free.

There is no direction for Iraq to go but upward and forward. In one of the leading evangelical churches in Baghdad, in which this author spoke on November 25th, 2003, the congregation began to clap and the pastor jumped out of his seat on the platform and hugged me when I announced what the American congress had just voted. He even asked whether I said $87 million or $87 billion dollars was the dollar amount that the congress had just approved as an aid package to Afghanistan and Iraq. It was actually $87 billion. Along with that announcement a specific detail included funding for 5,000 garbage trucks to remove the enormous amount of trash and garbage from the streets of Baghdad. The main streets were cleaned periodically, but the state of the side streets was a different story.

Now it is June of 2004. A new president-elect has come to power from the Iraqi governing council ahead of schedule. He attended President Reagan's funeral June 11, 2004, in Washington and was interviewed by the media several times. Mr. Iyad Allawi seems very optimistic, but also very realistic about the current situation of Iraq. He told BBC Television that military decisions taken after June 30 transfer of sovereignty must be approved by the new Iraqi government. Such statements are very encouraging because they represent Iraqis taking responsibility.

Yet, anyone has the right to wonder how the Iraqis can handle security when policemen and police stations continue to be decimated by insurgents across the country. Two stations were blasted, one in Baghdad and the other south of the capital. A car bomb outside an American base in Baghdad itself killed nine people Sunday, June 6th and injured thirty others.

Lakhdar Brahimi, who helped put together the interim government has been optimistic about the assuming of power by the new Iraqi government on June 30th. To be sure the radical Shiite cleric, Muqtade Al-Sadr continues to stir division, destruction and damage to both coalition forces and Iraq. Citizens are cooperating with the coalition forces, not only in the stronghold of Najaf and Falujah, but elsewhere as well. Yet hope is rising in the hearts of the population that Saddam's followers and occupational forces' days are to be over soon and they can move forward with America's help to become a democratic modern nation.

In an age of instant news, instant ball game replays, instant coffee and fast-food stores, people have become accustomed to fast-paced solutions to problems. Such may be true in the western world and particularly in America, but it is not so in most countries of the world. You will appreciate the evaluation of this fact by the following illustration.

In many developing countries, when one asks for something to be done, the answer is "tomorrow." In countries where they are moving forward, time is more valuable and when such a question is asked, the answer is, "Give me five minutes." In the developed countries one would say, "Just a minute." But in America the response, astonishingly is, "Just a second." Therefore, the most valuable commodity in the world, which is time, is looked upon with different eyes depending on what part of the world, geographically, a person is located. The above statements are directed at those who keep complaining that things are not going as fast as they should in Iraq. That would be a true evaluation if the situation were in America, the "can do nation." However, most of the Iraqi's are content with the progress that is being made in their country. The enormous American investment in their infrastructure and the freedoms they are beginning to enjoy throughout the country are deeply appreciated by the citizens.

D. What about the Weapons of Mass Destruction?

This chapter is entitled "Iraq—Yesterday, Today and Tomorrow." At this moment the question which must be posed concerns itself with the topic of WMD (Weapons of Mass Destruction.) It is universally agreed that back in 1990-91, when the winds of war over the Gulf were blowing fiercely, sinister Saddam was about to come up with an atomic weapon. Subsequent to the Gulf War of 1991, weapons' experts concluded that had he been allowed six months to a year of freedom from war the Iraqi atomic scientists would have produced a small atomic weapon. It is necessary to refresh the mind of the reader that even as far back as 1986 the Oziraq reactor outside of Baghdad was designated for that purpose. However, the Israeli military destroyed it from the air before the atomic reactor was activated. Amazingly enough, between that time and 1991, the scientists switched to more ingenious methods of producing such a weapon. One of their inventions was a weapon which could be fired from a giant super-sized cannon.

At this date, February, 2004, media talking heads and political pundits wonder loudly why did Saddam Hussein reject the demands of the Coalition Forces to surrender and be exiled, instead of going to a war with a superpower which he could not possibly win, if such weapons were non-existent? To rephrase the problem, the media world is challenging our American administration that since such weapons were not found after a year of searching, therefore we should not have attacked Iraq.

The basic and fundamental issue of the war was that since the military regime of the "bully of Baghdad" had produced WMD's, and could unleash them on their neighboring countries and even the Western powers at will, he should be stopped. So, the question is very serious. Where are these weapons since they were not found? First, possibly the weapons were shipped to Syria and elsewhere. On the last week of April, 2004, the media was abuzz with the news that the country of Sudan was demanding that Syria's scud missiles must be removed from Sudan. Were these actually Syrian or Iraqi? The government of Sudan was fearful of America's retaliation. The fact is, historically Syria's information, whenever any subject is discussed, has always been dubious and very questionable. Consequently, their denial of having any such activity before the fall of Iraq cannot be trusted. Financial experts have already uncovered money trails which Saddam used through Syria to hide his billions. And three trucks loaded with gold bullion were seized by American forces near the Syrian border during a random border crossing checkpoint between Iraq and Syria early in the Iraqi war.

Additional information has been appearing in the media before the publication of this book to the effect that Saddam's intelligence operatives had paid U.N., American and British high-level personnel enormous bribes to cover up his schemes. One of the schemes was his siphoning oil and selling it illegally under the nose of the U.N. observers. Another scheme was to bribe willing U.N. members of the WMD inspectors, who would let his intelligence personnel learn of the next stopover in order that the areas of search would be cleared of nuclear and any such weaponry, as WMDs. Furthermore, some of the funds, which were supposed to be funneled to pay for humanitarian and medical purposes were used to pay even the son of the U.N. president, Kofi Annan. The names and the proofs are to be made public in short order.

The second possibility, which is more plausible, is that the corrupt administration in Baghdad ordered the destruction and dismantling of all such weapons in the hope of convincing the search teams that if Iraq does not have WMD's, therefore war should not be launched against Iraq. Of course, that would have allowed the continuation of the dictatorship of the "King of Terror" over his people. The truth is in the third revelation, which came to my attention through a Fox news report 5/9/04, that Saddam sent 408 of his nuclear scientists to Libya. Gadhafi tunneled a mountain to carry on the secret activity from 1998-2004. This revelation explained to me why America forced Libya to dismantle and give up their nuclear projects. Gadhafi came clean when he allowed the shipping of the weapons research systems to the U.S. in March 2004 as proof.

At any rate, may I say that if the gregarious and gracious George W. Bush, the illustrious president of the USA, had declared war on Iraq with the intention of liberating its downtrodden, oppressed, repressed and depressed people from a blood-thirsty and ruthless regime, he would have presented a better cause for the war than wanting to eliminate WMD's in Iraq. This is the conviction of the writer, which was substantiated in the last three trips to the British Isles where America's renown has been diminishing instead of growing. Many Britishers believe that we have bullied their Prime Minister, Tony Blair, into going to war for only one purpose, and that is to secure the oil fields for the West.

As of June 2004, the price of gas is $5.99 a gallon in London and only $2.09 in the U.S.A. The Anglo-American initiative in their conquest of Iraq and bringing democracy will guarantee the flow of cheaper oil than if we let another dictator or the Russians control Iraq! America's administration should be commended on the foresight to accomplish this before Americans would become hostages to crazy oil-producing countries, as we were in 1973.

On June 2, 2004, OPEC officials promised to increase daily production by 2,500,000 barrels a day to bring down the oil prices which had gone over $40.00 a barrel. They also fear a new interest in alternative energy sources which will diminish the need for fossilized sources. They cannot swim in oil; they must sell it.

History will verify that oil wars and oil politics have been going on for nearly a hundred years. The West's insatiable appetite for oil dictates to any country's administration a demand to guarantee the flow of oil at any cost. Who can forget for a moment the Middle Eastern oil embargo of 1973, when for six months long lines persisted at the pumping stations throughout the Western nations. Apparently, the common man is unaware that America produces more oil than any country in the world, followed by the Middle East. However, because it is cheaper to buy it from overseas than produce it in America, our oil wells have rarely been operating at 100 percent capacity. The logic is understandable and certainly acceptable.

Observation, reason and research prompts this writer to foresee that ten to twenty years from now the oil wells of the world will take second place to other sources of energy like solar, atomic, hydro-power, electric batteries, windmills and wave dispersion. The later is a brand new technology which uses the waves to create energy. The invention is led by a Yale graduate from Troy, Michigan.

The future of Iraq looks brilliant and bright. Many countries are already rushing in to play a major role in the industrialization of Iraq and the rebuilding of its infrastructure. Contrary to the media's pontifications, the country is not in ruins. As of February 20, 2004, USA Today reported that joblessness is only 28 percent, far lower than the World's Bank and the U.N. predicted. Oil exports are running 1.5 billion dollars, ahead of projections by U.S. authorities and Iraqi technocrats, who forecast 2004's revenue at 12 billion dollars.

The United States administration has the right to allow the countries which participated militarily in the liberation of Iraq to have the largest pieces of the gigantic pie. It is understandable that France and Germany scream "foul." But why should they be allowed in the rebuilding of Iraq when neither their men nor their machines participated in the bloody liberation of a country that owns the largest reserves of oil in the entire Middle East?

The educational future of the country of Iraq is as significant as its political system or as valuable as the oil wells over the desert sands. Surprisingly, the government of Hussein was able to maintain fifteen major universities and thirty-seven colleges and technical institutions. In fact, at the beginning of the school year 2002-03, there were 210,000 students involved in undergraduate studies on seventy various educational institutions of higher learning throughout the country. With the realization that Iraq has only 50 percent literate population, more institutions must be initiated and hundreds of Dr. Laubach-like courses taught to help the illiterate people learn to read and write simply and quickly.

Knowledge, these days, is no longer considered a luxury. Any individual in any location on the planet will be destined to a life of poverty and destitution without some kind of educational degree or a skill in some specialized field. There may come a day in which we will have jobless educated people. Here is an example. We found in the 1970's in Bangalore, India, where our family lived for a short period, that there was an over-abundance of educated people, especially engineers who were jobless. The number was estimated at five thousand.

Nevertheless, with that much brain-power, we knew that sooner or later something would develop in a positive manner. Today, Bangalore has become the "Silicon Valley." Outsourcing to India jumped 60 percent over 2002 according to a research magazine, "Data Quest"—140,000 jobs in America were outsourced to India, mainly in Bangalore. Still, there are 130 million jobs in America as of February 2004. Indian engineers and doctors dot the American landscape reminding everyone that job opportunities should not be limited to one's own country in this challenging twenty-first century.

Kuwait, Jordan, Bahrain, Dubai, Qatar and Israel are leading the way in industrialization, commercialism, education and progress in practically every field. Lebanon is recovering from the fourteen-year devastating civil war and trying to restore itself to its earlier prominence. The peoples of the other countries of the Middle East are envious of the success stories, particularly when television images provide evidence of these facts. Although fundamentalists, through intimidation and terrorism, keep trying to push time backwards to the days of Muhammad and the rise of Islam, the average Middle Easterner wants to live, study, work and think in terms of the twenty-first century and not in the eighth century and in today's culture, not the culture of Arabia.

The following is a case in point which has been printed in the papers, aired over the radios and viewed on television. February 11, 2004, the administration and parliament members of France voted unanimously to ban the wearing of religious symbols in the public place. That means a Jew cannot don a yarmulke. A Christian cannot wear a large cross. A Hindu will not be allowed to wear a turban. And a Muslim woman will no longer be permitted to wear a scarf over her head in public. There are over six million Muslims in France and they have been pushing for recognition of the fundamentalist view of Islam. Fear of what militant Islam can do in France prompted the French government to take a stand and demonstrate that they are a secular society. Inasmuch as the ban was mainly directed at the Muslim communities, it was also a statement against terrorism because terrorists spring from such fundamentalist and militant environments of Islamic beliefs throughout the world. France has also deported several mullahs who cause dissention by their sermons.

Yes, we are as a global village involved in a culture war, a clash of civilization and a conflict of philosophies. Let it be proclaimed, declared and announced that the world's people want peace, not war. We need harmony, not conflict. We must seek reconciliation, not vengeance. Too much blood has been shed and the entire human race screams daily, "We have had too much bloodshed, heartache and heartbreak, of my way over yours, of my religion is better than yours, of my political system is more desirable than yours, etc, etc, etc!"

Let the silent majority be heard as they proclaim, "We are for peace and strength, not war and weakness." Therefore, let us march to the sound of a different drum, the drum of celebrating life, liberty and the pursuit of happiness by the grace of our creator God, who loves us all and sent us that Good News in the person of the only true peacemaker the world will ever know.

This writer is still working on the manuscript of **Islam: A Threat or a Challenge** in Baghdad itself during March 2004. The country is moving forward, despite the constant terrorist activities which seek to destabilize the country. Improvements are seen everywhere and the people are happier, busier and above all tasting the fruit of liberty, justice, freedom and prosperity. Security is still lacking.

In the June 14th, 2004, issue of *People Magazine* it was refreshing to find an encouraging statement by Mr. Paul Bremer, the chief administrator of the Coalition Provisional Authority. He said, "We've made a lot of progress; we've done something like 18,000 individual reconstruction projects all over the country. . . .and are creating hundreds of thousands of jobs. (pp. 64-66)

Today, June 28, 2004, is a red-letter day for me as I am finalizing this chapter, as well as the entire book. This chapter alone has taken seven long months of research, labor, travel and consultation. It is also the day in which our U.S. administration surprised the world by transferring official sovereignty to the Iraqi interim government, led by President Ghazi Al-Yawer and Prime Minister Iyad Allawi. Seven months from now the people of Iraq themselves will vote for whom will rule over them in a new and democratic Iraq. The U.S. has proven once again to the entire world, as we did after World War II, that we do not desire to become a colonizing power. We are supporters and defenders of freedom. Now that we have a free Iraq, our role will be to help the new government and its people to be secure and experience liberty for now and future generations.

As we go to print July 1st, 2004, the world is watching on their T.V. sets, with mixed reactions, Dictator Saddam Hussain in a Baghdad court room answering questions prior to his judge and jury confrontation. The Coalition Forces surrendered him into the hands of the new interim government June 30. Saddam, belligerent and boisterous, insisted that he is still the president of Iraq. He berated the judges and announced that the Kuwaites were dogs and that he had the right to take back their country because it was originally a part of Iraq. Furthermore, he exclaimed that he had nothing to do with the gasing of thousands of Kurds. Rather he had heard about it over the radio! Although the American version of the Iraqi constitution abolished the death penalty, the new leadership re-instated it once they came to power. The potent proof which the court can bring against him, besides the documented elimination of opponents, and the burial grounds of the murdered masses, are the living people who will face him with their own eye-witness testimonies. A good number of these witnesses will show the world the cavity where their left ears were, because he ordered their extraction as a punishment for their going AWOL from his army.

E. Biblical prophecy and the future of the Middle East

Due to the deep and long interest I have had in prophecy and the Middle East, one more subject must be pursued. It is the astonishing Biblical reference to the future of Iraq penned down by Isaiah, the prince of prophets, 2700 years ago. Here is the fascinating declaration according to chapter 19:23-25:

In that day there will be a highway from Egypt to Assyria, and the Assyrian will come into Egypt and the Egyptian into Assyria, and the Egyptians will serve with the Assyrians. In that day Israel will be one of three with Egypt and Assyria, even a blessing in the midst of the land, whom the Lord of hosts shall bless, saying, "Blessed is Egypt My people, and Assyria the work of My hands, and Israel My inheritance."

Isaiah's prophecies in chapter 53 concerned the passion of Jesus the Messiah, which sat dormant for seven centuries before they were fulfilled precisely and in minute detail. Has the time come for Iraq's prophetic utterances to be consummated?

Assyria in ancient times occupied the northern part of Iraq and Persia, just as Babylonia covered the southern portion and Iran. Although several sincere attempts have been made in the last fifty-six years to unite the Arab countries, they all failed. Even after Syria and Egypt made an alliance in 1958 and called themselves the United Arab Republic, the alliance fizzled very quickly. When President Abdel Nasser, of Egypt, died in 1970, the dream of the United States of Arabia died with him. Yet the prophecy of Isaiah announces that Egypt, Iraq and Israel—which has been the greatest traditional enemy of the Arab world—will become allies and unite as a group of three friendly nations! I very sincerely lament the tragic truth that *most Arabs unite only on one issue, their hatred for Israel*!

Why is Egypt so important? Because it is the largest Arab country in the world with 70,000,000 population.

Thus, it represents the twenty-two Arab countries and their people of over 250,000,000. The incredible future miracle of God describes how He, in the end times, will bring the Arabs and the Jews, the warring children of Abraham, together in peace and harmony. *"My people"* is the exclusive and reserved title which God used over the centuries for Israel will now be bestowed upon Egypt. Subsequently, one is to understand that Isaiah, the prophet, predicts explicitly and reveals clearly that Egypt will be given such a lofty and towering title as Israel in the end times. Will it happen in our lifetime or as many Biblical students of prophecy believe only in the millennium?

Another mysterious matter deals with Iraq, ancient Assyria, as a third party to this triumvirate of nations. It seems to me that the messianic age would certainly be upon us if and when this takes place. The reason is obvious when one studies the history of the Israelites. You see, Israel, the Northern Kingdom, was decimated by Assyria, which was the northern part of today's Iraq, in 722 B.C. Thereafter, the ten tribes were taken into captivity to Assyria. The Southern Kingdom, known as Judah, was destroyed by Babylon, Iraq's southern geographical location at that time in 587 B.C. Nebuchadnezzar destroyed Jerusalem and took the best of the citizens into captivity to Babylon.

Therefore, two out of the three traditional enemies of Israel, namely the Babylonians and the Assyrians, will become friends and allies of Israel. The Egyptians, the third ancient enemy, made peace with Israel in my lifetime in the year 1978. The peace treaty was accomplished under the leadership of President Jimmy

Carter of the U.S.A., President Anwar Sadat of Egypt and Prime Minister Menachim Begin of Israel.

Is it a mystery to notice that Egypt is never mentioned as a partner in the coalition of the Armageddon wars, according to Ezekial 38:1-6 and 39:1-6? Iraq will be next to make peace with their cousins. Historians have researched into the roots of the people of Iraq and discovered that the "ten so-called tribes" of Israel are actually part of today's Arab population of Iraq! That is why I say "cousins."

Humanity must look forward with joyous anticipation when the ancient enmity will be forgotten and true friendships established among these ancient enemies. What a day it will be when no more belligerence, bloodshed, brutality and animosity are practiced. But hope, love, peace and justice will be the order of the day through the Prince of Peace, the peacemaker, the passionate Messiah!

Yes, no effective solution has ever been found by any committee or country, president or potentate, king or commoner, not even the U.N. to solve the Arab-Jewish dilemma. But the conqueror of hate and death will accomplish the impossible goal—Jesus the Messiah. How? By changing hearts, minds and attitudes through the work of the Holy Spirit. Take notice of this unfulfilled promise from Isaiah 2:4.

He shall judge between the nations, And shall rebuke many people; They shall beat their swords into plowshares, And their spears into pruning hooks;

Nation shall not lift up sword against nation, Neither shall they learn war anymore.

Let us join our hearts in earnest prayer to the Heavenly Father and say a resounding "Amen, O God, hasten the day, please!"

We have not made a particular religion superior to another religion. No other religion is recognized except the True Religion. It invites people to a more sublime and nobler pathway. How then can We ever inspire a religion for whom We did not send a messenger and in which none of the true believers could trust?

Suffice it to say that the True Religion is the religion of love, brotherhood, compassion and peace. We have entrusted it to Our worshipers through The True Gospel as a persuasive proclamation. We have supported it with The True Furqan as an extraordinary revelation. Whosoever puts his trust in any other religion except the True Religion, it will not be recognized. At the end of the trail he will find himself among the regretful.

We have conveyed The True Furqan to remind you of the True Religion and to approve the veracity of The True Gospel. The purpose is to demonstrate its superiority over all religions no matter whether the hypocrites agree or disagree.

O, people everywhere: do not promote wickedness and animosity. Do not even take vengeance upon your enemies because a kind deed cannot be on the same level as an unkind one. Therefore, reinforce deeds which are more wholesome and treat the one with whom you have hostility like an intimate friend. (The True Furqan "The Sacrifice" 54:4-6,10)

CONCLUSION

The previous nine chapters by no means completely cover the manifold issues and topics discussed in this book. Neither this writer nor any other is presumptuous enough to think that any book he or she writes is an exhaustive or final word on that specific subject.

Furthermore, it is appropriate in the context of the 21st century where the Global Village is facing a new type of warfare, namely nuclear, biological and chemical terrorism, to wonder what can be done to solve this savage and colossal world-wide problem. Inasmuch as mankind is never satisfied with the status quo, no matter how excellent it is, a solution or several solutions should be examined. It is mystifying indeed to look into the biblical record of the creation and discover that even Adam and Eve, while in the perfect environment of the Garden of Eden, still were not totally satisfied. Yet, the ambition and longing of individuals and societies for a tranquil, purposeful and productive co-existence with their fellowman is still the ultimate hope for the human race. Plato's Utopia keeps eluding mankind everywhere and anywhere!

Consequently, it is the opinion of this author that the following suggestions may expedite our journey toward such a worthy goal despite the fact that these suggestions may not necessarily be the ultimate answer—peace and justice for all.

1. Exchange students should go beyond Western Countries and include Muslim countries. Since 1991 Russian exchange students have been flooding the U.S.A., so the Chinese before that. Civic organizations can contribute immeasurably, such as Rotarians, Civitans, Lions, Masons and church organizations.

2. Exchange pulpits of Jewish Rabbis, Christian Pastors and Muslim Mullah's once a year, or every six months. A meal should be served after the sermon, since most worship services are at noon or evening. Afterward an hour could be spent in dialogue with questions by the audience led by a panel of experts and a moderator.

3. Hold public forums, discussions, dialogues and debates in a Civic Center, public library or on a college campus. Such activities should be well advertised to attract as many members of all three groups of religionists. Conclude with prayer for peace, love, justice and understanding.

4. Sponsor a massive letter campaign to Muslim governments and embassies to stop persecution of minorities within their countries for the well-being of the citizens and to alter the world opinion from thinking that Muslim countries are historically violent. Announce that the 100 killing verses in the Quran are out of date, but were valid in early Islamic history for Muslims of that day.

5. Ban all terrorist groups from every country which is a signatory to the United Nations "Bill of Human Rights" and arrest or eliminate their members. Terrorists are not freedom fighters when they terrorize the legitimate governments and harm innocent people.

6. Release the tens of thousands of Prisoners of Conscience immediately from every prison of all the Muslim and non-Muslim countries world-wide.

7. Provide monthly U.N. sponsored conferences on racial, religious and economic rights and responsibilities in every country of the U.N. to cover all of the 216 countries. Urge the media to reduce glamorizing criminals, terrorists and suicide bombers. Demand that their names and how many victims they have killed and injured be eliminated from their reporting. We must stop making criminals and violent people famous, but infamous. The evil deed should be reported, but not the wicked individual's name, neither his nationality nor his religious affiliation.

Finally, the guarantee for peaceful co-existence and tolerance will result when we fundamentally and sincerely love our Heavenly Father, then express that love to our fellowman through the grace of the Lord Jesus Christ, the True Peacemaker. I learned to tolerate the Israelis in particular and Jews in general when I was transformed from a Palestinian Christian by culture to one by experience.

Please consult the amazing book, The True Furqan, chapter 2, where one can see how the Spirit of God can make the impossible possible. Yes, an Arab can love a Jew and visa versa whenever each individual experiences the miracle of salvation through Messiah Jesus.

We can and must forgive each other. We can and must stop living in the past. We can and must start living here and now with a heartfelt commitment to building a new future of love and peace for our children and grandchildren, instead of destroying them with hateful hearts and vengeful attitudes. True love can conquer all. I am personally proof positive to that fact, so are many others in the tiny land of the prophets and the apostles, the Holy Land and throughout the world.

BIBLIOGRAPHY

Abdul-Rauf, Muhammad, Dr. *History of the Islamic Center.* Washington, D.C.: The Islamic Center, 1978.

Abdulati, Hammudah. *Islam in Focus.* Salimiah, Kuwait: International Islamic Federation of Student Organizations, 1990.

Adams, Moody. *Farrakhan, Islam & the Religion that is Raping America.* U.S.A.: The Moody Adams Evangelistic Association, 1996.

Ahmed, Akbar S. *Islam Today.* London, NY: I.B. Tauris Publishers, 2001.

Ali, Michael Nazir. *Frontiers in Muslim – Christian Encounter.* Oxford, U.K.: Regnum Books, 1987.

Allegro, John. *The Dead Sea Scrolls.* London, England: Penguin Books, 1956, reprinted 1964.

Al-Ashqar, Umar Sulaiman, Dr. *The World of the Jinn and Devils.* Trans. Jamaal al-Din M. Zarabozo. Boulder, CO: Al-Basheer Company, 1998.

Al-Masih, Abd. *The Gospel Questions the Qur'an.* Villach, Austria: Light of Life, 1998.

_____ *The Great Deception*. Villach, Austria: Light of Life, 1995.

Al Saffee & Almahdy. *The True Furqan*. Enumclaw, WA.: WinePress Publishing, 1999.

Al-Qaradawi, Yusuf. *The Lawful and the Prohibited in Islam*. Plainfield, IN: American Trust Publications, 1994.

Ali, Michael Nazir. *Frontiers in Muslim-Christian Encounter*. Oxford: Regnum Books, 1987.

Andersen, Christopher. *George and Laura*. New York: Harper Collins Publishers, 2002.

Andrew, Brother with Verne Becker. *For the Love of my Brothers*. Minneapolis, MN: Bethany House Publishers, 1998.

Baker, Dwight L. *Understanding Islam: An Approach to Witness*. Waco, TX: Baptist Literacy Missions Center at Baylor, 1989.

Bennett, Ramon. *Philistine, The Great Deception*. Jerusalem, Israel: Arm of Salvation, 1995.

Braswell, Jr. George W. *Islam, its Prophet, Peoples, Politics and Power*. Nashville, TN: Broadman Press, 1996.

Brooks, Geraldine. *Nine Parts of Desire, The Hidden World of Islamic Women*. New York, NY: Anchor Books, 1995.

Copleston, F. S. *Christ or Mohammed: The Bible or the Koran?* Harpenden, Herts, England: Nuprint Ltd, 1989.

Coughlin, Con. *Saddam, King of Terror.* New York, NY:
HarperCollins Publishers, 2002.

Dashti, 'Ali. *23 years – A Study of the Prophetic Career of
Mohammad.* London: George Allen and Unwin, 1985.

Engdahl, F. William. *A Century of War.* Germany: Ebner
Ulm, 1992.

Faizi, S.F.H. *Sermons of the Prophet.* New Delhi, India:
Kitab Bhavan, 1997.

Fry, C. George & James R. King. *Islam, A Survey of the
Muslim Faith.* Grand Rapids, MI: Baker Book House,
1982.

Gabriel, Mark A., Ph.D. *Islam and Terrorism.* Lake Mary,
Florida: Charisma House, 2002.

Goldsmith, Martin. *Islam & Christian Witness.* InterVarsity
Press: Downers Grove, IL. 1982.

Grant, George. *The Blood of the Moon.* Brentwood, TN;
Wolgemuth & Hyatt, 1991.

Haddad, Yvonne Yazbeck and John L. Esposito, editors.
Muslims on the Americanization Path? Oxford: 2000.

Hamada, Louis Bahjat. *Understanding the Arab World.*
Nashville, TN: Thomas Nelson Publishers, 1990.

Hawatmeh, Abdalla with Roland Muller. *The Man From
Gadara.* Canada: 2003.

Hisham, Ibn. *The Life of Muhammad.* Vol. 1. Villach, Austria: Light of Life, nd.

Hismah, Ibn. *The Life of Muhammad – The Persecuted Prophet in Mecca.* Vol. 1. Villach, Austria: Light of Life, 1997.

Hughes, Thomas Patrick. *A Dictionary of Islam.* New Delhi: Asian Educational Services, 2001.
Ibraham, Ishak. *Black Gold and Holy War.* Nashville, Tennessee: Thomas Nelson Publishers, 1983.

Johnson, David Earle. *Princes of Islam.* U.S.A.: David Johnson Books, 2002.

_____ *Conspiracy in Mecca.* Lincoln, NE: Universe, Inc, 2001.

Kassis, Hanna E. *A Concordance of the Qur'an.* Berkeley, California: The University of California Press, 1983.

Korkut, Dede, M.D. *Life Alert – The Medical Case of Muhammad.* Enumclaw, Washington: WinePress Publishing, 2001.

Kubo, Sakae & Walter F. Specht. *So Many Versions?* Grand Rapids, Michigan: Zondervan Publishing House, 1975, 1983.

Lee, Arthur Paterson. *The Controversial Jesus.* Belleville, Ontario, Canada: Guardian Books, 2000.

Mahfouz, Naguib. *Palace of Desire.* New York: Anchor Books, 1992.

Manser, Martin H., ed. *Chambers Dictionary of Synonyms and Antonyms.* W & R Chamber Ltd, 1990. Reprint, 1989.

Mark, Brother. *A 'Perfect' Qur'an or "So It was Made to Appear to Them"?* 2000.

Markham, Ian and Ibrahim M. Abu-Rabi, editors. *11 September.* Oxford: One World, nd.

Masih, Abd al. *The Gospel Questions the Qur'an.* Villach, Austria: Light of Life, 1998.

McGeveran, William A. Jr., ed. *The World Almanac and Book of Facts 2002.* New York, NY: World Almanac Books, 2002.

Mikhail, Labib, Dr. *God's Last Messenger.* Springfield, VA: Blessed Hope Ministry, 1998.

_____ *Islam Muhammad and the Koran.* 1996.

Mordecai, Victor. *Is Fanatic Islam a Global Threat.* Talor, SC: 1997.

Mustafa, Dr. *Against the Tides in the Middle East.* Casselberry, Florida: International Evangelical Resource Centre, 1999.

Nehls, Gerhard. *Christians Ask Muslims.* Cape Town, South Africa: Life Challenge, nd.

Parrinder, Geoffrey. *Jesus in the Qur'an*. Toronto, Ontario, Canada: Fellowship of Faith, 1965.

Parshall, Phil. *Bridges to Islam - a Christian Perspective on Folk Islam*. Grand Rapids, Michigan: Baker Book House, 1993.

_____ *Inside the Community, Understanding Muslims through Their Traditions*. Grand Rapids, MI: Baker Books, 1994.

Pickthall, Marmaduke, ed. *Holy Quran*. Karachi, Pakistan: Taj Company, Ltd., n.d.

Poston, Larry A. with Carl F. Ellis, Jr. *The Changing Face of Islam in America*. Camp Hill, PA: Horizon Books, 2000.

Price, Randall. *Unholy War*. Eugene, Oregon: Harvest House Publishers, 2001.

Qutb, Sayyid. *Islam and Universal Peace*. Plainfield, Indiana: American Trust Publications, 1993.

The Gospel of Barnabas. Oxford: Clarendon Press, 1907.

Robinson, Neal. *Christ in Islam and Christianity*. New York: State University of New York Press, 1991.

Sakr, Ahmad H., PhD. *Feast, Festivities and Holidays*. Lombard, IL: Foundation for Islamic Knowledge, 1999.

Shorrosh, Anis A., Dr. *Islam Revealed - A Christian Arab's View of Islam.* Nashville, Tennessee: Thomas Nelson Publishers, 1998.

Star, Leonie. *The Dead Sea Scrolls – The Riddle Debated.* Crows Nest, NSW, Australia: ABC Enterprises, 1991.

Tanagh, Samy. *Glad News! God Love You My Muslim Friend.* Santa Ana, CA: Calvary Chapel, 1999.

Thirty Days Muslim Prayer Focus. Youth With a Mission, 2003.

Tisdall, W. St. Clair. *Christian reply to Muslim Objections.* Villach, Austria: Light of Life, 1980.

Warraq, Ibn. *Why I Am Not a Muslim.* Amherst, New York: Prometheus Books, 1995.

Wilson, Marvin R. *Our Father Braham, Jewish Roots of the Christian Faith.* Grand Rapids, MI: William B. Eerdmans Publishing Company. 1989.

Woodberry, J. Dudley. *Muslims and Christians on the Emmaus Road.* Monrovia, CA: MARC, 1989.

Woodberry, J. Dudley and Russell G Shubin. *Why I Chose Jesus.* Article in Missions Frontiers Magazine. March 2001, pp. 28-33.

Ye'or, Bat. *The Dhimmi, Jews and Christians under Islam.* Cranbury, NJ; Associated University Presses, 1985.

ANIS A. SHORROSH

Zacharias, Ravi. *A Shattered Visage*. Grand Rapids, MI: Baker Books, 1993.

Order Form

To order additional copies, fill out this form and send it along with your check or money order to: Truth in Crisis, PO Box 949, Fairhope, AL 36533
Cost per copy $15.00 plus $5.00 P&H.

Ship _____ copies of *Islam: A Threat or A Challenge* to:

Ship _____ copies of *The True Furqan* to:

Name_____

Address:_____

City/State/Zip:_____

Please tell us how you found out about this book.
☐ Friend ☐Internet
☐ Book Store ☐Radio
☐ Newspaper ☐ Magazine
☐ Other _____